LOVE DON'T NEED A REASON

Before you start to read this book, take this moment to think about making a donation to punctum books, an independent non-profit press,

@ https://punctumbooks.com/support/

If you're reading the e-book, you can click on the image below to go directly to our donations site. Any amount, no matter the size, is appreciated and will help us to keep our ship of fools afloat. Contributions from dedicated readers will also help us to keep our commons open and to cultivate new work that can't find a welcoming port elsewhere. Our adventure is not possible without your support.

Vive la Open Access.

Fig. 1. Hieronymus Bosch, *Ship of Fools* (1490–1500)

LOVE DON'T NEED A REASON: THE LIFE & MUSIC OF MICHAEL CALLEN. Copyright © 2020 by Matthew J. Jones. This work carries a Creative Commons BY-NC-SA 4.0 International license, which means that you are free to copy and redistribute the material in any medium or format, and you may also remix, transform and build upon the material, as long as you clearly attribute the work to the authors (but not in a way that suggests the authors or punctum books endorses you and your work), you do not use this work for commercial gain in any form whatsoever, and that for any remixing and transformation, you distribute your rebuild under the same license. http://creativecommons.org/licenses/by-nc-sa/4.0/

First published in 2020 by punctum books, Earth, Milky Way.
https://punctumbooks.com

ISBN-13: 978-1-953035-14-1 (print)
ISBN-13: 978-1-953035-15-8 (ePDF)

DOI: 10.21983/P3.0297.1.00

LCCN: 2020947355
Library of Congress Cataloging Data is available from the Library of Congress

Book design: Vincent W.J. van Gerven Oei
Cover image: Barry Callen, portrait of Michael Callen. Courtesy of the artist.

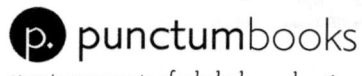

spontaneous acts of scholarly combustion

HIC SVNT MONSTRA

Love Don't Need a Reason

The Life & Music of Michael Callen

Matthew J. Jones

p.

Contents

Preface: I Almost Missed the Epidemic	21
Kerosene Lantern: An Introduction	32
Small Town Change	48
No, No	64
Innocence Dying	78
Nobody's Fool	92
Where the Boys Are	110
Living in Wartime	132
We Know Who We Are	142
How to Have Sex in an Epidemic	156
Lowlife	180
Purple Heart	202
The Flirt Song	218
One More Lullaby	234
Take It Easy	252
They Are Falling All around Me	272
Sometimes Not Often Enough	288
On the Other Side	300
Goodbye	314
The Healing Power of Love	328
Michael Callen's Legacy: A Conclusion	338
Bibliography	353

Acknowledgments

I found my way into this project quite by accident. As a doctoral student at the University of Virginia, I took a course called "Music and Sexuality" with music scholar Fred Maus, who became my dissertation advisor, dear friend, and trusted mentor. During the Fall 2010 semester, I searched the literature for a potential seminar paper topic that would synthesize my interests in popular music, queer studies, ethnography, archival work, and accessible scholarly writing. After observing that very little seemed to have been written about music and HIV/AIDS, especially after the early 2000s, I compiled some existing research in the various fields that comprise HIV/AIDS studies, especially HIV/AIDS and the arts, and began to read. Again and again, I saw the name Michael Callen in footnotes and parenthetical asides. Always acknowledged as an important force in AIDS activism and lauded as a gifted singer-songwriter, Callen was conspicuously absent from what I call "The Master Narrative of AIDS Activism," which is dominated by the AIDS Coalition to Unleash Power (ACT UP), sometimes at the expense of other figures and organizations with very different aims.

A self-professed YouTube junkie, I scoured the site for music videos, live performances, and interviews, anything that might give me some context, history, and information, about this mystery man. YouTube user BettyByte had uploaded a number of clips featuring Callen's activism and music, including an intriguing segment of an interview in which Callen poignantly asked the camera, "What ever happened to our great gay imagination?" My curiosity piqued, I sent BettyByte a message and soon received what I would come to know as the arch response style of Michael Callen's surviving partner, musical collaborator, and executor of the Callen estate, Richard Dworkin. Eagerly, I wrote back like a dutiful graduate student, introducing myself and the nature of my project. Soon, I boarded a train from Charlottesville to New York City to meet Richard and discuss Michael's work. In many important respects, this is a book about human relationships and love. And it simply would not exist without Richard.

An accomplished drummer in his own right, Richard has played for decades with The Microscopic Septet and a number of blues, jazz, and rock musicians ranging from the relatively obscure like Buena Vista (a San Francisco-based trio of gay men who sang Motown, R&B, and soul covers) to rock singer-songwriter Alex Chilton (1950–2010), R&B legend Nona Hendryx, and many others. Over the years, ours became an important professional relationship as Richard facilitated access to people and materials that would shape this book. He also graciously shared his private archive of home videos, unreleased recordings, photographs, and memories of Michael. Now, Richard is a close and cherished friend with whom I still share dinners of take-out Chinese and Pepperidge Farm cookies when I am in New York, and lively conversations about gay history, the politics of HIV/AIDS, and our shared love of music over social media when I am not.

In the summer of 2013, Richard invited me to a fundraiser for the Callen-Lorde Community Health Center called "Walk on the Wild Side" at the Central Park Zoo. During our subway ride, we chatted about HIV/AIDS, Michael's music, and the direction of my research. He grew quiet, and I decided to let the moment breathe, trusting my instincts rather than my training in ethnographic methods. After a few minutes, he touched my hand and, with tears in his eyes, said, "We have been waiting for someone to tell this story." As I would discover over the years, the wounds of the AIDS crisis remain tender for Michael's chosen family. Likewise, members of his biological family had been repeatedly mistreated by reporters who, as Barry Callen, Michael's older brother, told me, wanted to manipulate the family and capture their tears for the camera. Those who knew Michael fiercely protect him and his legacy. Through Richard, I met people who knew, loved, and worked with Michael. Almost everyone I contacted graciously and enthusiastically agreed to be interviewed in person, over the phone, via Skype and social media, and email; to read drafts of this book; and to share their stories, talents, pictures, videos, and other mementos of Michael. In alphabetical order, they are: Jon Arterton, Richard Berkowitz, John Bucchino, Robert Butler, Barry Callen, Richard Dworkin, Aurelio Font, Jim Fouratt, Mindy Schull Gillert, Joel Jason, Buddy Johnston, Grant King, Marsha Malamet, Holly Near, Tim Miller, Suede, Douglas Sadownick, Sarah Schulman, Joseph Sonnabend, Sean Strub, Terry Tincher, and Cliff Townsend. Their willingness to trust me to tell Michael's story is a gift I treasure. I, too, am fiercely protective of Michael's legacy.

Finally, I would be remiss if I didn't acknowledge the network of people in my life who have supported, encouraged, challenged, and loved me at every step on my circuitous way. My parents, Linda and Anthony Jones—sometimes I wonder what y'all think about this wandering-wondering, opinionated, musical, verbose child you produced, but at the end of the day, you've been by my side through every twist and turn. I love you both more than I can say.

My sisters Bret Walden, Ben Phillip, Alex Howle, and Eric Martin (1978–2018, I miss you every day). The Cville Gaggle: Mike Hill, Tim Lyons, Ben Blackman, Jake Treskovich. My fellow PhDIVAS: Emily Gale, Carrie Allen Tipton, Nancy Riley, Liz Ozment. The UVA MusGrads and MusGradAlumni and the graduate students in musicology at UGA, especially Josh Bedford, CJ Komp, and Mary Helen Hoque. My Ohio queer kids: Mason Schmikla, Abigail Karr, Darryn Edwards, Joshua Jones, who reminded me every day of the importance of intergenerational queer bonds; my "visiting" academic family: Allison Wanger and Sara Marzioli, who kept me sane during those difficult contingent years at Miami University of Ohio.

The faaaaabulous editorial and creative team at punctum books, who believed in this project from proposal to publication — Vincent and Eileen, thank you both from the bottom of my heart.

My mentor, musicology hero, and friend Susan Thomas — it's been a long road since that MA thesis on Rufus Wainwright! I wouldn't be the scholar, teacher, and person I am without you. I don't tell you that often enough, but it's the truth.

Fred Maus, my PhD advisor who fought for my research on music and HIV/AIDS because he believed in it and believed in me. Thank you.

The fiercely loyal Jana Braziel and Nadine Hubbs — thank you both for your continued advocacy and support. Jacky Avila, Richard Berkowitz, and Sean Strub graciously provided feedback on an early draft of this manusript. The musicology faculty at the University of Georgia and the music faculty at University of Virginia who helped mold this first-generation student into a musicologist. My former colleagues at the Institute for Women's Studies at the University of Georgia and the Department of Global and Intercultural Studies at Miami University of Ohio; and my new colleagues as St. Francis Episcopal School in Houston — Thanks, y'all!

Kaye Chastain, you taught me to love language back in Jasper, GA; Faye Kesler introduced me to musicology at Berry College; Ivan Frazier helped me understand musicmaking as an embodied experience; and David Haas doesn't know this, but I have framed in my house a music history exam he graded when I was an very lost, overwhelmed undergraduate transfer student at UGA and was seriously considering throwing in the towel on college completely. His short note praising my essay on the development of the orchestra after Wagner turned me around. The small things really do stick with us.

There are more baristas and bartenders than I can remember, all around the country, who kept the coffee coming while I wrote and rewrote, then poured wine while I stressed about finding a publisher and worried about being taken seriously as an academic once I left my contingent faculty position. Sometimes a stranger makes the best listener.

Joan Clawford (2000–2020), my beloved kitty companion, who moved from Georgia to Virginia to New York to Georgia to Ohio and finally to Texas. Meow.

Finally, all the scholars who work in contingent positions and outside academic institutions. Contingency sucks. It is a cancer, eating away the bones of the academy. Contingency is a bad neoliberal solution to a complex neoliberal problem. It's abusive, and I am in awe of the brilliant work done under conditions most inhumane. We are more than tenure-track job titles, or their absence. We are more than our CVs. We are more than cover letters that get tossed out because of a typo. We are more than tears spilled in fear and frustration. We are more than interchangeable bodies to teach classes according to the numbers on an administrative spreadsheet. The system is so deeply broken. Higher ed is burning. Persevere in your work. Find better options, pay, and locations. There are so many more ways to be a thinker, writer, and scholar than graduate school trains you to imagine — which is, perhaps, the most bitter irony. But, no matter what, do not let the machine grind you to dust.

I feel like one of those Academy Award winners who can't stop babbling, even as the orchestra strikes up and they grab the crook to yank me from the stage. So, thank you with love, gratitude, and music.

Matthew J. Jones, PhD
August 2020
Houston, TX

Nothing's lost forever. In this world, there is a kind of painful progress. Longing for what we've left behind and dreaming ahead.

At least I think that's so.

Harper Pitt (Tony Kusher's Angels in America*)*

*This book is dedicated to Dickie D,
and All the Ones Who Aren't Here*

*And to Linda and Anthony Jones, Kaye Chastain,
and Eric C. Martin (1978–2018)*

PREFACE

I Almost Missed the Epidemic

I'm not being coy or cagey. As an accident of age and geography, I more or less missed those years between 1981 and 1996 commonly described as the "AIDS crisis" in the US. I was born in 1978 and grew up in Jasper, a rural North Georgia town with a population, circa 1980, of 1,556, nestled in the Appalachian foothills of Pickens County (population, circa 1980, 11,625). When the Centers for Disease Control and Prevention (CDC) in Atlanta noticed the first cases of pneumocystis pneumonia (PCP), which is "almost exclusively limited to severely immunosuppressed patients," and Kaposi's sarcoma (KS), a typically benign skin cancer, among "previously healthy homosexual male[s]," I was toddling around my parents' small living room.[1] My first memory of AIDS is a *Reader's Digest* cover that, retrospectively, I know came from 1987. At the time, however, AIDS was little more than a fire-engine red word emblazoned on the cover of a magazine that, at nine years old, I didn't read, and at forty-two, I still don't. HIV/AIDS only became meaningful, tangible, and real later.

1 Centers for Disease Control and Prevention, "Pneumocystis Pneumonia — Los Angeles," *Morbidity and Mortality Weekly Report* 30, no. 21, 5 June 1981, 1–3; Centers for Disease Control and Prevention, "A Cluster of Kaposi's Sarcoma and Pneumocystis Pneumonia among Homosexual Male Residents of Los Angeles and Orange Counties, California," *Morbidity and Mortality Weekly Report* 32, no. 23, 18 June 1982, 305–7.

In the spring of 1993, my eighth-grade class at Pickens County Middle School was segregated by sex then herded into separate classrooms for the annual sex education program, a three-day experiment in terror featuring slideshows of worst-case nineteenth-century scenarios: sex organs gushing thick yellow-green discharge; festering chancres, boils, and blisters; the necrotized ruins of untreated syphilis; and stern admonitions against indiscriminate sex, equated with different kinds of disease and death. I don't know what the young women in my school learned — whether they were told to fear their sex and their reproductive capacities; to guard their virtue against the voracious appetites of their male peers; to use condoms or take birth control — but given the extraordinary rates of teen pregnancy in my hometown and others like it, I assume that they, like us boys, learned very little practical information. I was left with some psychic scars after a freewheeling Q&A. Amid the nervous laughter of adolescent boys giggling into knowledge of themselves, I sat, front row center, eyes fixed on the blackboard awaiting the inevitable. From the back of the room, a boy I once kissed on the elementary school playground asked, "What about queers? What do they do?" Rubbing both hands along the sides of the lectern like a Baptist preacher revving up a salvation machine, the mouse-haired representative of public health scanned the room as she delivered her stern homily: "Boys, whatever do you do, do not *choose* to be gay. You will get AIDS. And you will die." And that was that.

The next year, I met my first boyfriend, a high-school senior who played trombone in the marching band, wrote poetry, chain-smoked cheap cigarettes, and led me to two life-altering realizations: how to kiss and how I liked my coffee (cream, no sugar). Our relationship was innocent, sexless, and magical, but as often happens in a homophobic culture, it was stamped out. My parents forbade me to see him ever again. He graduated, moved to Atlanta, then relocated to Miami with a new lover. I know that he came back to Jasper twice. Once, I caught a glimpse of him standing in a crowd during an outdoor community festival. Over the crest of a nearby hill, I saw him turn and leave just as I finished my trombone solo in our high-school jazz band's funkless rendition of Blood, Sweat, and Tears's "Spinning Wheel." On the day I graduated high school in the spring of 1997, he covertly grabbed my hand, kissed my cheek, and whispered "I love you" before disappearing into the buzzing hive of families crawling on the bleachers in the hot Georgia sun. In 1999, I received a phone call from a mutual acquaintance who told me that the first boy I loved had been in the hospital with pneumonia and had died. One of his last acts was to instruct this friend to track me down and to send his love to me. Though he had crossed my mind many times, I never reached out to him after he left Jasper. I suppose on some level I took life, living, for granted, perhaps imagining that our paths would cross someday in our old hometown and that we'd grab a beer, catch up, and reminisce. The shock of his death left me numbed and disoriented. This was the first major loss of my young queer life, someone my age, someone gay, someone I knew intimately and loved fiercely. I hung up the phone and collapsed into my sorrow. A few days later, I attended his funeral and was struck by the silence. Southern funerals are somber occasions, to be sure, but they also occasion loquacity. People tell stories and share fond memories of the dead over piles of food brought in by friends, family, and neighbors. His family spoke in hushed, euphemistic tones, offering only cryptic clues about his sudden death. As a gay man who grew up in the shadow of the epidemic, I intuited from his sunken cheeks and sallow complexion — the stigmata of plague — all that his shame-silenced family would not say. He had died of AIDS.

My adult life has been fundamentally and undeniably shaped by the ongoing global AIDS pandemic, as it is for most gay men of my generation. In the back of even our most liberated minds, each love affair or liaison cues a little voice that sings out against the grain like a Liza Minnelli song, *"Maybe this time…?"* The losses are innumerable. According to the World Health Organization, almost forty-million people have died of AIDS-related illness since the early 1980s.[2] So many, in fact, that the largest piece of public memorial art ever created — the NAMES Project AIDS Memorial Quilt, a fifty-four ton tapestry of more than 48,000 panels representing more than 100,000 individuals, or less than twenty percent of all AIDS deaths — can no longer be displayed in its entirety in one place.

Love Don't Need a Reason: The Life and Music of Michael Callen represents one effort to grapple with AIDS from the perspective of a trained historian and cultural critic of popular music, sexuality, and politics. It tells the story of Michael Callen (1955–1993), a white, college-educated, cisgender gay man from a Midwestern working-class background who literally changed the way we have sex in an (ongoing) epidemic.

Throughout the research and writing of this book, I consulted publicly available collections, most importantly The Michael Callen Papers at the The New York City LGBT Community Center National History Archives. The Michael Callen Papers (henceforth, MCP) comprise thirty-two boxes of paper materials, ranging from high school theater programs to book drafts, mountains of medical bills and hundreds of letters. There are forty-two video tapes of media appearances, live performances, speeches, news reports, and activist videos; and 317 audio recordings of answering machine messages, taped interviews and phone conversations, rehearsal tapes, demos, live and studio recordings. I wanted to pour over every item while I was in the archive. However, during the period of my research, the Center's archive was only open to scholars for two hours a night, two nights a week. Because I was a graduate student in Virginia, living on a meager teaching stipend, I had to take on extra teaching duties at the University of Virginia as well as evening and weekend work with high school and community musical theater programs to save enough money to temporarily relocate to New York from Charlottesville in order to work with the collection in a way that was time and cost effective.

---

2   UNAIDS, "Global HIV & AIDS Statistics — 2020 Fact Sheet," http://www.unaids.org/en/resources/fact-sheet.

Throughout my research, I have been unable to secure research and travel funding, whether during my employment at two major universities or as an "independent" scholar. I raise the issue of economics and research not out of bitterness or self-pity but because I learned from it. I learned what institutions value when they dole out research grants, and I learned what I value — telling Michael's story, no matter what obstacles present themselves. I also learned that Michael, too, struggled to fund his own artistic projects, piecing together the budget to record two albums piecemeal from paid speaking and singing gigs, a day job, ingenuity, and the kindness of supportive friends, family, and strangers. Queer history and HIV/AIDS history remain DIY endeavors.

In the archive, I had to make strategic decisions. Using my iPhone 6S, I scanned every document in all thirty-two boxes, literally tens of thousands of pages. I opted to watch only videos labeled as musical performances since a single two-hour tape would gobble up an entire night of valuable scanning time. Likewise, I only listened to audio recordings of musical performances, scanning documents and pausing to make notes on the evolution of Michael's musical style as well as audience banter, song information, and set lists. I did sometimes savor what Maryanne Deyer calls "the potential of the thing that is paper," the materiality of the materials: a notebook with missing pages and ghostly grooves left behind from whatever had been written on top of them, and forty-year-old letters, typed, folded, touched, read and reread, annotated with pencil as Michael composed his reply — those marks now fading.[3]

I also consulted private archives — though that word seems somehow too formal for the array of cherished, quirky things people who knew Michael shared with me: home videos, photographs, letters, diaries, scrapbooks, articles from now-defunct

---

3 Maryanne Dyer, "Papered Over, or Some Observations on Materiality and Archival Method," in *Out of the Closet, Into the Archives: Researching Sexual Histories*, eds. Amy L. Stone and Jamie Cantrell (Albany: SUNY Press, 2015), 65–95.

magazines, sex toys, kitchen gadgets, and, of course, anecdotes and memories. There were what Ann Cvetkovich calls "archives of feelings," of joy, love, hope, anger, and trauma.[4] Cvetkovich writes that trauma "serves as a point of entry into the vast archive of feelings, the many forms of love, rage, intimacy, grief, shame, and more that are part of the vibrancy of queer cultures."[5] Trauma's unusual archive consists of materials that "in pointing to trauma's ephemerality, are themselves frequently ephemeral. [...] personal memories, which can be recorded in oral and video testimonies, memoires, letters, and journals. [...] objects whose relation to trauma might seem arbitrary but for the fact that they are invested with emotional, and even sentimental, value."[6] These objects hum with feeling. For me, a member of the generation after Michael's, they provided entry into a gay world that was lost because of AIDS. For the people who shared these objects, they were reminders of a collective trauma — the loss of friends, lovers, chosen families, and entire ways of life that they had worked to build in the 1970s.

While archival research and close listening are important components of my work on Michael Callen, archives do not tell the whole story. To balance and contextualize these fragmented pieces of Michael's life, I conducted extensive oral history interviews with his friends, family, and fellow musicians. My conversations with different narrators took place in a variety of locations, some physical, including living rooms, kitchens, cafes, restaurants, gay bars, and around the piano at Uncle Charlies (where I played on Wednesdays and Sundays), The Monster, and The Duplex in New York City; and others remote, over the phone, Skype, email, or Google Voice.

Oral history has long been a central technique for doing queer history. Because they "often go unmentioned in mainstream historical texts," Boyd and Ramírez argue that queer oral

---

4 Ann Cvetkovich, *An Archive of Feelings: Trauma, Sexuality, and Lesbian Public Cultures* (Durham: Duke University Press, 2003).
5 Ibid., 7.
6 Ibid.

histories have both "an overtly political function and a liberating quality."[7] Because they are "intense interactions," queer oral histories often lead to bonds of friendship or political commitment, which has certainly been the case for me. Queer oral histories also make "historical and generational discontinuities explicit" since "across all racial, national, religious, and economic groups," LGBTQ+ folks experience "different degrees of both acceptance and rejection: within our blood families, at our employment sites, within our particular neighborhood, town, city, school, and so on."[8] Across various groups, there are important differences in language and rhetoric, inclusivity, and comfort with explicit discussions of sex and eroticism. The knowledge produced in queer oral history "can be painful or uncomfortable in unpredictable ways [because queer narrators] risk opening themselves up to vulnerability or trauma" and the researcher can be traumatized by hearing stories of disease, violence, and death.[9] As an HIV-negative researcher writing a story about HIV/AIDS, I remained keenly aware that these narrators were reliving not only Michael's life but also his death, and that his specific death occurred in the general context of many, many others — a cultural trauma Dagmawi Woubshet describes as a "compounding poetics of loss."[10]

Trust is also a necessary component of queer oral history, a topic Esther Newton addresses in her classic essay, "My Best Informant's Dress."[11] The shared experiences of same-sex desire, homophobia, and coming out; hiding in plain sight and learning the rhetorical-gestural languages of cruising; networks of friend-

7   Nan Alamilla Boyd and Horacio N. Roque Ramírez, "Introduction: Close Encounters," in *Bodies of Evidence: The Queer Practice of Oral History*, eds. Nan Alamilla Boyd and Horacio N. Roque Ramírez (Oxford: Oxford University Press, 2012), 1.
8   Ibid., 13.
9   Ibid., 8.
10 Dagmawi Woubshet, *The Calendar of Loss: Race, Sexuality, and Mourning in the Early AIDS Era* (Baltimore: Johns Hopkins University Press, 2015).
11 Esther Newton, "My Best Informant's Dress: The Erotic Equation in Fieldwork," in *Margaret Meade Made Me Gay: Personal Essays, Public Ideas* (Durham: Duke University Press, 2000), 243–57.

ship and eroticism; diva worship of the same starlets; and the shared sense that AIDS cost us living links tour own shared past: all these variables cultivate "intimacy-as-trust with both narrator and researcher being more to one another than is the case during an exchange between two oral history collaborators who simply do not understand what it means to occupy similar positions."[12]

Because trauma is capricious and feelings are fragile, I approached with neither a journalist's hard-hitting agenda nor the cumbersome juggling act of the anthropological anxiety over emic (from within) and etic (from without). I preferred to *talk* rather than interrogate, to let the conversations go where they wanted to, guided by the caprices of memory and the dynamic between myself and the oral history narrator. I had to earn trust in order to gain access to the information that I wanted, but at the end of the day, I was also the one poised to benefit most from this work — whether in terms of economic, cultural, or forms of capital. I am, after all, the author of this book.

A refrain common to all of my interviews with gay men, who were the bulk of my informants, went something like this: *all of my friends from that period are dead.* I specifically remember talking with one of Michael's closest friends, performance artist Tim Miller, in 2011 when I drove him to the airport in DC after a tour stop in Charlottesville. "Talking about Michael," he said, "I always have to wonder 'why me? Why did I survive? Why am I HIV-negative?'" The members of The Flirtations, a gay *a cappella* group Michael co-founded in 1987, spoke openly about the trauma of losing not one but two members to AIDS — founding tenor TJ Meyers died in 1990, just after the group finished their first album, before Michael passed away in 1993. Holly Near told me about speaking to Michael from the road as he inched closer to death, telling him stories of her travels until he fell asleep and she hung up the receiver then wondering whether each call would be the last.

I never met Michael myself, but I've come to know him through years of reading and re-reading his words, talking to

12 Boyd and Ramírez, "Introduction," 9.

those who knew him well, and listening to his music. For three years, I lived in Oxford, Ohio and taught at Miami University of Ohio, the school from which his mother, father, sister, and brother all graduated. Oxford is just one town away from Hamilton, where Michael was raised, and about an hour from Rising Sun, Indiana, where he was born. This physical proximity to his hometown and birthplace allowed me to walk the same streets that Michael wandered; to see the halls of his high school; and to thumb the pages of yearbooks and hometown newspapers for traces of the life he lived before becoming one of the most important AIDS activists of the 1980s. I've often felt something like Michael's spirit or essence as I worked. I've transcribed his songs to play on piano and guitar and sung them in my apartment and, on occasion, in piano bars and coffee houses. In short, I've become friends with Michael in my own way. Consequently, I refer to him as Michael throughout this book. This decision may irk some readers as too informal or casual, too familiar for objectivity or analytical distance. To such criticisms I can only respond by saying that I fell in love with Michael's music, his writing, his activism, and his personality. Even beyond the grave, he remains, in the words of his friend and songwriting partner Marsha Malamet, "a total charmer." Michael's family of choice was huge, welcoming, and diverse, and through this work, I've been welcomed into that family. For that, I will be forever grateful.

Finally, working on this book demanded that I confront and reflect upon my own relationship to HIV/AIDS as a gay man who grew up in the shadow of the epidemic; whose notions of sex, intimacy, and gay identity continue to be shaped by closeness to and distance from AIDS (my apologies to Paul Attinello for the gratuitous play on the title of his important essay about AIDS and music); and whose survival in the age of AIDS can be traced directly back to Michael's activist work in the early 1980s.[13] Today, I am HIV-negative, on PrEP, healthy, and employed in a teaching

---

13 Paul Attinello, "Closeness and Distance: Songs about AIDS," in *Queering the Popular Pitch*, eds. Sheila Whiteley and Jennifer Rycenga (New York: Routledge, 2006), 221–34.

position outside of academia that affords and enables me to tell this particular story in this specific way. I hope that this book represents a responsible use of my privileges — a dutiful effort to preserve one important part of our queer history — promiscuous sex, sissies, plague, and all. Its flaws are a reflection of my own. Following the advice of a popular blog, I have tried to "Write Where It Hurts." I make no apologies for being "too close" to my subject, for loving Michael and the circle of friends I have made through him.

Audre Lorde encourages us to find power in the erotic, to give up "being satisfied with suffering and self-negation, and with the numbness which so often seems like their only alternative in our society."[14] I do not know if Michael ever read those same words, but they capture the essence of his attitude toward liberation for LGBTQ+ folks and for People with AIDS. Queer history and lifewriting are deeply personal endeavors. A major insight of intersectional feminist work is that "the personal is political." So much of our gay history was lost to AIDS, so many LGBTQ+ stories remain untold. That is personal and political to me. The AIDS crisis constitutes one of the largest cultural traumas of modern history but has seldom been acknowledged as such. This is beginning to change even as our communities still grapple with its losses. Survivors endure erasure by subsequent generations who are disconnected from their own collective pasts by neoliberal, normalizing agendas — a point articulated beautifully in recent books by Sarah Schulman and Jack Halberstam.[15] And young LGBTQ+ folks continue to live in externally imposed ignorance of themselves as people in history, as people with history, as people living history. One consequence of that ignorance is that feelings of isolation, shame, and loneliness felt by queer youth as the mature into their identities cross gen-

---

14 Audre Lorde, *Sister Outsider: Essays and Speeches by Audre Lorde* (Berkeley: Crossing Press, 2007), 58.
15 Sarah Schulman, *The Gentrification of the Mind: Witness to a Lost Generation* (Berkeley: University of California Press, 2013); Jack Halberstam, *Trans*: A Quick and Quirky Guide to Gender Variability* (Berkeley: University of California Press, 2018).

erational lines. Another is the troubling rise in HIV infections among young LGBTQ+ folks, especially young gay men of color. One of the legacies of Michael Callen's activism and his music is that he showed us "how to have gay, life-affirming sex, satisfy our emotional needs, and stay alive." It has been a humbling privilege and a labor of love to tell his story, and I hope that in doing so, this book continues Michael's mission.

Fig. 1. Michael Callen, Lake District, England (c. 1984). Photo by Richard Dworkin. © Richard Dworkin.

1

Kerosene Lantern: An Introduction

You do commit yourself,
Take the jagged knife
And cut away the bitter fruit
And listen to the voices saying,
"Remember not to hurt yourself.
— Judy Mayhan

You probably have not heard of singer-songwriter, author, and AIDS activist Michael Callen (1955–1993), yet like most people you probably benefit from his activist work every day. His accomplishments are impressive, but like him, they have been largely relegated to the footnotes of history. This is due to many factors: changes in the management of HIV infection over the past forty years, activist fatigue, trauma, and the sheer scope of the epidemic. It is also a result of what Christopher Reed and Christopher Castiglia have memorably called "de-generational un-remembering" and what Sarah Schulman describes as "the gentrification of the mind."[1]

It can be difficult for people who did not live through the US AIDS crisis (1981-1996) to fully grasp how *little* anyone knew about AIDS in the first few years of the epidemic and how fear of the unknown fueled hatred and discrimination toward people with AIDS (PWAS). Causal theories abounded as scientists and doctors tried to understand the increasing number of fatally sick young gay men among their clients. Was AIDS caused by environmental factors, drug use, chemicals in food, or a novel new virus? Conspiracy theories about AIDS as a government-made bioweapon proliferated, and conservatives rolled out their faithful, Christian standard: God's revenge against a sin. When Michael was diagnosed with immune deficiency in 1981, the term "AIDS" had not yet been named nor had the human immunodeficiency virus (HIV) been discovered. Rumors of a deadly gay cancer spread like a rhizome through urban gay America, initially primarily centered in New York, San Francisco, and Los Angeles, while most of the country carried on as usual, oblivious to an emergent epidemic. Michael, like so many others, was infected with HIV before he, or anyone else, even knew that a

---

[1] Christopher Castiglia and Christopher Reed, *If Memory Serves: Gay Men, AIDS, and the Promise of the Queer Past* (Minneapolis: University of Minnesota Press, 2012); Sarah Schulman, *The Gentrification of the Mind: Witness to a Lost Imagination* (Berkeley: University of California Press, 2012). Castiglia and Reed write, "The sweeping calls to unremember targeted the generation hardest hit by the onset of AIDS, cutting that generation off from younger gays and lesbians who might continue the visionary work undertaken in the late 1960s and 1970s. We call this temporal isolation de-generation. [...] We call the phenomenon of distancing the past "unremembering" for two reasons. Above all, the act of distancing the past is a perpetual process, not a once-and-for-all forgetting. [...] The other reason [...] has to do with the forms of temporal distancing that have accompanied the traumatic losses occasioned by AIDS and the policed conservatism that followed on the heels of those losses" (9-10). Schulman writes, "Gentrification is a process that hides the apparatus of domination from the dominant themselves. Spiritually, gentrification is the removal of the dynamic mix that defines urbanity — the familiar interaction of different kinds of people creating ideas together" (27). I will return to these ideas in the conclusion.

sexually active gay man (SAGM) could get anything worse than chlamydia, gonorrhea, herpes, or syphilis from sex, and of these, only herpes was more than a nuisance thanks to the development of antibiotics. It was a naive and ignorant time, in the fullest sense of those words.

HIV seemed to come out of nowhere, though we now know that it likely jumped from simian to human hosts in the early twentieth century, its spread facilitated by political unrest throughout the African continent, new forms of rapid, global transportation, and the loosening of sexual mores in the wake of a global sexual revolution.[2] HIV arrived in a perfect storm of circumstances then caught humanity unaware in the early 1980s. As primary care doctors struggled to treat ailing patients who died with frightening rapidity and researchers scratched their heads in disbelief, neoconservative governments led by US President Ronald Reagan (1911–2004) and British Prime Minister Margaret Thatcher (1925–2013) slashed budgets for scientific research and public

---

2   For an excellent history of HIV, see Victoria Harden's *AIDS at 30: A History* (Lincoln: Potomac Books, 2012). The classic "in the moment" account remains Randy Shilts's *And the Band Played On: Politics, People, and the AIDS Epidemic* (1987; rpt. New York: St. Martin's Press, 2007), though the book has been critiqued by Douglas Crimp ("Randy Shilts' Miserable Failure," in *Melancholia and Moralism: Essays on Queer Politics and AIDS* [Cambridge: MIT Press, 2009], 117–28) for its reliance on a false and ultimately homophobic narrative about "Patient Zero," Canadian flight attendant Gaëtan Dugas (1953–1984) who was (mis)credited as the man who brought AIDS to North America. Retrospective autopsy of preserved tissue samples found that Robert Rayford, who died in 1969, had HIV and likely died of pneumocystis pneumonia or another opportunistic infection. Furthermore, Dugas actually volunteered his detailed sexual history to CDC investigators and met with them several times for an important early cluster study which demonstrated that HIV/AIDS was transmitted via sex and bodily fluids. David France's *How to Survive a Plague: The Inside Story of How Citizens and Science Tamed AIDS* (New York: Knopf, 2016) is an excellent activist history and companion piece to the documentary of the same name. And there are dozens of AIDS activist memoirs, including Richard Berkowitz's *Stayin' Alive: The Invention of Safe Sex* (New York: Basic Books, 2003); Sean Strub's *Body Counts: A Memoir of Politics, Sex, AIDS, and Survival* (New York: Scribner Books, 2014); and Paul Monette's *Borrowed Time: An AIDS Memoir* (San Diego: Harcourt, Brace, and Jovanovich Publishers, 1988).

health programs. Budget cuts and bureaucracy blocked access to crucial funding for research at the exact moment when *more* money was necessary, and the blood of millions of people who died of AIDS-related illness stains their legacies.

From his initial diagnosis until his death in 1993, Michael remained skeptical of the medical and political establishment's rush to embrace the "single-virus theory" to explain AIDS. Initially, his skepticism drew its inspiration from the feminist healthcare movement of the 1970s. Feminist healthcare advocates empowered patients to become experts in their own care, to ask difficult questions about medical treatment and diagnoses of their doctors, and to push back against conventional wisdom by educating themselves about their bodies and women's health concerns. Such resistance was necessary due to medical science's deeply entrenched misogyny and its long historical reliance on male cadavers for research and male subjects for medical studies. Later, communities of color would launch their own critiques of the whitewashing of scientific and medical research, resulting in important discoveries about rates of illness and disease as well as drug therapies and interactions in the bodies of different racial groups in addition to the role of social, cultural, and economic factors in the overall picture of patient health.

In 1982, Michael joined one of the first support groups for gay men with AIDS where he met Larry Goldstein. Having been diagnosed with Kaposi's sarcoma (KS, a typically benign skin cancer found in older Mediterranean men) in 1978 and because KS was one of the hallmark opportunistic infections (OIs) of AIDS, Goldstein was retrospectively diagnosed as having AIDS by 1979. So, he had been living with AIDS for four years — already a long-term survivor, that is, someone who had been living with AIDS for more than three years.[3] Michael witnessed with his own eyes,

---

3 Michael told this story to NPR's Terry Gross in a *Fresh Air* interview on November 16, 1990 (henceforth, MC and TG [1990]), and it appears in Michael Callen's *Surviving AIDS* (New York: Harper Perennial, 1990), 66. Given that the latency period, after the initial acute phase of HIV infection, can last as long as ten years, Goldstein could have been infected as early as 1969. Goldstein lived for nine years, though Michael was unsure if his death was

very early in the AIDS crisis, that long-term survival was possible, that AIDS was not always immediately fatal. These early experiences later became, in his own words, an obsession.[4] In an era when knowledge about AIDS was partial and changing every day, it was imperative to Michael that PWAs stay abreast of the latest medical developments and that he and other activists disseminate information using broadcast and print media like the *People With AIDS Coalition Newsline* newsletter, the robust gay press, and old-fashioned word-of-mouth as well as to mainstream media outlets. Michael empowered PWAs to become their own experts, to self-advocate, to question authority and knowledge, and to demand that their physicians explore every alternative.

Michael's physician, renowned researcher Joseph Sonnabend, ran a private clinic for gay men, among whom he diagnosed extraordinary rates of chlamydia, gonorrhea, herpes, parasites and amoebas, and hepatitis. Based on first-hand knowledge of his patients' medical histories, Sonnabend hypothesized that repeated, chronic infection by common viruses and bacteria, combined with poor sleep and nutrition, recreational drug use, and other factors, including perhaps a novel virus, suppressed the immune system over time and wondered whether what would soon be called "AIDS" was the end result of such chronic damage. He also wondered if, given rest and time, the immune system might recover. He called his a "multifactorial theory,"

---

related to AIDS or some other cause. He writes: "Although I lost touch with him, I learned through friends that Larry Goldstein had died in 1988. But none of them knew whether he died of AIDS. For all I know, he was hit by a cab! New York City has always been potentially lethal" (69n3).

Throughout this period, the Centers for Disease Control and Prevention periodically updated their clinical definition for AIDS, sometimes based on new data and sometimes due to direct-action protest by activist. In general, AIDS has been defined by the presence of HIV in the blood, a T-Cell (CD4 Helper Cell) count below 200 cells per cubic millimeter of blood (1000 is the norm for an unimpaired immune system), and the presence of a variety of opportunistic infections including pneumocystis pneumonia and Kaposi's sarcoma.

4 Callen, *Surviving AIDS*, 10.

and it inspired Michael. Whatever the underlying cause or causes of this epidemic of immune deficiency, Michael believed that

> gay men needed to be warned in no uncertain terms that if they continued to pursue lifestyles that abused their immune systems, they might die. Gay men would have to radically alter their sexual behavior. And this impossible task would have to be accomplished virtually overnight. Someone needed to issue the call to arms for a *second* sexual revolution.[5]

In November 1982, Michael, Sonnabend, and Richard Berkowitz, another of Sonnabend's patients, published "We Know Who We Are" in the *New York Native,* a New York City gay newspaper, and the paper's editor gave the article a subtitle, "Two Gay Men Declare War on Promiscuity." The publication of "We Know Who We Are" resulted in a "fire storm of protest."[6]

Michael also held views that were, at various times, considered heretical by the AIDS establishment. He was a critic of Dr. Anthony Fauci (then a clinical researcher at the National Institute of Allergy and Infectious Disease at the National Institutes of Health) and of several powerful HIV/AIDS organizations and activists groups, including Gay Men's Health Crisis (GMHC). The discovery of HIV in 1984 turned the tide of scientific research against the multifactorial theory. Even as Michael was skeptical of the single-virus theory he, like many other PWAs, willingly cooperated with doctors and research scientists in their quests for treatments and a cure. A self-described "HIV factory," Michael's own HIV-rich blood was used in research to develop the first HIV antibody tests.[7]

---

5   Ibid., 6.
6   Ibid.
7   Michael Callen, "Are You Now, or Have You Ever Been," *People with AIDS Coalition Newsline,* January 1989, 34–36. At the end of Callen's editorial is a note from Joseph Sonnabend that reads, in part, "Michael Callen has AIDS. Michael Callen had cryptosporidiosis in 1983. His T-4 lymphocytes have been abnormal since 1982. He has had shingles, and he has had thrush since 1983. He has Kaposi's sarcoma. He is also HIV-seropositive — in fact, to such

Over the years, Michael's HIV skepticism became an albatross, a boon, and finally, a kind of stigma. Although he remained a leader in the AIDS movement until his death, and his influence is palpable into the present day, Michael faced marginalization and hostility from the emergent AIDS establishment for his "heretical" beliefs. As Michael recalled, "a GMCH board member referred to our 'vigilante impulsivity' and claimed that we were urging gay men to 'follow along in self-flagellation.'"[8] Michael saw his actions as a fight for his own life and the lives of other PWAs. As historians, scholars, documentarians, and activists begin to write the history of the first years of the epidemic, it is essential that Michael Callen's work be acknowledged, contextualized, and preserved.

As one of the first prominent PWAs in the US, Michael put his own human face on the epidemic at a time when fear, ignorance, and stigma surrounding AIDS lead to widespread panic. PWAs risked losing their jobs, their homes, and their friends and families should their illnesses be made public. Many PWAs went to great length (whether by choice or societal compulsion) to disguise their illness by putting makeup over visible KS lesions; to put on weight to offset the detrimental effects of wasting; to speak of their illness in euphemism; or to attribute their condition to another health problem. With a thoroughly Midwestern clarity of moral purpose and unwavering determination, Michael confronted AIDS directly. An effective orator and spokesperson for the AIDS Self-Empowerment Movement, he spoke and wrote with great passion and brutal candor about living with AIDS, and his words moved people. Michael appeared on local, regional, and national news media programs including *The Phil Donahue Show, Geraldo, Good Morning America, Fresh Air,* and *The Regis Philbin Show*; the nightly news programs of ABC, CBS, NBC, and PBS; Vito Russo's influential series *Our Time*; and dozens of promotional and informational videos about HIV/

---

a degree that his serum has been used as a control in developing tests. HIV is regularly and easily cultured from his blood" (36).

8 Callen, *Surviving AIDS*, 7.

AIDS for healthcare and activist organizations. He even made cameos as a "safer-sexpert" in several adult gay films![9] Like his friend and fellow activist from San Francisco, Bobbi Campbell (1952–1984), Michael was truly a 1980s "AIDS Poster Boy," though he more often felt like a trained, dancing bear who was expected to keep his mouth shut and play the distraught and pathetic PWA when the cameras were rolling.

In spite of tremendous personal risk, emotional strain, and vicious criticism, Michael fought for PWAs, sometimes at the expense of his own health and wellbeing. Michael exemplified an ethic of PWAs helping other PWAs, a self-empowerment movement focused on creating the community's own media, organizations, and research rather than looking for governmental intervention, as was later the goal of groups like ACT UP (the AIDS Coalition to Unleash Power).

A community organizer, Michael helped create and establish several important AIDS support service groups including Gay Men with AIDS (GMWA), People with AIDS Coalition, New York (PWAC-NY), the People with AIDS Health Group (with Joe Sonnabend and Tom Hannan), and the Community Research Initiative (CRI, with Sonnabend). CRI emerged "as a measure of [the] intense frustration [of PWAs and their physicians] with the failure of the Federal AIDS treatment research effort to find anything of value for people with AIDS."[10] As Michael explained to NPR's Terry Gross in 1990,

> Those of us living with AIDS were so frustrated that we came up with an idea that was radical in its simplicity. [...] We

---

9 In *The Gentrification of the Mind*, Schulman recounts a memory shared with her by dancer Scott Heron. She writes, "Scott Heron told me that the porn theater on Fourteenth Street and Third Avenue, which is now a CVS drugstore, used to have a loop of AIDS activist videos running in the skanky basement [...]. Scottie says that among all the porn loops in the basement booths, there was one clip of Michael Callen, one of the inventors of safe sex, talking about how he was going to beat AIDS, talking about his new book, *Surviving AIDS*" (55).
10 MC and TG (1990).

felt that our physicians, our community physicians who were actually keeping us alive on a daily basis [...] should group together with [PWAs] and other research experts to design our own clinical trials. [...] The advantage or the major difference between community-based research movement and the way drugs are tested here in America is that we believed that if PWAs have a say in designing the protocols, in saying what risks they are willing to take and what risks they are not willing to take, we will have better enrollment and better compliance with the protocols, which will mean that the scientific value of data generated by community-based research will be of a higher quality.[11]

He also worked alongside Mathilde Krim (1926–2018) and Joseph Sonnabend, co-founders of what would become the American Foundation for AIDS Research (AmFar) and participated in a few of ACT UP/New York's early direct-action protests. An architect of the AIDS Self-Empowerment Movement, Michael co-authored the PWA manifesto known as "The Denver Principles" (1983), and his moving testimony on behalf of the AIDS community brought a Congressional delegation to tears, prompting

---

11 Ibid. Michael further explained how CIR differed from federal research programs through their focus on the control and prevention of opportunistic infections, research into immune modulation, and their emphasis on informed consent. The "community-based research movement takes [informed consent] very seriously and ensures that people considering entering one of its trials know everything there is to know in simple, understandable language." In *Surviving AIDS,* he explained that "when we first proposed the idea of community-based research, everyone said that it was too ambitious, it couldn't be done. We were told that medical centers, with their monopoly on drug research, would never allow such upstart competition. Once again, skeptics have been proven wrong. There is now a network of more than forty community-based research centers in the United States, with similar organizations being set up in other countries. If the community-based research movement accomplishes nothing else, its successful conduct of the research that led to FDA approval of aerosolized pentamidine, for the prevention of pneumocystis pneumonia that is the number-one killer of people with AIDS, more than justifies the backbreaking effort it took to launch it" (10).

New York Representative Geraldine A. Ferraro to enter his remarks into the *Congressional Record*.[12] And he delivered speeches at AIDS rallies, gay pride events, and professional conferences around the world.

Michael wrote, co-authored, and edited three important books about AIDS. Widely considered the first safe-sex guide, *How to Have Sex in an Epidemic: One Approach* (1983) was written with fellow PWA Richard Berkowitz, whom he met through their mutual physician, Joseph Sonnabend. The booklet is noteworthy for its comprehensive risk-assessment approach, and its suggestion that gay men use condoms, which initially struck many gay men as absurd. Until then, condoms were seen as a tool for pregnancy prevention, something only straight people needed to worry about. However, gay men's willingness to engage in a great sexual-social revolution in the 1970s laid a foundation for sexual innovation that made them willing to adapt to new and changing conditions for pleasure.[13] The authors of *How to Have Sex in an Epidemic* said their methods would likely work no matter what one believed caused AIDS, and their revolutionary suggestion that gay men should use condoms to interrupt transmission of known infectious agents *prior* to the discovery of HIV continues to save lives in the twenty-first century. The "terrible triumvirate," as Michael, Richard Berkowitz, and Joe Sonnabend were called in the *New York Native*, has also been vindicated as doctors now recognize that comorbidities, history of disease (especially STIs), drug use, and number of partners — that is, multiple factors — shape an individual's risk for HIV infection or transmission and play a role in the overall health of PWAs.

Hope was central to Michael's activist ethos. He edited a two-volume series called *Surviving and Thriving with AIDS: Hints for the Newly Diagnosed* (1987, 1988) which contained articles

12 See Geraldine A. Ferraro, "The Trauma of Living with AIDS," *Congressional Record* 129, no. 69 (28 May 1983), http://michaelcallen.com/mikes-writing/congressional-record-on-aids/.
13 See Crimp's "How to Have Promiscuity in an Epidemic," in *Moralism and Melancholia*, 43–82.

about the latest mainstream and alternative treatments available to PWAs.[14] He also took a serious look at his own life as well as the lives of other long-term survivors he met in his travels and through his activist work. In 1990, Harper/Collins published Callen's *Surviving AIDS*, a memoir about his experience as a PWA that includes interviews with other long-term survivors. In the preface to that book, Callen attributed his survival to "luck, Classic Coke, and the love of a good man" as well as "good old-fashioned grit."[15] Jeffrey Escoffier complied an anthology of Michael's safe-sex writing called *In My Time: Essays on Sex, Science, and AIDS*, and it is regrettable that this collection has never been published. However, a manuscript copy of this anthology has been instrumental in my research for this book.

Finally, Michael was an accomplished singer, pianist, and songwriter. As a child in Hamilton, Ohio, he studied violin, sang in church and school choirs, and taught himself to play piano while starring in school musical theater productions. His efforts earned Michael a music scholarship to attend Boston University, though he dropped music to study English and Creative Writing. He continued to dream of being a performer and, after college, moved to New York City to pursue that goal in 1977. Inspired by the Women's Music movement, Michael intended to create gay music for gay male audiences, despite the admonishment of friends who assured him that commercial success was inevitable if only he would downplay his sexuality. Headstrong and possessed of a clear vision of himself as a gay artist, Michael refused to play it straight, even if fame and fortune eluded him as a consequence. He earned critical accolades for his performances at cabarets and piano bars around the city, fronted a short-lived a cappella group called Mike & the Headsets, and had a prolific period as a songwriter in the early 1980s when he completed many of the songs that would appear on his later studio albums, *Purple Heart* (1988) and *Legacy* (posthumous, 1996).

---

14 Michael Callen, ed., *Surviving and Thriving with AIDS: Hints for the Newly Diagnosed*, 2 vols., (New York: People with AIDS Coalition, Inc., 1987, 1988).
15 Callen, *Surviving AIDS*, 1–11.

In 1982, he formed Lowlife, a gay and lesbian rock-and-roll band, with his lover and drummer, Richard Dworkin, bassist Pamela Brandt (1947–2015), and guitarist Janet Cleary. Lowlife toured the East Coast for several years before disbanding in 1986. In 1987, Michael experienced a serious AIDS-related illness which forced him to confront the fact that he might die without leaving behind a record of his own songs. He went into the studio to record the critically acclaimed *Purple Heart,* which he and Richard Dworkin released on their own Significant Other Records in 1988. The album included his AIDS-themed songs "Living in Wartime," "How to Have Sex," and "Love Don't Need a Reason." He co-wrote the latter with Marsha Malamet and Peter Allen (1944–1992), and it became the official anthem of AIDS Walk charity events around the country. It endures as Callen's most well-known song and has been recorded by dozens of artists.

In 1987, Michael co-founded one of the most beloved gay acts of the era. The Flirtations toured the globe, released two albums before Michael's death (*The Flirtations* [1990] and *Live: Out on the Road* [1992], as well as the group's final effort, *Three* [1996]), and even appeared in Jonathan Demme's *Philadelphia* (1993). Additionally, The Flirts (as they were affectionately known) conducted workshops on issues like gayness, coming out, living with AIDS, multiculturalism, and diversity on college campuses, at high schools, and even at some elementary schools. As his health declined, Michael performed less often with the group, eventually announcing his retirement after a farewell performance at the historic Gay and Lesbian March on Washington in April 1993. During the last year of his life, Michael devoted his energy to recording vocal tracks for what he knew would be his final album. A sprawling two-disc tribute to his artistry, his gayness, and his politics, *Legacy* featured a panoply of luminaries from the worlds of gay and lesbian music including Cris Williamson, Holly Near, and The Flirtations alongside jazz giant Fred Hersch, synthesizer wunderkind Greg Wells, songwriter and pianist John Bucchino, and "The Mike-ettes," a trio of legendary backup singers: David Lasley, Arnold McCuller, and Diana Grasselli. Released posthumously in 1996, *Legacy* is a testament to Michael's talents as well as his determination to *live* with AIDS.

In recent years, a few books have appeared that engage with Michael's life and activist work. Martin Duberman's *Hold Tight Gently: Michael Callen, Essex Hemphill, and the Battlefield of AIDS* (2014) is a dual biography of Black American poet Essex Hemphill and white activist-musician Michael Callen.[16] While Duberman pays close attention to Hemphill's poetry, he gives only lip service to Michael's music across a scant few pages. Michael also figures prominently in Dennis Altman's *AIDS in the Mind of America: The Social, Political, and Psychological Impact of a New Epidemic* (1986), Richard Berkowitz's *Stayin' Alive: The Invention of Safe Sex, A Personal History* (2003), Sean Strub's *Body Counts: A Memoir of Activism, Sex, and Survival* (2014), and David France's *How to Survive a Plague: The Story of How Citizens and Science Tamed AIDS* (2016). However, their focus is Michael's legacy as an AIDS activist and none offer significant discussions of Michael's musical work or its intersections with his activism. These authors left open a door which I am happy to enter. *Love Don't Need a Reason* tells the story of Michael Callen's life through the lens of his music, and in doing so, adds a new layer of complexity and nuance to the story of AIDS activism in the first fifteen years of the epidemic.

Because *Love Don't Need a Reason* is a biography rather than an argument-drive monograph, I have tried to operate between disciplinary grooves rather than write as a musicologist or as a historian or as an ethnographer, and so on. I've supplemented my musicological toolkit with insights gleaned from HIV/AIDS studies, itself an interdisciplinary field comprising queer, feminist, and critical race theory; illness, disability, and social movement studies; literary theory; history; media, manuscript, and archive studies; oral history; biography and autobiography; literature, theater, and poetry; medical humanities, virology, epidemiology, and public health. In the course of writing *Love*

---

16 Martin Duberman, *Hold Tight Gently: Michael Callen, Essex Hemphill, and the Battlefield of AIDS* (New York: St. Martin's Press, 2014).

Don't Need a Reason, I've confronted gnarly questions related to his music; my field research (primarily in-person and telephone oral history interviews punctuated with more haphazard casual conversations in person, over email, and through social media); and my own engagement with the songs he wrote and performed as well as the era (from 1978 to 1993, the years of my birth and his death) that we simultaneously inhabited. Studying Michael's songs and performances demanded an approach beyond "just" the music that could transcend disciplinary barriers, because Michael resisted traditional boundaries in life, in activism, and in song. Callen's identities as a gay man, a PWA, an activist, and a musician were thoroughly intertwined. His music engages with political topics including masculinity, the place of queer children in the biological family, elective queer kinship, multiculturalism, gay history and experience, and HIV/AIDS as a biomedical, political, economic, and cultural reality. *Love Don't Need a Reason* is the result of thinking across these boundaries.

Fig. 1. Michael Callen (r) and Barry Callen. Courtesy of Barry Callen.

2

Small Town Change

I'll never understand why I never found a helping hand.
All the people, they just watched as I was leaving.
They said I was small town change.
— David Lasley & Don Yowell

Clifford "Cliff" Leroy Callen (1925–2007) was born in Moores Hill, Indiana, one of five children of Manie Edward (1885–1945) and Stella Florence (née Frazier, 1887–1959). In 1943, he graduated high school at the height of World War II, but at seventeen, Cliff was too young for combat duty. So, he joined the Merchant Marines. Soon, the "small-town farm boy [found himself] thrown to the wolves in New York City."[1] The city was exciting, and Cliff would have stayed in New York but for his father's untimely death and his mother's ailing health. Reluctantly, he returned to Indiana and took charge of his family's affairs. He sold their family farm then used the money to move his mother and

---

1 Barbra Callen, letter to Michael Callen, 23 October 1977, typewritten original, the Michael Callen Papers at The LGBT Community Center National History Archive (henceforth, MCP).

sister out of the countryside and into town, so they would be closer to a community of people, friends, doctors, and importantly, his own work. In 1949, Cliff took a job as a welder at General Motors's Fisher Body, enduring ten-hour shifts, seven days a week, and a grueling ninety-mile round-trip commute to the plant in Fairfield, Ohio. At home, he cared for his mother and sister, "raised a garden, cooked the meals, did the wash, cleaned the house, and whatever else needed to be done."[2]

In 1949, Cliff met Barbara Ann Walker (1933–2015), the daughter of itinerant Pentecostal gospel musicians Chester E. "Chet" (1908–1968) and Wilma (née VanTyle, 1904–1981) Walker. Eventually, Mr. Walker "sort of [ran] away from singing" and became an ordained minister through a correspondence course.[3] To earn a living, he toiled in a chair factory for thirteen years and then at a machine shop, from which he eventually retired. Mrs. Walker worked in a nearby creamery, but even with two incomes the Walker family's financial situation was precarious and their home life unstable. Because her family moved twenty-two times in the first eighteen years of her life, Barbara joked that her mother's preferred method of house cleaning was to "find a new house and just move into it!"[4] Although the Walkers were devoutly religious, they were also heterodox, and Barbara was free to walk her own path to salvation. On Sunday mornings, "the family would leave the house to go to church, and everyone would go to a different church! Daddy would go to the Holiness; Mother would go to the Baptist. [Barbara] would go to the Methodist, and [her] brother would go to Church of Christ. And nobody thought anything about it."[5] Although her parents allowed Barbara to attend the church she preferred, they still required her to observe strict Pentecostal traditions. She could not cut her hair or wear it down or drink soft drinks (for fear they would lead to alcohol), and she had to wear modest dresses that

2   Ibid.
3   Barbara Callen, interview with Michael Callen, 24 February 1992, audio recording, MCP (henceforth, BC and MC [1992]).
4   BC and MC (1992).
5   Ibid.

covered her legs practically to the ankle. Throughout her life, Barbara maintained her Christian belief in the inherent equality of all people, reminding others that, "the man in the gutter [is] just as much loved by God as anyone else."[6] Later in life, her second son would test the elasticity of her beliefs and the mettle of her motherly love.

Dating proved to be difficult for the young couple, not because of the Walker's religious beliefs but due to Cliff's work schedule. After working all day at GM, then attending to his mother and sister, he would drive thirty more miles to Rising Sun to see Barbara, often arriving after 9:30 pm and sometimes even later. While these late-night rendezvous rubbed against the grain of courtship norms and the Walker's sense of propriety, from Barbara's family's perspective, Cliff's age was a bigger obstacle. At twenty-five, he was considerably older than sixteen-year-old Barbara, and the Walkers worried that a worldly man who had been in the Merchant Marines and who had once lived in New York City might be too experienced for their naïve daughter. Their worries were unnecessary, for Barbara's convictions, especially those about sex, were set firm in the bedrock of her faith. She "would only go so far but no farther," allowing kissing and some heavy petting but no sexual contact or anything remotely risqué.[7] In a mid-twentieth-century small town, a young woman's reputation was a serious matter. Few wanted to risk being labeled "easy," or worse yet, pregnancy out of wedlock, which could ruin their chances for marriage. In time, Barbara's family grew to love Cliff, and the young couple married in 1952, settling first in Rising Sun. With its population of 2,500 nestled on the banks of the Ohio River in southeastern Indiana, Rising Sun was, as their eldest son, Barry, later described it, "the kind of town where famers go to die."[8]

---

6   Ibid.
7   Ibid.
8   Barry Wayne Callen, interview with the author, 21 September 2013 (henceforth, BWC and MJ [2013]).

Like many women of her generation, Barbara dreamed of being a housewife and mother. She also shared with other women her age a near perfect ignorance of her reproductive system and sex. When she had her first period at age eleven, Barbara thought she was dying. Her mother assured her that menstruation was "very natural and normal," but she did not explain much else.[9] Cliff had to teach Barbara about sex, and she later recalled that "he was very gentle about it. Very kind. Very caring."[10] When she had difficulty getting pregnant, Barbara worried that there was something wrong with her body. But on 24 February 1954, Clifford and Barbara welcomed their first child, Barry Wayne Callen. Barbara believed that she could not get pregnant while breastfeeding, so she was surprised to find that she was with child again only a few months later. A second son was born on 11 April 1955 at Margaret Mary Catholic Hospital in Batesville, Indiana. They named him Michael Lane Callen.

The psychological and physiological stress of having two infant children negatively impacted Barbara's health. Dizziness, bouts of sweating, and anxiety overwhelmed her at times, and she felt powerless to do anything about it. Barbara's emotional instability and unpredictability made the already difficult work of mothering nearly impossible, and family members, including her husband, wondered if she even wanted to be a mother and questioned her love for her two baby boys. At times, Barbara feared that she was having a nervous breakdown and grew paranoid that Cliff would leave her. Although it was not widely discussed or understood in rural Indiana in the 1950s, in retrospect, Barbara's symptoms align with a clinical diagnosis of postpartum depression, and the intense social pressures to behave according to the norms of new motherhood must have exacerbated her distress. Eventually, she saw a psychiatrist who prescribed tranquilizers and other medications to stabilize her mood. Within a few years, her depression faded, and Barbara

9   BC and MC (1992).
10 Ibid.

Fig. 2. The Callen Family Home, 66 Warr Court, Hamilton, OH. Photo by Author.

could fully enjoy motherhood. On 10 December 1958, she gave birth to a daughter named Linda Jo.[11]

In 1960, the Callen family relocated to Hamilton, Ohio, a blue-collar suburb of Cincinnati. Founded as a military outpost on the US Western frontier in 1789 and named for then Secretary of the Treasury Alexander Hamilton, the small city was conveniently located near Ohio's important automobile factories and Miami University in nearby Oxford. Both would play important roles in the Callen family's destiny. Lucrative manufacturing jobs lured workers from Appalachia and nearby rural areas in search of greater economic prospects. The influx of mountain folk earned for Hamilton the pejorative nickname "Hamiltucky" because "one out of three residents had migrated north from Kentucky to work in the auto plants. The joke was that they settled in Hamilton because their cars broke down on the way to Detroit!"[12]

11 Linda politely declined to participate in my research and asked that details about her life be omitted. I have respected this request except in cases where an archival source, such as a letter, or event requires significant discussion of her.
12 BWC and MJ (2013).

Clifford and Barbara purchased a small house at 66 Warr Court in the new Twin Brook subdivision. While waiting three months for construction on their new home to finish, the Callens rented an apartment that turned out to be a roach-infested death trap. A slow carbon monoxide leak from the furnace eventually made everyone sick, an experience that haunted Michael; he was repeatedly plagued by fears of strangulation and the memory that he had nearly died as an infant.[13] They moved to 66 Warr Court over the Labor Day holiday, and Barry and Michael started school the next day. Gradually, the Callen family settled into a new suburban normal.

As the Callens acclimated to their new life, broader cultural changes were afoot in the US. Buoyed by the postwar economic boom, the middle class rapidly expanded. Returning WWII and Korean War veterans (the white ones, that is) went to college on the GI Bill and purchased homes at greatly subsidized rates in new housing developments far from city centers.[14] For newly affluent (and mostly white) Americans, these changes engendered new notions of family — a "nuclear" unit built around a breadwinning father, a dutiful and well-heeled mother-homemaker, and two or three children, all housed within a modest yet modern single-family home. Across the 1950s, the ideology of normative nuclear families displaced other modes of kinship based on extended family networks and communal childrearing in the US cultural imaginary.[15]

Ideas of masculinity, too, mutated in the nuclear age, and what it meant to be a man in the mid-twentieth century was a question with few definitive answers. Marriage, procreation,

---

13 BC and MC (1992).

14 The politics of the GI Bill and affordable housing were highly racialized and are the subject of a number of recent works that look at "redlining" in cities and the racial biases that precipitated white flight to the suburbs. In "the Case for Reparations," *The Atlantic*, June 2014, Ta-Nehisi Coates makes an elegant and rigorously informed argument that such practices were rooted in deep American racism. https://www.theatlantic.com/magazine/archive/2014/06/the-case-for-reparations/361631/.

15 For more, see Elaine Tyler May's *Homeward Bound: American Families in the Cold War Era*, 20th anniv. edn. (New York: Basic Books, 2008).

occupational mobility, and home ownership functioned as important signs of success for white American men. Breadwinning — providing for the needs of the entire nuclear family on a single income — became both an aspiration for these men and a measure of their manhood. Popular sociologists like William H. Whyte (author of the 1956 best seller *The Organization Man*) worried that corporate culture threatened men's vitality. Separated from communal, artisanal, and trade-based economies and customs, The New Man of the 1950s purchased his pass into masculinity with his college degree and high salary rather than earning it through traditionally manly displays of prowess and skill. A kind of "male panic" ensued — though it might more accurately be described as a divergence — as new and sometimes competing forms of masculinity coexisted in uneasy tension.

Men's roles within the home and family were also changing. Modern family psychology, epitomized by Dr. Benjamin Spock's *The Commonsense Book of Baby and Child Care* (1946), encouraged men to take an active interest in domestic life by engaging with their children, balancing work and home life, and making themselves physically and emotionally available to their wives, all for the health of the nuclear family. Popular television programs like *Leave It to Beaver* (1957–1963), *Father Knows Best* (1954–1960), and *Ozzie and Harriet* (1952–1966) reinforced a stratified, middle-class gender ideology and facilitated a cultural shift from the stern and patriarchal father figure to the modern benevolent "dad."

Cliff Callen embodied the contradictions and frustrations of his era. On the swing shift at Fisher Body, he welded doors for automobiles, seven days a week in exhausting ten-hour stints. Outside of work, however, he was "a real lover of reading [who] was very much into intellectual discourse," especially politics and philosophy.[16] Cliff passed his love of books, reading, and politics down to his children. The dinner table was often a hotbed for discussion and debate, especially between Michael and his father. While he labored to build a better future for his fam-

---

16 BWC and MJ (2013).

ily, Cliff dreamed of being a self-made man with his own business, a small store or perhaps even a restaurant in Arizona, far away from the Midwestern cold and industrial labor. He always "had some goal or other that he'd like to have reached, and every time he tried to reach it something happened to take that success away."[17] So, Cliff hitched his hopes to the wagons of his three stars: Barry, Michael, and Linda.

With the support of his family, however, Cliff did fulfill his dream of getting a college degree when he received a Bachelor of Science degree from Miami University by taking night classes. At some point in the 1970s, the entire Callen family was enrolled in university degree programs, making them all simultaneous first-generation college students. Barbara earned multiple degrees from Miami University: a Bachelor of Science in Art Education, a Bachelor of Science in Learning Disabilities/Behavior Disorders, and a Master of Education in Guidance and Counseling. Barry graduated from Miami University in 1976. Michael graduated from Boston University in 1977, and a few years later, Linda also studied at Miami University.

After he received his degree, Cliff wrestled with conflicting ideas about manhood and class status. A promotion to a management position at GM (facilitated by his college degree) would have eased the family's financial burdens considerably and enabled Cliff "to do something other than grovel for General Motors."[18] However, traditional manly pride won out over pragmatism. Clifford flatly "refused every chance to climb the corporate ladder [at GM because] he felt that would entail the 'sacrifice of his beliefs and his morals' [and] would force him […] to treat employees below him in a 'degrading and demeaning' manner that would make them 'feel like just so many cattle.'"[19] The patri-

---

17 Barbara Callen, letter to Michael Callen, 5 October 1974, typewritten original, MCP.
18 Ibid.
19 Michael Callen, quoted in Martin Duberman, *Hold Tight Gently: Michael Callen, Essex Hemphill, and the Battlefield of AIDS* (New York: The New Press, 2014), 3. Barbara Callen also recounts this experience in her letter 23 October 1977 letter to Michael.

arch's unwillingness to change impacted his wife and children. Because he was "obsessed with the idea that [like his own father] he would predecease [his wife]," Cliff "forced [Barbara] to go to college and get a teaching certificate."[20] With clockwork regularity, terrific fights erupted between husband and wife each semester. The stress caused Barbara to put on considerable amounts of weight and according to Michael, it exacerbated her existing depression and anxiety, leading to another nervous breakdown.

While mid-century men wrestled with new masculine mores, women faced their own gender trouble. Even in a blue-collar town like Hamilton, women who left the domestic realm often faced brutal criticism. Other women "put [Barbara] down for working with or trying to help other people's kids when maybe [her] own [children] have their unmet needs, too."[21] Still Barbara enjoyed teaching elementary students with special needs. She adored her students like her own children and was their staunch advocate and ally for thirty years.

Whereas her own mother's work outside the home had not kept the Walker family from the brink of ruin, Barbara's second income afforded her family an extra layer of financial security, though it came at the cost of her emotional well-being and her dream of being a stay-at-home mom. Nevertheless, the Callens, like most working-class families, still struggled to make ends meet. Even so, music and the arts were important priorities in their home. "We come from a sort of 'Daddy Sang Bass, Mama Sang Tenor' background," Barry told me before describing a life filled with music, literature, and art even when money was tight.[22] Their multi-instrumentalist mother played organ, xylophone, accordion, autoharp, and the family piano, which was painted her favorite color — pink. After putting the children to bed, Mrs. Callen would play piano or organ and sing for an hour each night, and as the children grew older, family music-making became a favorite pastime. Barbara also performed for

20 Ibid.
21 Barbara Callen, letter to Michael Callen, 5 October 1974, MCP.
22 BWC and MJ (2013).

church and community events and was a member of the Hammond Organ Club of Hamilton. Although she never learned musical notation, Barbara composed religious songs and children's music, which her sons — especially Michael — mocked mercilessly but lovingly. Barry and Linda each sang and played the guitar, while Michael received intermittent vocal training off starting at the age of 7, including a year and a half at the Cincinnati Conservatory of Music, and he sang in church choir where he was labeled "leather lungs" by the choir director. Through the Title I Education Program, Michael "received violin lessons from age 13 through 15 and was awarded a scholarship to study (from 15 to 16) at Miami University," though his "inability to read music [...] finally caught up with [him] and [he] forewent further training."[23] Michael also taught himself to play piano, and he inherited both his mother's ability to yodel and her knack for songwriting.[24]

Early in life, Michael learned that his music could have an impact on other people. As a toddler, he entertained his mother by pulling pots and pans from the cupboards and drumming on them with kitchen utensils as mallets and drumsticks. As a mischievous youngster, he frequently snuck into the living room early in the morning, flipped the switch on the family's Hammond organ, and blasted low bass notes which rattled the whole house. "I thought I was having a heart attack!" Barry laughed as he recalled his younger brother's antics, but "Mike would wake us up with that note!"[25]

Among the family's most cherished possessions was a big cabinet stereo with wire mesh speakers and a record player. Music poured out of the stereo at all hours, and their family's eclectic record collection included "lots of folky, lefty stuff" like Peter, Paul, & Mary — music which Michael later credited with cultivating his social consciousness — Broadway original

---

23 Michael Callen, résumé, 1977, typewritten original, MCP.
24 Barry Callen released his first album, *The Gospel of Fun*, in 2011.
25 BWC and MJ (2013). Barry also wrote about this incident in a letter to his brother dated 29 March 1993, typewritten original, MCP.

cast soundtrack albums; classical music, pop, and light jazz; and even a record of Zulu drumming and chanting.[26] Scattered among the discs was Julie Andrews's *The Lass with the Delicate Air* (1958), which included Michael's childhood favorite song "Pedro the Fisherman." A home video recorded in New York City in the early 1980s captures Michael waxing rhapsodic about the impact Andrews had on his singing. "The thing Miss Andrews did for me unaware was strengthen my falsetto," he tells the camera. "I was always getting smacked for singing in her register and sounding like a woman, but it's how you strengthen your falsetto."[27]

However, an accidental encounter changed Michael's musical life forever, for there on the small screen, he found his spirit diva: Barbra Joan Streisand. Flipping the TV one night, he happened to catch Streisand's *My Name Is Barbra,* an influential television special which first aired on CBS on 28 April 1965. "Instantly," Michael later recalled, "I *knew*."[28] Barry remembered that his brother "wanted to be her. He would *perform* her. He would play Streisand's songs over and over, act them out, be *beyond* campy."[29] Self-conscious and already aware that he was not like most boys in Hamilton, Michael identified in Streisand a fellow "misunderstood ugly duckling who would one day rise to stardom as a singer."[30]

Just as their interest in education and the arts differentiated the Callens from many of their Hamilton neighbors, so too did their Democratic politics. At the time, the two American parties were essentially reversing their polarities, with Democrats becoming the party of progressive stances on Civil Rights, Women's

---

26 Ibid.
27 "Mike at Jones St, early 80s," n.d., home video shot by Elliot Linwood McAdoo, Richard Dworkin's private archive (henceforth, RDA).
28 Ibid.
29 BWC and MJ (2013).
30 Michael Callen, "Birth Announcement," n.d., handwritten original, MCP. While undated, this essay is likely from 1988–1989, given that he mentions the recent release of *Purple Heart*. This appears to be a therapeutic exercise in "reassessing [his] memories."

Liberation, and labor issues while Republicans positioned themselves as the stalwart base of Richard Nixon's "Silent Majority."[31] Lost in a "sea of redneck Republicans," Clifford "took a lot of shit" for his staunchly Democratic views.[32] Caught between conflicting ideas, he sometimes expressed his frustrations through a stubbornness of will that his youngest son would one day inherit. Although Cliff did have a temper, according to Barbara, her husband "wouldn't lay a hand on anybody when he was angry," especially the children.[33] Most of the time, he left unpleasant disciplinary tasks to his wife, who later recalled that she "would have to be clear to the end of [her] rope before Cliff intervened."[34] Michael, however, remembered his father as "smelly and tired [from work] and grumpy," a stern disciplinarian.[35]

As young kids, the Callen brothers perceived their family's money troubles on some level and became "little hustlers [...] always hustling for money."[36] Together, Barry and Michael devised a clever entrepreneurial endeavor: Twin Brook International. Named after their subdivision community and staffed by neighborhood kids, Twin Brook International offered an array of community events, programs, and services. For a small fee, residents could read Twin Brook's very own newspaper, visit a neighborhood museum, and attend theatrical productions put on by the kids. The Callen brothers were also not opposed to a little subterfuge to make a buck. Nearby, construction crews were at work on a new subdivision, and the boys reckoned that the workmen would be hungry and thirsty after toiling long hours in the sweltering summer sun. So, they filled a wagon

---

31 For more on this shift, see Rick Perlstein's *Nixonland: The Rise of a President and the Future of America* (New York: Charles Scribner and Sons, 2009) and *The Invisible Bridge: The Fall of Nixon and the Rise of Reagan* (New York: Simon and Schuster, 2015).
32 Jeffrey Escoffier and Michael Callen, "My Rise from Complete Obscurity: An Interview with Michael Callen," in *In My Time: Essays on Sex, Science, and AIDS*, ed. Jeffrey Escoffier, 1993, unpublished manuscript, RDA.
33 BC and MC (1992).
34 Ibid.
35 Escoffier and Callen, "My Rise from Complete Obscurity."
36 BWC and MJ (2013).

with popcorn and Kool-Aid, which they sold by the bag and by the glass. Unbeknownst to the workmen, these thoughtful children added an enormous amount of extra salt to the popcorn to drive up their thirst and super-saturated the refreshing Kool-Aid with sugar to make them want even more. The strategy paid off, and the boys walked home with plenty of coins jingling in their pockets.[37]

Between Clifford's irregular hours and Barbara's school commitments, maintaining the Callen family's version of the American Dream required help from the children. As a teenager, Michael assumed what he considered to be a disproportionate amount of household duties because, he later wrote, "as a fag, I was the only one who could cook and clean."[38] On a typical day, Michael went to school, ran home to make dinner, returned to school for extra-curricular activities, came back home to finish his homework, then did the dishes, laundry, and other household chores. On Fridays, Michael took his father's paycheck and did the family shopping. The stress was intense, and it impacted his familial relationships. In Michael's estimation, his mother treated him "horribly" during this period as a result of her depression, the stress of working, and the added difficulty of finishing her degrees; his brother was "lazy," and his sister was "helpless."[39] Even so, his love and loyalty for family endured. Later in life, Herculean feats of multitasking would become a hallmark of Michael's social justice work and cooking for his loved ones remained a lifelong passion.

In spite of the added responsibilities and stress, Michael maintained an excellent academic record in high school. No matter how much Michael succeeded, however, his father "withheld praise, always saying [he] had to do better" and took every opportunity to remind his three children that they were just "poor, white trash."[40] Less outspoken than her husband and

---

37 Ibid.
38 Callen, "Birth Announcement."
39 Ibid.
40 Ibid.

possessing what Michael described as a "deeply Christian [but] simple faith [with] a very clear sense of right and wrong," Barbara offered quiet encouragement, instilling in all her children a conviction to "stand up for what is right."[41] Both Callen brothers took these lessons to heart. As teenagers, they canvassed neighborhoods for the Democratic Party during election seasons, and as adults, both brothers retained a strong sense of social justice. "One of the bricks my parents gave me, a very useful brick," Michael would later say, "was to stand up for what you thought was right."[42] This "deep Midwestern lesson" would later lead Michael Callen to the forefront of AIDS politics.[43]

---

41 Escoffier and Callen, "My Rise from Complete Obscurity."
42 Deborah Wasser, dir., *Legacy*, 1993, RDA. This is an independent documentary film about Callen's final recording sessions that was used to help raise money for the completion of the album. It compiles footage from across Michael's life and career.
43 Ibid.

Fig. 1. Michael Callen, yearbook photo (c. 1965). Courtesy of Barry Callen.

3

No, No

> *From the moment we are born*
> *And maybe even before*
> *We are taught that we must choose*
> *To be either/ or.*
> *The pink and blue conspiracy*
> *Is lesson number one*
> — Michael Callen

Queer icon and author Quentin Crisp once quipped that "there is no sin like being a woman," and for effete boys in rural areas, this was especially true.[1] While there exists a certain social space for the tomboy, who may or may not be a butch lesbian hiding in plain sight, there is no parallel safety zone for the sissy. And there was no doubt about it: Michael was a *sissy*!

Michael's effeminacy manifested early. He idolized wisecracking female figures like Granny Clampett, the acerbic matriarch portrayed by Irene Ryan (1902–1973) in *The Beverly Hillbillies* (1962–1971). In second grade, he donned Granny Clampett drag, including stockings, a dress, and a hat, for several Twin Brook International dramatic productions, throwing himself into the part with gusto. He "liked being that character even when he

---

1 Quentin Crisp, interview in Rob Epstein and Jeffrey Freidman, dir., *The Celluloid Closet* (New York: HBO, 1996).

wasn't in the play [...]. He kinda wanted to be her."² Although no one on Warr Court "knew what a diva was," they recognized that Michael "wanted the spotlight [and] the majority of the attention."³

Home movies capture the clangorous tension between Michael's effete mannerisms and the normative masculinity of other sons of Hamilton. In grainy black-and-white footage, a grinning Michael leads a parade of Twin Brook children down Warr Court. With his "wrists flopping" and triumphantly twirling a baton, Michael is "in pig heaven," the only boy marching with the girls while Barry, "in full military drag," brings up the rear with the other boys.⁴ While Michael's gender-deviant behavior was endearing, albeit a little odd, to those around him when he was a young child, the novelty faded as he grew older. "When someone's a sissy in third grade, it isn't a problem," his father reasoned. "But if they are a sissy at the time puberty sets in, that's when you get to worry."⁵ And Cliff and Barbara were starting to worry.

Michael was worried, too. His earliest memories juxtaposed the verdant yard of the Callen family home with his private internal struggles. He was "tortured and tormented about feeling acutely different and knowing that something was really out of whack," but he did not know what it was.⁶

In the 1960s, homosexuality was considered a mental illness by the medical and psychiatric communities and a major moral dilemma by conservative religious leaders. Even people who were not virulently homophobic heaped prejudice onto LGBTQ+ folks through their pitying attitudes, their prayers for

2   Barry Wayne Callen, interview with author, 21 September 2013 (henceforth BWC and MJ [2013]).
3   BWC and MJ (2013).
4   Michael Callen, interview in Kenneth Paul Rosenberg, dir., "Why Am I Gay? Stories of Coming out in America," *America Undercover,* ep. 10, HBO, 10 August 1993 (henceforth MC and KPB [1993]).
5   Clifford Callen, interview with Michael Callen, 26 February 1992 (henceforth CC and MC [1992]), audio recording, Michael Callen Papers at The LGBT Community Center National History Archive (henceforth MCP).
6   MC and KPB (1993).

Fig. 2. Michael Callen (c.1960). Screenshot of home movie shot by the Graves family.

change, and, most damningly, their silences. Most parents were ill-equipped to discuss sex and sexuality in general, let alone homosexuality. Occasionally, Cliff attempted to breach the subject of Michael's effeminacy with his wife, who usually rebuked him. "Don't say anything about it, or you might make it worse!"[7] At one point, Michael's parents asked his elementary school teacher to keep track of which children their son socialized with during recess. After learning that the majority of his friends were girls, Cliff laid down the law. "It's time for you to start playing kickball."[8] In the hyper-masculine, gender-stratified, mid-centu-

7   CC and MC (1992). Clifford Callen also wrote about this to his son in a letter dated 13 November 1979. Typewritten original, MCP.
8   Barbara Callen, interview with Michael Callen, 24 February 1992, audio recording, MCP (henceforth, BC and MC [1992]). In the interview, Barbara refutes that she and her husband asked Michael's teacher to spy on him. In the corresponding 1992 interview with his father, Michael asks for verification of his memory. Clifford says he cannot corroborate Michael's memory,

ry Midwest, sports were *de rigueur,* but Michael had no interest in any of it and continued to be his flamboyant, authentic self.

Once, Cliff and Barbara even sought divine intervention to ensure their budding sissy turned out to be a "normal" boy. When Barry was eleven and Michael ten, their mother dressed them in their Brooks Brothers suits, drove to Rising Sun, and dropped them off, alone, to visit her parents. The Walkers then took their grandsons to a private home that had been converted into an evangelical Pentecostal church. "They'd torn out the interior and replaced it with pews, a lectern, and a big cross on the wall behind it."[9] The boys had never seen anything like it! Grandfather Walker introduced his grandsons to a woman minister. Before they could recover from that shock (the had only known ministers to be men), she began to wail in a "screechy hillbilly accent."[10] As the minister revved up the salvation machine, her small congregation got the spirit, speaking in tongues, testifying, and leaping about the church. Grandfather Walker removed his prosthetic wooden leg, knelt on his "good" knee, and prayed: "Dear Lord, save these young boys from the Great Whore of Babylon in Hamilton! From vice and evil ways!"[11] The minister called for the congregation to cast out Satan from the young boys by the laying on of hands, and twenty or thirty "old, diseased, poor, scary-looking" worshipers swarmed Michael and Barry.[12] The chaotic scene was antithetical to Barry and Michael's "idea of church [which] was very middle class: people show up in a suit and tie; sing; listen; stand up; sit down; shake hands; goodbye. No feathers ruffled."[13] The Pentecostal service

but he adds that time and two other children may have obscured his ability to remember all the details.

9   BWC and MJ (2013).
10 Ibid.
11 Ibid.
12 Ibid.
13 Ibid. In *Surviving AIDS* (New York: Harper Perennial, 1990), Michael notes that the family attended a Methodist church in Hamilton. In *Hold Tight Gently: Michael Callen, Essex Hemphill, and the Battlefield of AIDS* (New York: The New Press, 2014), Martin Duberman identifies the family as Baptist.

confused and frightened both of them. After the service, however, Barbara picked up her two sons and drove them back to Hamilton as if nothing out of the ordinary had happened. No questions asked.

In retrospect, Barry believes that he and Michael were ambushed. "Mom knew what had happened," he told me.[14] Because the adults in their family already suspected that Michael was gay, they "wanted to pray the gay out of him, and they threw [Barry] in just to make sure [Michael's] gay hadn't rubbed off."[15] Residual trauma and resentment from the experience impacted Michael's relationship with his family, both personally and musically. From that point on, he refused to participate in family music-making at reunions and holidays that typically featured a "big Southern feast and singing lots of hymns and that kind of stuff."[16] He also renounced all religious ideology, identifying as an atheist for the rest of his life, often to his mother's chagrin and occasionally her fierce denial.

Michael's first inklings of same-sex desire arose early in childhood. He longed just to be near an older neighbor boy in Rising Sun. As he progressed into adolescence, Michael desperately wanted to be with men, but he also feared them. With every passing year, the feelings intensified, yet lacking a vocabulary with which to describe his desires, Michael remained silently "tortured by [his] sexual attraction to men."[17] At some point, he noticed that two men had moved into the neighborhood, and they seemed *different* from the other residents of Twin Brook. He observed them carefully, at a distance, until he could take action. He tore pieces of paper into little strips and wrote a note on each one: "I'm different. Are you? Can you help me?" Michael planted these notes around their house, under flowerpots, in the

---

14 BWC and MJ (2013).
15 Ibid.
16 Ibid.
17 MC and KPB (1993).

shrubs, and in the mailbox. Then, he waited for an answer that never came.[18]

Sometime later, during a game of canasta with three girlfriends, a tough neighborhood girl with a beehive hairdo "narrowed [her] eyes, pointed at [Michael], and declared with great authority, 'if you don't stop acting like a girl, you're gonna turn into a *homosexual*.'"[19] Michael "broke out into a cold sweat."[20] Although he did not know the precise meaning of the word, the palpable revulsion in her voice indicated that "a homosexual must be *the* most horrible thing anyone could ever be — so horrible that no one had ever spoken of it in [Michael's] presence."[21] Still, he felt "calmed to finally have it named."[22]

Desperate for information, Michael turned to books, gathering what he could from the outdated tomes in the Hamilton Public Library, a common stage in the coming out process that anthropologist Kath Weston terms "tracking the gay imaginary."[23] In an old psychology textbook, he found homosexuality listed alongside murder, pedophilia, and kleptomania and read that gay men often "lurk around public restrooms and seduce little children."[24] A clandestine copy of Dr. David Reuben's *Everything You Always Wanted to Know about Sex But Were Afraid to Ask* reinforced the homophobic idea that gay men were little more

---

18 Tim Miller, interview with author, 8 April 2019. Tim also recounted this story in the liner notes to Michael's final studio album, *Legacy* (1996).
19 Michael Callen, "Birth Announcement," n.d., handwritten original, MCP.
20 Callen, *Surviving AIDS*, 2. Duberman's account of the "canasta" story varies in some details: "Mike was playing canasta with some older family friends one day — cheating and winning, 'screeching' (his description) with delight — when one of the women put down her cards, gave him a stern look, and said, 'If you don't watch out, Michael, you're going to become one of those homosexuals,'" (1). Duberman's version is derived from documents in the MCP. My account comes from *Surviving AIDS*.
21 Ibid., 2.
22 Callen, "Birth Announcement."
23 Kath Weston, "Get Thee to a Big City: Sexual Imaginary and the Great Gay Migration," *GLQ: A Journal of Gay and Lesbian Studies* 2/3 (1995): 253–77, esp. 257–58.
24 David Schmidt, interview with Michael Callen, 12 November 1987, typescript, MCP (henceforth, DS and MC [1987]).

than "pathetic psychopaths who hung out in public restrooms writing lurid notes to each other on toilet paper."[25] Because it was one of the first popular sex manuals and sold over 100 million copies, Reuben's book shaped mainstream cultural attitudes about sex and sexuality. Unfortunately, the early editions were informed by the ideologies of a pre-Stonewall, homophobic culture built on heterosexual privilege. "Homosexuality seems to have a compelling urgency about it," Reuben opined, without stopping to consider the social, legal, and political factors that created this "urgency" in the first place.[26] The author also argued that "homosexuals thrive on danger" and ranked those who "combine homosexuality with sadistic and masochistic aberrations [...] among the cruelest people who walk this earth. [...] [T]hey filled the ranks of Hitler's Gestapo and ss."[27] Reuben's ac-

25 Callen, *Surviving AIDS*, 3. David Reuben's *Everything You Always Wanted to Know about Sex: But Were Afraid to Ask* (New York: David McKay Publishers, 1969) was instrumental in shifting attitudes about sex in the US. It was also a product of its time and reflects certain prejudices, especially toward gay people. It has been revised many times, most recently in 2000, to reflect further shifts in our cultural understanding of sex and sexuality.

The 1969 edition contains the following description of two gay men cruising in a public men's room: "Generally the circumstances are far from romantic. According to one homosexual, it goes something like this: 'Whenever I feel like sex, I walk into a men's room, find an empty cubicle, go in, take down my pants, and sit on the toilet. Then I wait. It never takes very long. Pretty soon another guy sits down in the next cubicle. I watch his feet. If he's a gay guy, he'll slide his foot over and kind of nudge mine. That means he's 'cruising.' If I'm interested, I nudge back. Then we get started. I always use a piece of toilet paper to write some kind of note — usually I just say, 'Do you suck?' Sometimes if I have plenty of time, I add something else like, 'How big are you?' I throw the paper on the floor, he picks it up, comes over into my cubicle, and sucks my penis. That's how it ends — sometimes I suck his penis but usually I just got home" (133).

26 Reuben, *Everything You Always Wanted to Know about Sex*, esp. ch. 8, "Male Homosexuality," 129–51.

27 Ibid. These tone-deaf assessments are of a piece with those of the larger culture in the era. Reuben also conveniently overlooks the Nazi persecution of homosexuals, the destruction of Magnus Hirschfeld's Institute for Sexual Science in Berlin, and the assassinations of prominent gay Nazi leaders. The first edition of *The Diagnostic and Statistical Manual of Mental Disorders* (1952, henceforth, DSM) classified homosexuality as a paraphilia, an intense

count of the "almost unbelievable variety of ingenious" sex acts that gay men perform on one another under "circumstances [that were] far from romantic" shocked and titillated Michael, and the author's description of gay intimacy as devoid of feeling and sentiment resonated with the young reader's lonely sense of himself as the only person in the world who had same-sex attractions. Michael wondered if he would ever find love or intimacy in a world where gay men rarely saw one another's faces or exchanged names, much less built lasting emotional bonds. Maybe Reuben was right, Michael thought. He was a doctor, after all. Maybe "a masturbation machine might do it better."[28]

In a place like Hamilton, media, news, and filmic images of gay life were hard to find. Even if Michael had been able to access the available archive of LGBTQ+ images, they certainly

---

sexual arousal to atypical objects, fetishes, fantasies, and other behaviors. Subsequent editions including the *DSM-II* (1968) and *DSM-III* (1980) listed homosexuality alternately as a sexual orientation disturbance or "ego-dystonic homosexuality." Works of popular psychology described homosexuality in ambivalent or pejorative terms. In 1956, *Time* characterized gay men as psychic masochists who "wallow in self-pity and continually provoke hostility; to ensure more opportunities for self-pity [sic] he 'collects' injustices — sometimes real, often fancied." ("Curable Disease," *Time* 68, no. 24 [10 December 1956], 76). The article concludes with advice "not to attempt the impossible, and suggests these criteria by which [analysts] can judge whether a prospective patient offers reasonable hope of cure: he must have inner guilt feelings that can be put to use in treatment; he must accept the treatment voluntarily and actively want to change; he must give up his habit of using homosexuality as a weapon against his family, which (unconsciously) he always hates. The analyst must not begin by attacking the homosexual head on — or the patient will at once cry that he is being persecuted. Yet the analyst must convince him that his self-damaging tendencies will engulf his whole personality, if they have not already done so. There are, says the article, no 'healthy homosexuals.'" Ten years later, *Time* revisited the subject of homosexuality in America, but the magazine's perception of gay life had changed little (see "The Homosexual in America," *Time* 87, no. 3 [21 January 1966], 52–57). The unnamed author concluded that while society might treat gay communities unfairly, such sexual deviance "deserves no encouragement, no glamorization, no rationalization, no fake status as minority martyrdom, no sophistry about simple differences in taste — and above all, no pretense that it is anything but a pernicious sickness."

28 Ibid.

would not have quelled his fears; they might have even made him feel worse. Mid-century theater, literature, and film portrayed sexually "deviant" characters as pathetic subjects in need of medical intervention, miserable saps on an inevitable path to suicide, or dangerous monsters who deserved imprisonment or death.[29] With no gay role models and few media representations of homosexuality to guide him, Michael groped along his path toward a gay identity, counting the days until he could finally leave the Midwest.

As he grew into a young man, his sissy behavior became a source of derision and, occasionally, violence. At school, other boys subjected him to a daily litany of homophobic verbal assaults, calling him "faggot" and "sissy." Sports were akin to religion in the Midwest which meant "there was no excuse good enough to get you out of gym [where he had to play] baseball and other butch things [Michael] hated."[30] So "frightening, and embarrassing" scenes played out on the "dreadful, dreadful sports field."[31] The locker room, too, elicited paralyzing anxiety. Fearful that a single glance might betray him, or that he might get an erection in the showers, Michael lollygagged about in an attempt to be the last one in the shower. However, his peers perceived Michael's attempts at invisibility as lingering in the locker room, which only made him more conspicuous.[32] Boys would chide

---

29 Vito Russo, *The Celluloid Closet* (New York: Harper and Row, 1987). Plays and later film adaptations of Lillian Hellman's *The Children's Hour* (1934, 1961), Tennessee Williams's *Cat on a Hot Tin Roof* (1955, 1958) and *Suddenly, Last Summer* (1958, 1959) confirmed the idea that the only good homosexual was a dead one. Such representations of homosexuality colluded with and derived from a longer history of depictions of socially and sexually deviant men and women who were punished for their transgressions. Movies like *Some Like It Hot* (1959) made same-sex desire and gender nonconformity the butt of endless jokes. *Tea and Sympathy* (1953, 1956) was ostensibly more sensitive. Its young male protagonist struggles with the norms of masculinity, but ultimately, he masters the codes and butches himself up. So, the threats of homosexuality and male effeminacy are tamed when they are not destroyed.
30 MC and KPB (1993).
31 DS and MC (1987) and MC and KPB (1993).
32 MC and KPB (1993).

him, physically attack him, and flick him with wet towels which left painful blisters on his skin. On more than one occasion, boys from the Hamilton Methodist Youth Fellowship would, in Michael's own recollection, "circle around and piss on me."[33]

The bullying was relentless, and the pressures were intense. However, Michael felt that "it was not possible to talk to anyone about what was happening [to him] because [he] had the sense that people would take [his abusers'] side, that people would say 'well, if you have these feelings, then they deserve to pee on you' or 'no wonder people are punching you out.'"[34]

What's more, the abuses were not limited to those inflicted by his classmates. Michael's high school choir teacher, Sam Shie (1943–2012), allegedly pressured him to engage in some kind of sexual activity.[35] In Michael's account, the married older man "tried to rape me, and then he tried to kill me" after the young student rebuffed his teacher's advances.[36] As retaliation, Shie extorted Michael, withholding solos as a way to pressure Michael to keep the incident a secret. Shie allegedly resorted to intimidation and physical violence. When the teacher later learned that Michael had received a music scholarship, Shie "wrote [the school and] asked them to revoke it."[37] Michael later wrote that

---

33 Ibid. In 2013, Barry told me that these boys were members of the local Methodist Youth Fellowship and that his brother had actually given him the names of the offenders before his death in 1993. The scars of such brutalities remain tender for the Callen family as well as for Michael Callen's queer friends and family outside of the Midwest.

34 Ibid.

35 Independently, Barry Callen and Richard Dworkin related this story. There is a written account of Shie's life and an abuse scandal unrelated to Callen in Peter Davis, *Hometown: A Portrait of an American Community* (New York: Simon and Schuster, 1982).

36 Callen, "Birth Announcement."

37 Ibid. In high school, Michael received two scholarships. One paid for music lessons at Miami University in Oxford, OH, and another from Boston University, where he initially enrolled as a music major in 1973. Michael's account does not specify which school Shie contacted but given that Shie was an Ohio native and a graduate of OSU, it seems likely that he would have tried to pull strings at Miami University rather than Boston University. However, the historical record is unclear.

Shie "had people beat me up, and I couldn't tell anyone."[38] Terrorized and traumatized, Michael quietly dropped out of choir during his senior year and tried to focus on college, never revealing the abuse to anyone but his brother until many years later. Michael would forever remember Shie as his "first exposure to pure evil."[39]

Michael also recalled that on two occasions his father slapped him across the face for his effeminacy: once for girlishly prancing through the house and another time for singing a Leslie Gore love song in his shrillest voice and keeping the male love-object pronouns in the lyrics. "I don't ever want to hear you sing high like that again," his father warned.[40] From that moment on, Michael made a "clear, conscious choice" not to be anything like his father and to "torture [his] father with even more falsetto singing and sissy mannerisms."[41] Years later, Michael confronted his parents about these incidents. Barbara doubted that they had ever happened, and Cliff concurred, saying that he had no memory of slapping Michael. However, he also tried to respect Michael's memory, admitting that "it could have happened."[42]

Regardless of whether these events occurred as Michael remembered them, Barry observed the ways that Michael and his parents kept hurting one another, never intentionally but because their personalities were so similar. Michael inherited his father's stubbornness and his mother's spitfire personality — a dangerous combination that led to frequent disagreements in the small house at 66 Warr Court.[43] Throughout his life, Barry would often serve as the bridge between Michael and their parents, though he never capitulated to Cliff and Barbara's homo-

38 Ibid.
39 Ibid.
40 CC and MC (1992) and Jeffrey Escoffier and Michael Callen, "My Rise from Complete Obscurity: An Interview with Michael Callen," in *In My Time: Essays on Sex, Science, and AIDS*, ed. Jeffrey Escoffier, 1993, unpublished manuscript, Richard Dworkin's private archive.
41 BC and MC (1992).
42 CC and MC (1992).
43 Barry Wayne Callen, interview with author, 30 August 2020 (henceforth BWC and MJ [2020]).

phobia. He was his brother's champion. "Michael was the person I loved most in the world," Barry told me in 2020. "That has never changed."[44]

At Taft High School, Michael made friends with a group of kids that his high-school best friend, Terry Tincher, described as the more free-thinking contingent in the chorus and theater programs.[45] Terry recalled the day he met Michael in the school gymnasium during an assembly. As Tincher entered wearing all white — shoes, a t-shirt, and the painter's overalls that were then in vogue — Michael spotted him and called out, "Look, it's the White Tornado!" (White Tornado was the branding slogan for Procter and Gamble's Ajax ammoniated cleaner). They were thereafter inseparable. His friends were awestruck by Michael's ability to "spontaneously create art out of experiences," his quick wit and quirky personality, and his ability to type 150 words a minute, which made him popular when term papers were due.[46]

66 Warr Court became home base for this motley crew of kids. "Cliff would be in [his] brown reclining chair and never move [as] a tornado of kids came through. Mike was always being outrageous; maybe somebody was playing the piano."[47] After school and on weekends, they would pile into a friend's van and drive to one of the shopping malls around Cincinnati. On Michael's cue — usually a predetermined code word which he would yell — they would all fall to the ground in the middle of a store or pedestrian walkway, much to the consternation and confusion of adult onlookers. Such antics, while tame by today's standards, felt transgressive and even dangerous in the 1960s and early 1970s but were really just innocent fun to alleviate the tedium of life in a small town.

Terry believes that everyone in their circle of friends knew that Michael was gay, but "people didn't talk about it. It was the 1970s, and we were in this little milquetoast town in the mid-

---

44 BWC and MJ (2020).
45 Terry Tincher, interview with the author, 22 June 2017 (henceforth, TT and MJ [2017]).
46 Ibid.
47 Ibid.

dle of Ohio. We were probably thinking way 'earlier' than that," by which he meant that their ideas about gender and sexuality were, like those of most Americans, far behind the cutting edge of urban sex radicals, feminists, and Gay Liberationists.[48] Publicly, Michael kept trying to play it straight. With each passing year, however, he found the charade more difficult to maintain. The weekly ritual of Friday night dates elicited anxiety and disgust. Physical intimacy with women made him squeamish. So powerful was his revulsion to heterosexuality (but importantly, *not* to women outside of sexual situations) that Michael could only endure a goodnight kiss by silently counting the seconds until the young woman pulled away. Ironically, his deviance from Hamilton's normal mode of masculinity may have made him more attractive. Barry recalled that "three of the most beautiful girls in our high school came to the house regularly because they wanted to date him and fuck him."[49] Once, a group of teenage girls chased him around the house "while trying to pull down his pajamas and bite him on the ass, pull him down, and kiss him," Barry laughed. "God! It wasn't fair!"[50] However, everything about Michael's relationship to his own sexuality was about to change.

---

48 Ibid.
49 BWC and MJ (2013).
50 Ibid.

Fig. 1. Michael in high school production of *Tobacco Road* (c. 1972). Courtesy of Barry Callen.

4

Innocence Dying

> *Out of the south and into the bars,*
> *fragile child carrying the scars*
> *of a redneck father*
> *who never bothered to love him.*
> — Michael Callen

Michael had never traveled more than fifty miles from Hamilton, but he longed for change and a new life far away from his small hometown. Leaving Ohio, he knew, was key to his survival. In 1973, Michael flew to Boston to audition for a music scholarship at Boston University, where he inadvertently got his first glimpse of one of the quintessential aspects of twentieth-century urban gay life.

Waiting nervously outside an audition room on the music building's fourth floor, Michael took a bathroom break. Inside, all of the stalls were occupied, and several men lingered in the small space. The atmosphere felt charged with electric, nervous energy, and Michael quickly surmised that these men were there "to relieve themselves in several senses."[1] Unwittingly, he had just stumbled upon his first "tearoom," a public toilet where

---

[1] Quoted in Martin Duberman, *Hold Tight Gently: Michael Callen, Essex Hemphill, and the Battleground of AIDS* (New York: The New Press, 2014), 4–5.

men rendezvous for quick, usually anonymous, sexual encounters. Entering a stall, he saw walls

> covered with gay graffiti — "meet me here 7-8-73." Two large holes had been drilled between the stalls and Mike became aware that through the holes "two eyeballs on either side" were looking at him. Then a mouth appeared where an eyeball had been. Mike immediately got an erection and started to sweat. A note on toilet paper arrived from underneath the stall: STICK IT THROUGH. He did — and instantly ejaculated.[2]

It was a scene straight out of *Everything You Always Wanted to Know about Sex, but Were Afraid to Ask*, yet afterward, Michael's body felt "at peace for the first time ever."[3] His head still spinning from the tearoom encounter, Michael sang his audition material and was awarded a music scholarship.

Michael left for Boston after graduating from Taft High School in the spring of 1973 — coincidentally, the very year Gay Liberation activists successfully lobbied the American Psychological Association to remove homosexuality from its list of psychopathologies. The move to Boston would provide not only psychic and physical distance from his family and the bullies who terrorized him in Hamilton but also an opportunity to start over. In a new city, a thousand miles from home, Michael could reconstruct a new identity "from the shambles of what was left after eighteen years in Ohio."[4]

According to his college transcripts and a résumé he typed in 1977, Michael took several semesters each of German, Latin,

---

2 Ibid., 5.
3 Ibid.
4 David Schmidt, interview with Michael Callen, 12 November 1987, typescript (henceforth, DS and MC [1987]), Michael Callen Papers at The LGBT Community Center National History Archive (henceforth, MCP). Callen describes this "first" experience differently in several sources. In the Schmidt interview, he notes that it occurred *after* moving into his dorm, i.e., in the fall of 1973. However, other, earlier documents in the MCP locate the event during his scholarship audition, which would have been in the fall of 1972 or the spring of 1973.

art history, and creative writing alongside the usual first-year sequence of music classes including harmony, counterpoint, and music history, in addition to private voice lessons with Wilma O. Thompson (1915–2000). He was a member of Boston University's Stage Troupe, which produced plays and musicals like Harvey Schmidt and Tom Jones's *The Fantastiks* (1960), Richard Brinsley Sheridan's *The School for Scandal* (1777), Edna St. Vincent Millay's *Aria da Capo* (1920), and a short-lived production of Steven Schwartz's *Godspell* (1971), directed by Michael.[5]

While Boston was exciting and new, this first year away from home proved to be the most difficult year of his young life. A first-generation college student from a small Midwestern town, Michael felt the aches familiar to those who are the first to leave home and begin a different sort of life. Sometimes resentful, homesick, and frightened, he wrote to friends back home about the stresses and tribulations of "trying to live in two places at once," as he struggled to maintain closeness with his family and, at the same time, to establish his independence.[6] He had suicidal thoughts, depression, anxiety and even contemplated dropping out of school. Ultimately, however, he knew that he could not turn back, admonishing himself to "shit or get off the pot. It was either LIVE — really live (like make a new life, new friends, new responsibilities, new commitments) or come back to Hamilton…and, do what?"[7] In the summer of 1974, Michael made the "monumental decision to stay in Boston," find an apartment, and bravely stare down his future.[8]

Feeling constrained by the music program's emphasis on classical and concert music, or as Michael put it, "finding these particular arts not so fine," he dropped his music major during his second year at Boston University and declared a new focus in English Literature and Creative Writing "by default. […]

---

5 Michael Callen, résumé, 1977, typewritten original, MCP.
6 Michael Callen, letter to Barb (childhood friend, not his mother), 9 August 1977, typewritten original, MCP.
7 Ibid.
8 Ibid.

When in doubt, major in English!"⁹ As an English major, he studied the classics of Antiquity, Shakespeare, and other great (usually male) authors. He also took a course on Emily Dickinson (1830–1886) and even signed up for a poetry seminar with Anne Sexton (1928–1974), though the author's suicide meant they never met. Michael also made his first contact with other LGBTQ+ students in Boston.

Gay students in Boston-area colleges and universities benefited from a degree of openness that differed from other cities, though this did not mean an absence of homophobia. On 4 December 1969, just a few months after the Stonewall uprising, students at Boston University established the city's first gay student organization, The Boston University Homophile Club (BUHC).[10] By the fall of that year, lesbians in Boston had founded their own chapter of the Daughters of Bilitis. Soon, gay and lesbian students at nearby Harvard and MIT established their own homophile clubs, and there was considerable overlap in the membership of all these organizations.[11] There was also a Boston chapter of Gay Liberation Front, and the city was fortunate to have a robust gay press. Launched by the Boston-based Fag Rag

9   Ibid.
10 Boston University Homophile Club, "Your Love Is a Sin, a Crime, a Perversity," 1970, typewritten original, the William J. Canfield Papers at Northeastern University, featured in "We Raise Our Voice: Celebrating Activism for Equality & Pride in Boston's African-American, Feminist, Gay & Lesbian, & Latino Communities," online exhibit, *Northeastern University Libraries, Archives, and Special Collections*, https://voices.library.northeastern.edu/.
11 While such organizations are common on college campuses in the twenty-first century, this was not so in the 1960s and 1970s. Founded in 1966, Columbia University's Student Homophile League, one of the first LGBTQ+ student organizations in the country, refused to submit lists of member names to the school's administration out of concerns for student safety, and as a result, the organization was refused official status, given no funding from the university, and prohibited from using campus spaces to hold meetings. As recently as the 1990s, LGBTQ+ students and faculty groups at major universities like the University of Georgia held their meetings in secret, behind closed doors, and literally with the blinds closed to prevent prying eyes or outing participants. Annette Hatten addressed the experiences of UGA's first LGBTQ+ faculty group in a speech during the organization's annual reception at the University of Georgia in 2014.

Collective in 1971, *Fag Rag Quarterly,* a radical leftist newsletter with a national readership, was vehemently "denounced on the floor of the US Congress as 'the most loathsome publication in the English language.'"[12] The weekly *Gay Community News* first hit newsstands in 1973 and maintained a national readership throughout the decade.

Compared to other American cities, Boston had a distinctive, intellectual gay subcultural and activist style. "New York was sexier, and [San Francisco] was really sexy, but Boston was smarter," according to Michael Bronski. "Boston really generated *ideas.*"[13] Boston's gay community left an indelible mark on Michael for years to come, and so, too, did its feminist movement.[14] As part of his project of self-education, Michael read

---

12 Leon Neyfakh, "How Boston Powered the Gay Rights Movement," *The Boston Globe*, 2 June 2013, and see Jim D'Entremont, "Pilgrim's Progress: Boston's Gay History," *The Guide*, November 2007, archived at https://web.archive.org/web/20160203060339/http://archive.guidemag.com/magcontent/invokemagcontent.cfm?ID=211D6820-56B6-41CB-8DF1503C48C70284

13 Quoted in Neyfakh, "How Boston Powered the Gay Rights Movement." For more on Boston's political history, see Jim Vrabel, *A People's History of the New Boston* (Amherst: University of Massachusetts Press, 2014).

14 Since the American Revolution, Bostonians have played vital roles in social justice movements from abolition and suffrage, labor organizing, Women's Liberation, and gay rights. Feminism found especially fertile soil in Bean Town. First-wave feminist leaders like Elizabeth Cady Stanton (1815–1902) and Julia Ward Howe (1819–1910) spent formative years in the city, laying the groundwork for women's suffrage while rubbing elbows with New England literati like The Alcotts and Ralph Waldo Emerson. In 1964, a group of Black American women formed Mothers for Adequate Welfare to advocate for poor and working women, and Emmanuel College hosted the first feminist conference in 1969. From this conference came Bread and Roses, the nation's first socialist women's organization. In 1971, the Boston Women's Collective published the first edition of *Our Bodies, Our Selves,* a cornerstone in the women's healthcare movement, and Female Liberation churned out mimeographed copies of *The Second Wave: A Magazine for the New Feminism* from 1971 to 1984. In 1977, The Combahee River Collective issued the first version of its seminal manifesto, effectively establishing what would come to be called "intersectional" feminism by addressing the exclusion and erasure of women of color and lesbians from the agendas of the National Organization for Women (NOW) and other predominantly white, straight feminist groups.

radical feminist theory. Author-activist Gayle Rubin's seminal essay "The Traffic in Women: Notes on the Political Economy of Sex" (1975) galvanized his political consciousness. However, he still saw himself as a musician. "Music is at present the sole joy of my existence," he wrote. "If I have a soul at all, it's in my music."[15]

Although he knew of the existence of the BUHC, Michael had never attended a meeting, and thus entertained fantasies of shameful, clandestine gatherings shot through with fear and anxiety. Spotting an advertisement for a gay and lesbian student picnic in *The Boston Phoenix*, his "jaw dropped [at] the notion that you could be out in college and use college facilities."[16] What's more, the gathering was scheduled to take place on the commons by the Charles River, right across from Michael's dorm on Bay State Road! On the afternoon of the picnic, he nervously "circled around until somebody named Marty Algaze came over and said, 'I think you're looking for us.'"[17] Within three months, Michael was president of the organization. His meteoric rise through the ranks resulted neither from political acumen nor leadership aspirations but, as Michael later explained with characteristic candor, because "nobody else was stupid enough to do it."[18]

While committed to Gay Liberation, BUHC was hindered by the perennial ebb and flow of busy student schedules. It was also plagued by internal conflicts stemming from larger tensions between lesbian-separatist feminists and gay men. Separatist feminists envisioned a distinct lesbian culture without the influence of men and patriarchal thinking while other gay men and lesbian women had begun to worry that the goals of the gay movement were moving from sexual *revolution* to just sex. The

---

15 Callen, résumé.
16 Jeffrey Escoffier and Michael Callen, "My Rise from Complete Obscurity," in *In My Time: Essays on Sex, Science, and AIDS*, ed. Jeffrey Escoffier, unpublished manuscript, 1993, Richard Dworkin Private Archive (henceforth, RDA).
17 Ibid.
18 Ibid.

tensions were real and threatened the future of the BUHC. During the first meeting of Michael's brief presidency,

> the lesbians came specifically so they could walk out. And I got very badly burned early. Politics is who steps up to bat. People would sign up for committees [...] and not show up and never call back, and I'd end up doing everything.[19]

By the end of the semester, Michael worried that "gay politics attracted egomaniacs and people that really needed therapy, people that were working out their deep problems in public."[20] His nascent political career ended almost as quickly as it began. He abandoned the gay student group and gay politics more generally, dismissing both as nothing more than "a smelly fart."[21]

Coming Out Backwards

Although Michael shied away from political activism, he undertook an extracurricular regime of self-education and edification in gay history, literature, visual art, dance, music, and sex. "If it had anything remotely gay about it," he later recalled, "I would buy it or see it."[22] His explorations of gay culture lead to an epiphany, namely that "the horrible things mainstream society was saying about us — things [he] had internalized — were not true."[23] Inspired by Gay Liberation ideology and the feminist adage that "the personal is political," Michael began a process that he later described as "coming out backwards."

Michael's journey out of the closet began not with overt political organization (his brief stint with the BUHC notwithstanding) but with public sex and cruising. After a tryst in a tearoom, the man in the adjacent stall passed Michael a note scrawled on toilet paper. The short message read, "Did I see you at the bath-

19 Ibid.
20 Ibid.
21 Ibid.
22 Ibid.
23 Michael Callen, *Surviving AIDS* (New York: Harper Perennial 1990), 3.

houses?" Callen scribbled back his response, "What's a bathhouse?" The two men exited to rendezvous on the street, where the stranger "explained that there were places that gay men went which were sort of a quasi-gymnasium/health club where there were cubicles and stuff."[24] This short conversation served as Michael's entrée into the orgiastic world of gay bathhouses where he participated in "a noble experiment [through membership in] a brotherhood of lust. Where else [...] could a Wall Street stockbroker and a Puerto Rican delivery boy, each divested of the costumes and privileges of rank and class 'come together' as equals? The situation seemed positively *charged* with radical potential."[25]

While perhaps romanticized and quixotic in his memory, Michael's bathhouse adventures prompted insights of a more personal, thus political, nature. One evening, a man remarked that Michael seemed like he was "built to get fucked" then proceeded to prove the point. "Voila! [Mike] had a moment of

---

24 DS and MC (1987) and Escoffier and Callen, "My Rise from Complete Obscurity."
25 Callen, *Surviving AIDS*, 4. This quote echoes the opening of Laud Humphreys's *Tearoom Trade: Impersonal Sex in Public Places* (Piscataway: Aldine-Transaction Publishers, 1970), an infamous and iconic work in LGBT studies, notable for its ethnography of men engaged in cruising and public sex. Questions surrounding the ethics of Humphreys's research have never been fully resolved. I have no evidence as to whether Callen read *Tearoom Trade*, but his language here evokes the opening lines, "At shortly after five o'clock on a weekday evening, our men enter a public restroom in the city park. One wears a well-tailored business suit; another wears tennis shoes, shorts, and teeshirt; the third man is still clad in the khaki uniform of his filling station; the last, a salesman, has loosened his tie and left his sports coat in the car" (2). While the baths provided a relatively safe place for men to have sex with other men, they served other purposes as well. Some baths were social and cultural hubs that featured movie nights, dances, and live entertainment. "The Divine Miss M," Bette Midler herself performed at New York's Continental Baths with a very closeted Barry Manilow accompanying her at the piano. In the 1970s, some bathhouses offered health services that were difficult or embarrassing for men to otherwise obtain, including important STI/STD screening and treatment. And finally, for young men with few other options or places to go, bathhouses, like YMCAs and other sex-segregated spaces, offered safe, inexpensive places to sleep. For a few dollars, a patron could check into a cubicle or private room.

'sheer revelation.'"[26] He had discovered anal sex. He did it many more times that first night and from that moment on "made a habit of announcing to a potential trick [...] that he was a 'stone bottom,'" playfully inverting the language of untouchable "stone butch" lesbian masculinity to describe his preference for being penetrated.[27]

The final step in Callen's retrograde coming out was to go to a gay bar. Back in Ohio, bars were places "truckers hung out and drank cheap beer," so the existence of bars for gay men struck the naïve college student as especially novel.[28] Bars were, generally speaking, of little interest to Michael, who didn't drink alcohol or dance. Because there was less verbal foreplay before getting down to business, the baths just made getting laid much simpler. Still, he dragged himself out to explore the bar scene. While no record exists of the specific bars he frequented, there are a few famous Boston destinations like Playland Café (21 Essex St., the city's oldest gay bar in operation 1937–1998), Jacque's (79 Broadway, which opened in 1938 and for a while catered exclusively to lesbians), and The Other Side (78 Broadway, owned by the same management as Jacque's, 1965–1976) that he would have had the opportunity to patronize.

Emboldened by feminism, Gay Liberation, and his first romance, Michael "came out with a vengeance" during his junior year and grew "bitter, abrasive, rigid, and impatient," going to battle with "everyone, especially [his] family" in the process.[29] On a Saturday night in 1976, Michael called his brother. "Barry, I have something to tell you," he began. "I'm gay." Although Michael was "capital G-A-Y, dressing like Granny Clampett, singing like Streisand," Barry was caught off guard by his younger

---

26 Duberman, *Hold Tight Gently*, 6.
27 Ibid. The classic text about the "stone butch" is Leslie Feinberg's *Stone Butch Blues: A Novel* (Ann Arbor: Firebrand Books, 1993). Before hir (this is Feinberg's preferred pronoun) death in 2014, Feinberg updated the novel for its 20th anniversary. It is available for free download at https://www.lesliefeinberg.net/.
28 DS and MC (1987).
29 Callen, *Surviving AIDS*, 3.

brother's revelation.[30] "So, you're happy?" he replied, assuming this was one of Michael's oddball jokes. At the time, Barry was a self-described Christian who was "praying for God to take [his] strong sexual drive away," and he could not fathom that his brother was homosexual.[31] "I knew he was weird but didn't know he was gay!"[32] Barry spent the evening wondering whether Michael was having "unnatural sex, but then [he] thought, 'What do you know about natural sex? You're a virgin!'" A few hours later, Barry picked up the phone. "I love you," he told his brother, "and I always will."[33]

Still, the mechanics of gay sex remained baffling to Barry, and Michael seized this opportunity to scandalize his brother by describing gay sex in exacting detail. "Let me explain it to you so you can understand," he began, savoring every syllable. "Sometimes I put my dick in their ass and their mouth and vice-versa."[34] Michael's coming out deepened the bond between the brothers, and Barry remained his younger brother's confidant and champion. Barry's support gave Michael the courage to tell their mother, who responded with less enthusiasm, pleading with her son that "whatever you do, do not tell your father."[35] Michael refused to hide his identity from his father, and in a sitcom-worthy twist, Cliff responded by saying, "whatever you do, do not tell your mother!"[36] This comic episode aside, Michael's coming out strained his relationship with his father.[37] During

---

30 Barry Wayne Callen, interview with author, 21 September 2013 (henceforth BWC and MJ [2013]). Michael also talks about his coming out in DS and MC (1987), *Surviving AIDS,* and Escoffier and Callen, "My Rise from Complete Obscurity."
31 BWC and MJ (2013)
32 Ibid.
33 Ibid.
34 Ibid.
35 DS and MC (1987).
36 Ibid.
37 Ibid.

the ensuing "very ugly" period of two years, father and son refused to speak "because it was simply too painful."[38]

Reflecting on his life back in Hamilton, Michael concluded that he "had no sex life [there and] was only into unrequited love [because he] was repressing [his] natural N O R M A L sexual attraction to males."[39] Like many gay people, Michael's childhood and adolescence had left him feeling rather lonely. While he had dated girls back in Hamilton, he had done so only to kowtow to heteronormative pressures in his small hometown. A thousand miles from home and his old life, Michael was ready for a gay romance. Fate intervened when he met Richard Pillard (b. 1933). Born in Springfield, Ohio, Pillard graduated from Antioch College, went to the University of Rochester Medical School, and interned in Boston, eventually taking a faculty position in psychiatry at the Boston University Medical School. In 1958, he married Cornelia Livingston Cromwell with whom he had three daughters. The couple divorced a few years later. Pillard came out as gay, making him one of the first openly gay psychiatrists in the US, and began an important series of psychological studies that investigated the possible biological basis of homosexuality.[40] Michael fell for the older man, and they began a brief relationship that was undone by differences in age and the power dynamics between the college senior and a medical doctor and university professor. For now, however,

---

38 Ibid. and Callen, *Surviving AIDS*, 3. In a series of notes for a piece that was never written called "Mike Goes to the Baths" (c. 1984), Michael recalls the man's name, writing "I first got fucked by a man named Caleb on a trip to NYC from Boston. Historic. Weird feelings that this was where it had all begun for me — getting fucked, that is." This set of fragmentary notes evokes the spirit of Benjamin's *The Arcades Project*. It can be found online at http://michaelcallen.com/mikes-writing/mike-goes-to-the-baths/.
39 Callen, letter to Barb, 9 August 1977. Underline in original.
40 Pillard's initial suspicions about a biological basis for homosexuality came from his own family: both his brother and sister and one of his daughters identify as LGBTQ+, and Pillard believes his father might have also been gay. See Chandler Burr, "Homosexuality and Biology," *The Atlantic* 271, no. 3 (March 1993), 47–65. Also see Richard C. Pillard and James D. Weinrich, "Evidence of Familial Nature of Male Homosexuality," *Archives of General Psychiatry* 43, no. 8 (1986): 808–12.

he threw himself into love wholeheartedly, and even after they ended their romance, they would remain friendly for the rest of Michael's life.

In the spring of 1977, Michael traveled from Boston to New York City, where he visited sex clubs like the Mineshaft (835 Washington St.) and gay bathhouses like the Everard (28 W 28th St.) and the St. Marks Baths (6 St. Marks Place). At The Club Baths (24 First Ave.), he got fucked by a handsome redhead named Caleb, an experience that left him feeling like "a bottomless pit, so [he] stayed there to get fucked by as many people [as] wanted to fuck [him], which was a lot."[41] On the bus back to Boston, he felt a bit unwell but dismissed his symptoms as travel fatigue from sleepless nights. By the time he made it home, his fever reached 104, and he had severely bloody diarrhea. Puzzled by a diagnosis of shigellosis (an infectious disease caused by the bacteria *Shigella*), Michael's doctors asked if he had been out of the country [he had not] and recommended that he stay in the hospital a few days. However, Michael had other plans. He had graduated *cum laude* on 22 May 1977 and planned to move to New York within a few days. So, he yanked out his intravenous drips, dressed, checked out of the hospital, and left for New York, doubled over with cramps and diarrhea the entire trip. He moved into a tiny run-down boarding house on Christopher Street, and as soon as he was "able to stand up and get fucked," Michael went back to the Mineshaft.[42]

---

41 Michael Callen, interview, n.d., audio recording, MCP.
42 Ibid.

Fig. 1. Michael Callen headshot modeled after Barbra Streisand's *Memories* album cover (c. 1980). Richard Dworkin Private Archive.

5

Nobody's Fool

Now, some would say I'm just my father's son,
That I am cold and distant and hard on everyone.
Father to son, now son to lover,
I judge you and begrudge you the love you need.
I wanna be your fool.
— Michael Callen

New York City was the East Coast hub of gay life, and by the time Michael arrived in 1977, Gay Liberation was in full swing. In enclaves like the West Village, gay life achieved an unprecedented level of visibility due to the sheer numbers of LGBTQ+ people in the city. Gay-owned and gay-friendly bars, restaurants, bookshops, coffee houses, community organizations, and social groups flourished, providing community members safety, visibility, and opportunity. In the 1970s, gay sex was gay revolution, and urban gay male sexual culture developed in radical opposition to ubiquitous homophobia, draconian sodomy laws, medical mandates, and religious condemnation by embracing the pleasures and politics of the flesh. The influx of young, single, and horny gay men into New York ushered in a new culture of public and commercialized sex in cruisy areas like the Central Park Ramble, the Hudson River Piers, and a plethora of bathhouses, sex clubs, and gay bookstores throughout the city. Such sexual-cultural practices intentionally disregarded norms of compulsory heterosexuality. A popular t-shirt then worn by gay men captured the zeitgeist with a simple slogan: so many men, so little time.

Michael moved to New York ostensibly to pursue a career in music, and while he did write some songs and play a few gigs at piano bars, his musical efforts were half-hearted. His real passion was sex, *lots* of sex. For a young gay man in the late 1970s, New York City was *the* proverbial candy store, and Michael had an insatiable sweet tooth. Because a virile young gay man never knew where or when sex in the city might strike, Michael always carried with him the gay man's sexual survival kit: small packets of K-Y lubricant, a bottle of amyl nitrate poppers, two tetracycline pills, and Handi-Wipes to clean up after a tryst.

While the city presented unparalleled opportunities for sex, it also presented certain challenges for naïve and inexperienced young men, especially those with uncertain career aspirations and limited financial means. "Not only must one be on the way up at work," gay author Edmund White warned, but also "produce good conversation, good food, good sex, attract the right friends, dance all night, jog three miles, press 200 pounds, and have an opinion about Caballé's *pianissimo*. One must have the drive of a tycoon, the allure of a kept boy, the stamina of an athlete, the bonhomie of a man of the world." In White's final estimation, this "is not a formula for happiness. No one can embody all or even most of these virtues, and the failure to do so can produce grave self-doubts."[1]

Michael suffered from what he called "classic gay low self-esteem," a complex of self-doubts, anxieties, and fears that resulted from the friction between homophobic society (which regularly denigrates LGBTQ+ folks as second- and third-class citizens, when it recognizes their fundamental humanity and rights at all) and queer lived experiences. With the help of a psychotherapist, he battled his own internalized homophobia, sought to be assertive and present-focused, and learned to state clearly his needs and wants. His therapeutic journey also includ-

---

1   Edmund White, *States of Desire Revisited: Travels in Gay America* (Ann Arbor: University of Michigan Press, 2014), 380.

ed confronting his parents about their inability to communicate openly and their continuing refusal to accept his sexuality. The ongoing Cold War of words with his father was a major source of pain in Michael's life. No matter how hard he tried, Michael could not get through to his father.

In spite of the geographic and ideological gulfs separating them from their son, Barbara and Cliff maintained a lively written correspondence with Michael. From the late 1970s to the early 1990s, they exchanged impassioned letters often.[2] These letters offer a glimpse into the private workings of one American family dealing with homosexuality in the last decades of the twentieth century. Among the letters in the Callen archive from 1973 to 1993, two things stand out. First, father and son were equally stubborn. Clifford's resolve to avoid the subject of homosexuality met its match in Michael's insistence on its manifestation in every aspect of his daily life. Second, the members of the Callen family loved each other very much, evidenced by their willingness to exchange ideas about the nature of masculinity, family, and sexuality over three decades.

Throughout the 1970s and '80s, Michael and his father typed their letters, using the page as a scrim behind which they could, to some extent, hide. They subjected one another's letters to painstaking semantic analysis, ferreting out meaning in every textural detail. Their tone is often dispassionate, academic, and detached, though both Michael and Cliff erupt through the page with great feeling on more than one occasion. In person or over the telephone, however, aversion became an art. Their conversations consisted of polite exchanges of pleasantries about work, family members, or the weather. This pattern repeated in Barry's conversations with his father, and the two brothers used to get some catharsis by comparing the details of their respective conversations with their dad.

---

[2] There is a gap in the archival record at The LGBT Community Center National History Archive from 1981 to 1992, with few letters to or from members of the Callen family. Certainly, their relationship continued to change as they negotiated new pathways into loving one another.

By the end of the 1980s, Clifford started to write his letters by hand using a whimsical novelty notepad with "Cliff's Notes" at the top in the familiar yellow and black design of the popular *CliffsNotes Guides*. A different Cliff spills out onto these pages among words scribbled in his messy penmanship. His gruff demeanor softened over time. No longer a stern patriarchal *father*, Cliff became more of a dad and grandpa. These later letters tend to be brief yet more deeply personal, filled with touching observations about post-retirement life (Barbara played a good bit of Nintendo, it seems) and warm declarations of fatherly love. Though they are shorter, less critical, and sometimes perfunctory, each letter ends with the same closing: "Take care, and we will be talking. Love, Dad."

A common theme in their correspondence was the love that bound their family, but they also clashed over contentious issues, especially Michael's homosexuality. Cliff refused to *verbally* discuss it, yet his letters demonstrate that he was willing to face and discuss his son's sexuality in *written* form. During a particularly heated epistolary exchange in the last two months of 1979, father and son negotiated the boundaries of their relationship. Michael fired the first shot, writing that "therapy hasn't been successful unless you can tell your parents that you love them or to go fuck themselves."[3] Over several eloquent and impassioned pages, he condemned his family's tendency to "hint for love [then] wait around hoping someone will sense we are deep in the need — to be touched, to be reassured, to be talked to, brought up, brought down."[4] As his letter closed, Michael confronted his father's homophobia directly. Perhaps Cliff was embarrassed about having a gay son, Michael reasoned, but the path to reconciliation and healing could only begin with an open admission of these feelings. Michael believed that they could work toward a better relationship "together, out of mutual love."[5]

3 Michael Callen, letter to Clifford Callen, 7 November 1979, typewritten original, Michael Callen Papers at The LGBT Community Center National History Archive (henceforth, MCP).
4 Ibid.
5 Ibid.

Cliff preferred dispassionate, intellectual conversation over emotional exchanges, which he handled clumsily, and his rebuttal illustrates his taste for analytical discourse, even when the subject was his son's identity. First, however, he took a pot shot at the insights Michael gained from psychotherapy, noting its near complete bankruptcy as a helping profession. "If your therapist is telling you that you are not being assertive enough," he quipped, "he reads you differently than I do or ever have."[6] Then, he adopted a critical distance that allowed him to wipe away any residual confusion about his view of homosexuality. Mr. Callen felt that his son

> consciously and freely chose [the homosexual] lifestyle with the full realization and knowledge that the relationships of family and most friends would be adversely affected. [...] In short, Mike, you with more potential than I ever dream any son of mine could have, effectively caused to be closed many, if not most of the doors or opportunities to serve mankind, to the degree theretofore possible, or even likely.[7]

He even blamed Michael for resorting to "some subterfuge at times" in order to disguise his sexuality and he reiterated his wish to avoid the subject of Michael's sexuality completely. "A satisfactory relationship does not require complete agreement," he wrote. However,

> <u>all relationships must have reasonably outlined parameters within the basic tenets of each person's philosophy.</u> Outside these parameters there is too much conflict or not enough common ground on which to operate successfully. I feel that if you and I can agree on the above underlined sentence, we can function [...]. It is unlikely we will spend large blocks of

---

6 Clifford Callen, letter to Michael Callen, 13 November 1979, typewritten original, MCP.
7 Ibid.

> time together, so I don't feel I'm asking for the moon for you to 'play it straight' when we are together.[8]

Cliff proposed that they take pleasure in common interests and safe topics: entertainment, travel, family, shared past experiences, and future plans.

Although the twenty-first-century discourse of heterosexual privilege was not contemporary with the Callen family's correspondence, it is clear that Michael and his mid-century queer compatriots were working out the foundations of that concept in their personal relationships and their political thought. Michael attempted to explain systemic homophobia and the invisible, or unmarked, nature of heterosexuality to his father by providing a list of compulsorily heterosexual behaviors in which his parents engaged thoughtlessly and without comment, molestation, or protest from anyone:

> You touch mother. You discuss your marriage. You mention that you live together. That you have children. All these are silent expressions [...] of your basic heterosexuality. No one accuses you of slapping your sexuality in everyone's face just because [mother] wears a wedding band. And yet it says as much about your sex life as my admission of gayness says about [mine].[9]

By contrast, invisibility was the norm for gay men and lesbian women. "Nowhere in the mass culture," Michael reasoned, "can we see two men holding hands or kissing or in any way feeling good about themselves."[10] Headstrong, determined, and self-assured, Michael refused to relent. "I cannot isolate my gayness," he insisted. "I do not do so with my present and vital relationships, and I cannot and will not revert to hiding an aspect of my

---

8   Ibid. Underline in original.
9   Michael Callen, letter to Clifford Callen, 17 November 1979, typewritten original, MCP.
10 Ibid. Emphasis in original.

being of which I am very proud and which is one of the primary sources of pleasure in my life."[11]

Michael even tried to appeal to his father's political sensibilities by offering a brief summary of gay history from the nineteenth century through the 1969 Stonewall rebellion, hoping that this historic display of community pride might vanquish his father's homophobia. The eloquent passage in Michael's letter reveals the depth of his thinking about the relationship between sexuality, power, and the human capacity for growth through critical self-reflection:

> The only answer for us, father, is *education*. You are going to have to trace back the source and power of your negative reaction [to homosexuality] and brutally and painfully examine it to see what is reasonable and what is not. I mean emotionally reasonable as well as intellectually, although I repeat that I feel that the mind (your mind especially) is one of the ways to your heart. We can't always change how we feel, but we can change how we think, and <u>sometimes</u> that <u>can</u> change the way we feel.[12]

Finally, Michael made a heartfelt plea to his father's basic emotions *as a father*:

> When you think on the subject of gayness, you need not think much farther than me. Look closely at who I am. You saw me form. Am I much different now that you know than I was before you knew? What difference is there, if you perceive a difference? Is that difference for the better or the worse?
>
> I KNOW THIS IS HARD FOR YOU AND MY TRUE SOURCE OF SADNESS IS THAT TWO WHO OBVIOUSLY LOVE EACH OTHER SO MUCH MUST BE LOCKED IN THIS LIFE-AND-DEATH-LIKE STRUGGLE TOWARDS FREEDOM TO EXPRESS THAT LOVE FOR

---

11 Ibid.
12 Ibid. Emphasis added. Underline in original.

EACH OTHER. Society and socialization are standing between us — a civil war between father and son. I have fought alone for so long [...] and now, war weary, I am watching your suffering intensify.

The givens are that I am homosexual, and you are heterosexual. We must build love from that basic difference. Just remember, all we are talking about here is love.[13]

Clifford Callen would not waver. He vehemently disapproved of his son's *chosen* lifestyle and prohibited any discussion of homosexuality, claiming to get "physically nauseated when forced to *consider* the subject, much less talk about it."[14]

Although Cliff had encountered gay men during his time in New York with the Merchant Marines, and both he and Barbara knew of isolated gay or lesbian individuals, mostly older spinsters and confirmed bachelors, as a general rule homosexuality was "very abstract and very foreign" to them.[15] As was (and remains) the case for many parents, they assumed that all three of their children were heterosexual, inasmuch as they considered it at all. From this assumption came an array of other presumed "facts" of heterosexual life: the relative degree of masculinity/femininity which should correspond to a person's biological sex; personality traits and appearance; the biological sex, gender, and degree of masculinity/femininity of an individual's preferred partner; procreative decisions; the way you have sex; and the parts of your body you (and others) consider appropriately erotic.[16] From his parents' perspective, Michael's coming out

13 Ibid. Allcaps in original.
14 David Schmidt, interview with Michael Callen, 1987, typescript (henceforth, DS and MC [1987]), MCP. Emphasis in original.
15 Barbara Callen, interview with Michael Callen, 24 February 1992, audio recording, MCP; Clifford Callen, interview with Michael Callen, 26 February 1992, audio recording, MCP.
16 Eve K. Sedgwick, *Tendencies* (Durham: Duke University Press, 1993), 6–7. Sedgwick writes: "Think of all the elements that are condensed into the notion of sexuality identity, something that the common sense of our time presents as a unitary category. Yet, exerting any pressure at all on 'sexuality

Fig. 2. Barry, Michael, Cliff, and Barbara Callen, at Linda Callen's Wedding. Courtesy of Barry Callen.

"upset their plans [...]. It meant that they wouldn't have grandchildren. It meant that they didn't know what it would mean."[17]

Even though Michael could muster some degree of understanding of their beliefs, he never capitulated to his parents' prejudices. When Linda married in the early 1980s, she wanted her brother to sing at the ceremony, but their parents worried that he would show up with a male companion as a date. In a letter to his sister, Michael insisted that

> until things are worked out between Mom and Dad and I about whether my friends and lovers are allowed into 66 Warr Court — until I can be convinced that I can expect that anyone I would bring [there] would be treated with fundamental human dignity and respect [...] I will never again cross that doorstep myself. If who I truly am is not welcome

identity', you see that its elements include" all the items listed above and others. For Sedgwick, there is no "truth" in sexual or gender identity. They are part of the operations of heteronormative power in culture.

17 DS and MC (1987).

Fig. 3. Cliff and Michael Callen on the Beach (c. 1982). Richard Dworkin Private Archive.

> [...], then the silhouette of a son that they would like to perceive me to be has no place there either.[18]

With Barry and Linda also living away from home, Barbara was left to mediate the feud between father and son. One on hand, she strongly believed that homosexuality was morally wrong; on the other, however, she felt that the "biblical mandate for mothers to love their children [was] stronger."[19] During a trip to New York in June 1981, mother and son had a "good, honest 'gut-spilling'" which left both feeling optimistic.[20] In a three-page handwritten letter to her son after the visit, Barbara worked out her complex and contradictory feelings. "If we **truly** love someone," she wrote, we "must accept them as is."[21] Mrs. Callen believed that father, mother, and son could "work out (of compromise)

---

18 Michael Callen, letter to Linda Callen, 10 March 1981, typewritten original, MCP.
19 DS and MC (1987).
20 Barbara Callen, note to Michael Callen, June 1981, handwritten original, MCP.
21 Ibid. Boldface and underline in original.

[sic] ways to make it easier on each other."²² However, she knew that her son would have to initiate that compromise, given her husband's extraordinary stubbornness. Her letter closed with a heartfelt declaration of affection, praising Michael for growing into "the kind of person we raised you to be — kind, thoughtful, intelligent, and a unique individual — your own kind of person."²³ With a knowing wink, she added that "most of these attributes can be directly attributed to your father, as I'm sure you know."²⁴ In both his constitution and the strength of his convictions, Michael was truly the son of his father.

Please, Talk to Your Daddy

Second-wave feminism was animated by the notion that the personal is political, and the use of personal, lived experience as a key to unlock larger systemic forms of oppression worked its way into other forms of activism as well as the arts. Many songwriters and poets turn to their own experiences for inspiration. Anne Sexton (1928–1974) and Sylvia Plath (1932–1963) epitomized the "confessional" midcentury poet, and their respective battles with depression and eventual suicides seemed to solidify mis-readings of their art as direct reflections of their private lives. Songwriters like Joni Mitchell have resisted the "confessional" label, insisting that their works should be mined not for autobiographical trivia but for something that resonates in the listener's own life. There are degrees of theatricality in art and in everyday life, as Erving Goffman, Simon Frith, Philip Auslander, and others have shown.²⁵ There is the real artist, offstage, going about daily life, and there is an artistic persona or

---

22 Ibid.
23 Ibid.
24 Ibid.
25 See Erving Goffman, *The Presentation of Self in Everyday Life* (New York: Anchor Books, 1959); Simon Frith, *Performing Rites: On the Value of Popular Music* (Cambridge: Harvard University Press, 1990); Philip Auslander, *Performing Glam Rock: Gender and Theatricality in Popular Music* (Ann Arbor: University of Michigan Press, 2006).

star text created around the artist. Finally, there are infinite dramatic personae adopted in individual songs and performances, and this is as true for singer-songwriters as it is for composers of musical theater and pop stars. The semantics of musical performances and recordings can make it difficult to distinguish between one "lamination" (Goffman's term) or layer of a star persona and another, but all musicians utilize musical and non-musical elements to construct authenticity.[26] In the hands of lesser talent, such "confession" become mere journaling or reportage, but from gifted artists, the results can be sublime.

One of Michael's greatest virtues (and one of the things that could make him difficult as a child, friend, or lover) was his insistence on speaking his own truth, even when it revealed painful or embarrassing things about himself or those around him. It was also one of his greatest assets as a writer. He had a knack for capturing the nuances of conversational language in his lyrics and prose. Inspired by Joni Mitchell and Laura Nyro (1947–1997), whose music he admired, Michael began to use personal experiences as song material, making universal gay art rooted in his own gay truth, and this can be heard in one of his most beautiful ballads.

A masterful portrait of a family in crisis, "Nobody's Fool" is a domestic triptych in three irregular verses. Stretching his dramatic writing and performance skills, Michael sings the roles of Mother, Father, and their estranged gay Son.[27] The title echoes a line from one of his father's letters. Describing what he felt after learning that his son was gay, Cliff did not mince words:

---

26 For more on the musical and non-musical elements of genre, see Franco Fabbri, "A Theory of Musical Genres: Two Applications," in *Popular Music Perspectives,* eds. D. Horn and Phil Tagg (Göteborg and Exeter: International Association for the Study of Popular Music, 1981), 52–81.

27 Michael was experimenting with similar themes as early as 1980. In the MCP, I discovered a handwritten, unfinished lyric from 5 June 1980 on stationary from the Georgetown Dutch Inn in Washington, DC, that reads, in part, "Papa don't like me / He thinks I'm no good / Mom's disappointed / She never thought I would / Be who I came to be / She don't want me loving you / You weren't raised that way / What do you want me to do / What will the neighbors say."

"To be thought a fool is anger provoking to the greatest degree possible."[28] Michael used his father's anger as the point of departure for a deep exploration of the impact of his coming out, and to examine the chilling effect his father's rectitude had on the other members of their family. He captured the resulting breakdown of communication among members of this most loquacious family in terms that balance the personal and the political, the particular and the universal.

> Talk to your Daddy
> He misses you. He does–
> In his own way
> I know it was rough
> For you and your brother
> But do it for me
> Talk to your Daddy
>
> If you could see him
> Through my eyes
> Sometimes he tries so hard
> But he's old now
> And he's set in his ways
> And sometimes I worry
> He's just counting the days
> Please talk to your Daddy
>
> *
>
> Hello? Son?
> Yeah, your Mom said it was you
> How's the job?
> Who me? Hell, I'm just old
> And gettin' older
> How's the weather there?
> It's gettin' colder here

---

28 Clifford Callen, letter to Michael Callen, 13 November 1979, typewritten original, MCP.

Wish you could come home
And see your Mom
She sure misses you boys
What'd you say?
Mama, turn down that TV!
You know I can't hear
With all that noise
She sure misses her boys

Your brother called the other day
Said he got screwed out of a
Whole day's pay
Him and some foreman,
They got in a fight
That boy's got a bad temper
I told him it served him right

Your mother says I'm too hard on everyone
But I ain't nobody's fool
Do unto others
Before they do unto you
That's my golden rule
I ain't nobody's fool

How long we been talkin'?
I ain't made of money
Honey, come and say goodbye
Take care now and call your Mom
I'll let you go now
Anything you need…
Just let me know.

*

Now, some would say
I'm just my father's son
That I am cold and distant

And hard on everyone
Father to son, now son to lover
I judge you and begrudge you
The love you need

I wanna be a fool
I wanna be a fool
I wanna be your fool

> — "Nobody's Fool" (Tops and Bottoms Music, BMI)
> Courtesy of Richard Dworkin

In the first stanza, Michael sings quietly with measured precision. Careful pitch placement and clear diction suggest that the mother has carefully chosen her words, and yet her opening plea reveals just how difficult this situation is for her. Although "Talk to your Daddy" is a declarative statement, Michael's voice trembles slightly, and in that small gesture he reveals the mother's emotional burden as she serves as the go-between for her husband and son. Michael's expressive piano playing underscores the shifting affective state of each speaker. The first section begins with a stately piano figure, and throughout both Michael's playing, like his singing, remains hushed and deliberate, a sonic reflection of the mother's mindfulness of the impact of every word she utters.

The second section is spoken by the father. There is a rehearsed banality to his words, typical of a certain sort of phone call home in which "all the players [try] not to talk about what was really going on."[29] The father asks about work and the weather, the same sorts of "safe" subjects Cliff had suggested that he and Michael stick to in their exchange of letters. Specific rhetorical gestures distance the father from the situation as well as from rest of the family. He uses second-person possessive pronouns, emphatically referring to "your" mom, never "my wife," and to his other son as "your" brother instead of "my son." Whereas

29 DS and MC (1987).

the mother's singing in the previous verse was deliberate and precise, the father slides between pitches, sings through throaty *r* and nasal *n* consonants, utilizes a greater range of dynamic contrasts, and occasionally abandons singing for pure speech. Michael sings in his chest voice, a choice that makes the father seem more vocally masculine. Throughout this verse, powerful bass notes and agitated rhythms in the piano accompaniment reflect the father's stormy emotions. Powerful bass notes and agitated rhythms reflect the father's stormy emotions. This more unrestrained music is ironic, given how hard the father works to conceal his emotions through small talk. Like Michael's own dad, the father in the song seems most comfortable when discussing uncontroversial subjects. However, he gets caught up in the emotional swell of a story about a fight between his older son and a foreman at work. This provides cover for a revelation of his true feelings: "Your mother says I'm too hard on everyone, but I ain't nobody's fool." Rather than risk being duped by anyone, he espouses a decidedly offensive philosophy: "Do unto others before they do unto you. That's my Golden Rule." Yet his verses, like Clifford's own letters, end abruptly, with a bittersweet declaration of affection for his son: "I'll let you go now. Anything you need, just let me know."

In the last section, Michael adopts the persona of the narrator-son. Although some people might note similarities in the personalities and dispositions of father and son (coldness, distance, and being too hard on others), the son wants to break the chain that stretches "father to son, now son to lover." Rather than "judge and begrudge" his lover, the gay son resolves to be his lover's fool, indicated by a leap into his soaring falsetto on that word, the higher register seemingly more comfortable and authentic, perhaps a sonic expression of his gayness. The accompanying music is lighter, its rhythms gentler, and played in piano's treble register. The son experiences a cathartic transformation and embraces his full range of emotions. He allows himself to be loved, and quite possibly hurt, rather than live a life of manly stoicism.

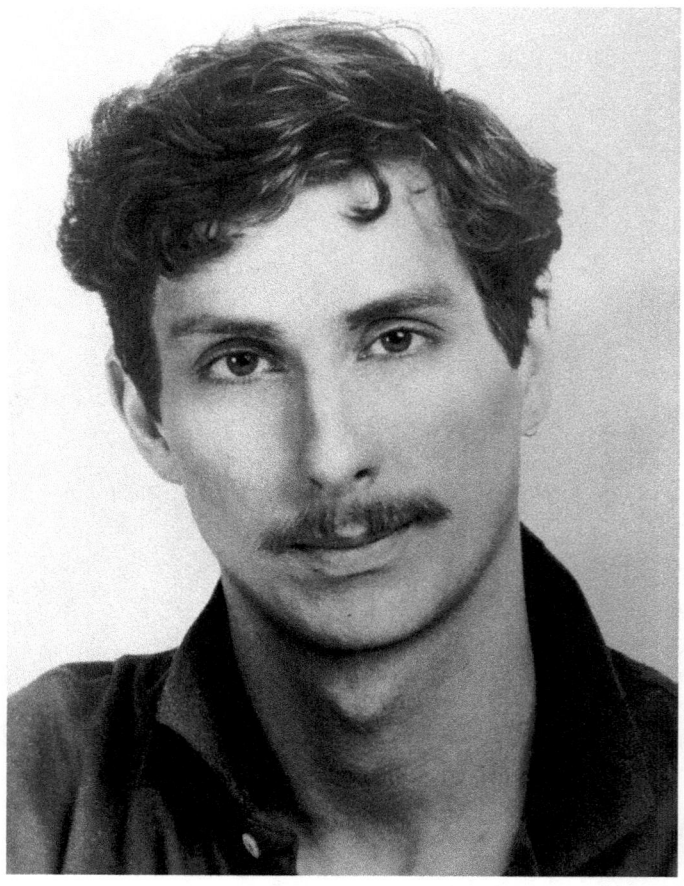

Fig. 1. Michael Callen Headshot (c. 1981). Richard Dworkin Private Archive.

6

Where the Boys Are

> *In a crowd of a million people,*
> *I'll find my valentine.*
> *Then I'll climb right up on his steeple*
> *and tell the world he's mine*
> — Neil Sedaka & Howard Greenfield,
> New lyrics by Michael Callen

Michael's first months in New York were trying as he navigated urban gay life and the stresses of New York itself. Living in the city brought with it a host of problems he had not encountered in either Hamilton or Boston. Of these, money was the most immediate. Having arrived with about $200 and no job prospects, Michael found a dilapidated room in a boarding house, paid a month's rent, and went to an employment agency to find work, with only twenty dollars left in his pocket. His first job placement was in a law firm with good pay, at $245 a week, and even a Christmas bonus. Furthermore, he could work nights, freeing up his days to focus on music. However, the job turned out to be a disaster. The firm used word processing equipment with which Michael was unfamiliar, and after he spent a sleepless night trying to memorize the complex manual, he was fired the next day and returned to the employment agency.[1]

---

1   Michael Callen, letter to Jon, n.d., typewritten original, the Michael Callen Papers at The LGBT Community Center National History Archive (hence-

While he looked for work, daily necessities still required money, too. He couldn't afford a telephone, which strained his relationship with Richard Pillard. At some point, Richard had loaned Michael $600, and now Michael worried about being in debt to his lover and about ever being able to pay him back. Strapped for cash, he eventually wandered up to Times Square, then a center for sex workers, where he gave a stranger a blowjob for four dollars, which he used to buy food. Because hustling depressed him and didn't provide a sustainable solution to his money problems, this was the only time Michael turned a trick to make a buck. He hoped things would take a turn for the better when he found another job, but he was fired during his first month after piercing his right ear (then a trend among out gay men in New York). Soon thereafter, Michael was "fagbashed" near the West Side Highway in a horrifying and traumatic encounter with an attacker who broke a two-by-four over his hip. Then, his apartment caught fire and nearly burned, and he awoke one night to find a rat slinking across him.[2]

It was all too much, and Michael began to question his decision to move to New York. Maybe he just wasn't cut out for life in the Big Apple. Maybe he should just go back to Hamilton.

After some difficult months, however, Michael adjusted to life in New York. He found a steady job as a legal secretary at Bradford National Corporation, moved into a nicer apartment at 18 Christopher St., and began to strategize his musical career.

In the late 1970s, New York was in the midst of a profound aesthetic shift, and Michael was living at ground zero of these new movements. Despite his proximity to the avant-garde downtown scene, however, Michael was out of sync with it. He didn't dance, drink alcohol, experiment with drugs, or care about edgy fash-

forth, MCP). The letter is undated, but on p. 9 Michael mentions that he has only lived in New York for two months, which means July or August 1977. Jon seems to be a friend from college.

2 Jeffrey Escoffier and Michael Callen, "My Rise from Complete Obscurity," in *In My Time: Essays and Sex, Science, and AIDS by Michael Callen*, ed. Jeffrey Escoffier, unpublished manuscript, 1993, Richard Dworkin Private Archive (henceforth, RDA).

ion. Musically, too, he was an anachronism. Michael's music had more in common with early-1970s Bette Midler than Patti Smith or the Talking Heads. His overtly gay version of the Middle of the Road (MOR) balladeering of New York compatriots Melissa Manchester and Barry Manilow was outmoded by downtown standards. And even these pop music luminaries responded to changes in musical taste, technology, and production by adopting contemporary aesthetics. Manchester dove headfirst into New Wave on *Hey Ricky* (1982), *Emergency* (1983), and *Mathematics* (1984) while Manilow updated his sound for the '80s gradually across several albums. Likewise, even pioneers of the singer-songwriter movement like Carole King (*Speeding Time*, 1983), Joni Mitchell (*Dog Eat Dog*, 1985), and Neil Young (*Trans*, 1982) experimented with synthesizers and new styles in the first half of the decade.

With the security of a day job, Michael took stock of his musical aspirations. "Lord knows why I never sang in Boston," he wrote to friends. "How ridiculous. How I ever justified it to anybody. God, you guys should have kicked me!"[3] However, he was optimistic. "I'm about 4 years behind in my career [but] I'm impetuous. I'm fast. It takes a lot of breaks here, but I feel now as if I can really start getting an act together [...] getting an accompanist, getting a musical director. I've got to do that for my sanity."[4] He typed up copies of his artistic résumé, posed for professional headshots, and even applied for a grant from The Glines, a non-profit for gay and lesbian artists that was founded in 1976 by John Glines, Barry Laine, and Jerry Gobin.[5] Eventually, Michael connected with like-minded musicians at Mickey's (44 W 54th St.), Reno Sweeney (126 W 13th St.), S.N.A.F.U. (676 6th Ave.), and The Duplex (61 Christopher St.), but the piano

3   Michael Callen, letter to Jon (n.d.).
4   Ibid.
5   The Glines is "devoted to creating and presenting gay art in order to develop positive self-images and dispel negative stereotyping." They brought Harvey Fierstein's *Torch Song Trilogy* to Broadway in 1981 and produced William Hoffman's *As Is*, one of the earliest plays about AIDS, in 1985. For more, see http://theglines.com/.

bars and cabarets — the places that would welcome his musical style — that had once dotted the Manhattan landscape were shuttering their doors as punk, New Wave, and emergent hip-hop styles revolutionized the city's music scene.

Although Michael had sung in choirs back in Hamilton and had studied voice at Boston University, he cultivated his vocal technique and style primarily through his own listening, mimicry, and synthesis. His mixture of Julie Andrews, Judy Garland, Barbra Streisand, and Bette Midler resulted in a dramatic but nondescript singing style: explosive and declamatory delivery of text, mile-wide vibrato, and overuse of belting. Like many young singers who possess extraordinary instruments but lack a clear artistic vision, Michael over-sang, reveling in the visceral pleasure of his voice, but he had yet to develop the vocal discipline and control that would elevate his singing to artistry or a signature style. Throughout his first years in the city, he worked on singing techniques by taking voice lessons with famed voice teacher Keith Davis (1909–1994), who coached Peter Allen (1944–1992), Barbara Cook (1927–2017), Gwen Verdon (1925–2000), Neil Sedaka (b. 1939), and other notables in the world of theater, opera, cabaret, and popular music. He also met pianist, singer, and arranger Buddy Barnes (1940–1992). Barnes, who would die of AIDS-related illness in 1992, had been jazz singer Mabel Mercer's (1900–1984) musical director from 1965 to 1972 and had since worked with other jazz and cabaret stars including Dorothy Loudon (1925–2003), Rita Gardner (b. 1934), and Sylvia Syms (b. 1934). The collaboration with Barnes pushed Michael to find his own voice.

A 26 May 1979 rehearsal tape captures Michael and Buddy Barnes at work on a set that included songs by Cole Porter, Kander and Ebb, "obscure 40s and 50s show tunes, and more current pop songs."[6] From his seat at the piano, Barnes advised Michael to reign in some of his over-the-top vocal mannerisms (vestiges of his deep admiration for Garland and Streisand) and

---

6 Michael Callen, résumé written at 29 Jones St., n.d., typewritten original, MCP.

"to let the song have a life of its own without injecting too much of your own emotion."[7] Each time they begin Kander and Ebb's "My Own Space" (from *The Act* [1977]), Michael dials back the "diva-isms," and his own beautiful and expressive voice starts to work for, rather than against, him. From Barnes, Michael learned to balance the yin and yang of his musical impulses as sensitive crooner and dramatic belter and to coax the feeling from a ballad. Still, his inner diva also worked her way into his performances, especially in his stage antics, props, costumes, and audience banter. On 27 January 1980, Michael made his New York City debut at The West Bank Café with Barnes at the piano.

- "New World Coming" (Barry Mann and Cynthia Weil)
- "Billie's Blues" (Laura Nyro)
- "Gotta Have Me Go with You" (Harold Arlen, *A Star is Born* [1954])
- "Here's that Rainy Day" (Jimmy Van Heusen and Jonny Burke)
- "Pennies from Heaven" (Johnny Burke and Arthur Johnson)
- "Another Hundred People" (Stephen Sondheim, *Company* [1970])
- "I'm Calm" (Stephen Sondheim, *A Funny Thing Happened on the Way to the Forum* [1962])
- "Right as the Rain" (Harold Arlen and E.Y. Harburg)
- "Almost Like a Song" (Ronnie Milsap)
- "Big Time "(Michael Stewart and Jerry Herman, Mack & Mabel [1974])
- "6:30 Sunday Morning/Touch Me in the Morning" (Peter Allen; Ron Miller, and Michael Masser)
- "If I Had You "(Irving King (Jimmy Campbell and Reg Connelly, and Ted Shapiro).
- "Ridin' High" (Cole Porter)
- "Welcome Back Again" (Buddy Barnes and Rowan Brown).
- I'm Over You (Marsha Malamet)
    — Michael Callen and Buddy Barnes Setlist, c. 1980

7   Buddy Barnes and Michael Callen, rehearsal tape, 26 May 1979, MCP.

Reviews of Michael's earliest live shows were mixed. *Gay New York* praised him as "the personable new young man in town [who is] as talented as he is good looking," while *The New York Post* noted that he "gives off mixed identities [and] elicits mixed feelings, too [because] all of the personal disciplines that direct a performance are not jelled yet."[8] David Sloan of the *New York City News* heard in Michael a "fresh, *commercial* gay vocalist" who delivers "a kind of music-for-you-and-your-lover anthology, with flawless, torchy versions of some of the best popular ballads of the last three decades" alongside his own songs which "have a sophisticated, pop sheen." Although Michael's sets needed "one or two faster, punchier songs to lend variety and leaven the overall loaf," Sloan was confident that Michael had "the panache to pull off something more closely resembling an out-and-out rocker [...]. He will probably show us that and much more."[9]

Negative reviews bruised Michael's ego, and sometimes insecurity and anxiety prevented him from performing entirely. "I am not performing," he wrote to his parents, "because I cannot risk rejection. Is that the sickest? It's easier to keep saying I want to be a singer than to sing."[10] Dissecting his feelings with surgical precision, perhaps as a result of his time in therapy, he admitted his fears:

> Let's talk about terror. We all know terror. It comes in small, subtle ways. What if and what do I do when, etc. My terrors: that I'm not talented. That I am not attractive. That I am not as intelligent as I would like everyone to believe. Doubts. I need love. I need reassurance.[11]

---

8 Unknown, "Michael Callen," *Gay New York*, February 1980; Curt Davis, "A Mixed Bag, or a Mistaken Identity," *The New York Post*, 9 October 1981, MCP.
9 David Sloan, "A New Vocalist for the Rest of Us," *The New York City News* 11, no. 23, 1 December 1981, MCP.
10 Michael Callen, letter to Cliff and Barbara Callen, 7 November 1979, typewritten original, MCP.
11 Ibid.

Loneliness remained a major problem for Michael. In the absence of close friends and a lover in New York, he sometimes felt despondent. In early 1980, he began dating George Harvey, a closeted member of the New York Police Department. In June, Michael celebrated five months with George in several lengthy, handwritten lover letters. "If you cannot be here physically," he wrote, "at least I can share my love with you this way."[12] Michael surrounded himself with souvenirs of their nascent relationship and described the scene in meticulous detail. "You are everywhere around me. To my right, the card I received today [...] the lamp you gave me lights this table. Your picture is straight ahead [...]. On the mantle — a cheap glass vase I bought the last time we were upstate. The sleeping bag where we made love is now soundproofing my piano — the piano that conceived the song (it wrote itself) that you brought me."[13]

In another effusive twenty-one-page letter, Michael traced the outline of his hand and wrote that this is "the hand of a man who loves you. This hand has rubbed your forehead, rubbed your neck, your hands, and feet and legs. This hand has cupped your beautiful penis and balls and brough them to my mouth to kiss and drink. [...] I would love to walk down a beach with this hand holding yours."[14] On the same page, he kissed the paper, leaving a red lipstick print of the "lips [that] have kissed every inch of your body, as they would be doing now if you were here."[15] While Michael occasionally worried such professions of love would alienate George, he allowed himself to be vulnerable, even if a bit maudlin:

> You are my father. You are my son. You are my daughter; you are my mother. You are my lover.

---

12 Michael Callen, letter to George Harvey, 23 June 1980, handwritten original, MCP.
13 Ibid. This song is called "Just Know That I Love You." Michael's recording from the *Legacy* sessions in 1993 remains unreleased.
14 Michael Callen, letter to George Harvey, 18 June 1980, handwritten original, MCP.
15 Ibid.

Fig. 2. "Scenes from Our Marriage." Drawings by Michael Callen (c. 1980). The Michael Callen Papers, Box 1/Folder 12, the LGBT Community Center National History Archive.

> I am your father; I am your son; I am your daughter; I am your mother. I am your lover.
> Mother brother father daughter lover. We are lovers.
> [...]
> Before I would have run into some stranger's arms and said to myself that I just needed to get my load off. But not now. I like saving it for the man I love. I hope he has some for me. Especially the drops.[16]

Michael also included several "erotic scenes from our marriage," simple sketches himself, against a kitchen counter, and over the kitchen table. In the middle of the page, Michael wrote, "Remember?" These notes may seem a little childish in retrospect, but Michael was allowing himself to be emotionally vulnerable with another man — differentiating himself from the stoic model of manhood he had fought about with his father for so many years.

In 1980, Michael also joined the New York City Gay Men's Chorus (NYCGMC), under the baton of founding director Gary Miller (who led the chorus until 1998). In the chorus, he befriended Joel Jason, Bobby Butler, Chris Humble, and Aurelio Font. Michael would host rehearsals of the NYCGMC tenor section in his apartment. Gathered around the piano, the men worked on their music and forged friendships that lasted for years. Joel became one of Michael's closest friends as the two bonded over their shared love of sex, music, and cooking. He recalled showing up at Michael's apartment for rehearsal and finding dozens of stands of homemade pasta draped over every object and surface in the tiny space, from broom handles to the arms of chairs. The singers had to huddle into the cramped space to sing, careful not to disturb Michael's latest culinary creation.[17]

Michael's musical friends believed in his talent and helped him find himself artistically. They encouraged him to "cut the bull shit [*sic*]; [reminding him that] you're great; you're talented;

---

16 Ibid. By "drops" he means "drops of semen."
17 Joel Jason, interview with author, 23 May 2020.

Fig. 3. Michael and Friends (c. 1980), l–r: Chris Humble, Bobby Butler, Mark Howansky, Michael Callen, Joel Jason. Richard Dworkin Private Archive.

now get your ass out there. We'll be there."[18] Although friends and music professionals encouraged Michael's pursuits, they also suggested that he place a lighter accent on his sexuality in order to bolster his mainstream appeal. A great admirer of Cris Williamson, Meg Christian, Holly Near, and Sweet Honey in the Rock, whose recordings were immensely popular among lesbian and straight feminist women, Michael felt frustrated by gay men's reluctance to support gay male musicians. To him, gay men seemed less interested in "confessional" and intimate acoustic singer-songwriters, especially after the rise of disco. Nevertheless, gay culture, art, and theater had saved Michael during college, and he was determined to create music for gay audiences, regardless of its impact on his mainstream appeal.[19]

18 Ibid.
19 There were some openly gay men in the music industry, including Sylvester (1947–1988), Jobriath (1946–1983), Steven Grossman (1951–1991), and Michael Cohen (1951–1997). Sadly, none of these men achieved lasting success, and three (Sylvester, Jobriath, and Grossman) had died of AIDS-related ill-

ness by the 1990s. Cohen died in 1997, though his cause of death is unclear from the scant historical record of his career. Grossman's *Caravan Tonight* (1974) was the first major-label record to deal with openly gay themes. Cohen's *What Did You Expect? Songs About the Experience of Being Gay* (1973) tackles similar material. Sylvester was a flamboyant San Francisco figure who became, for a time, an international star with the success of songs like "Mighty Real" and "Disco Heat." He collaborated with renowned producer and composer Patrick Cowley (1950–1982), who also died of AIDS-related illness. Sylvester was an anomaly in the 1970s mainstream, a Black, femme, gender-non-conforming superstar, but Sylvester's management team tried to "straighten" his image as his fame grew. On *Sylvester* (1977) and *Step II* (1978), the singer appears in more conventionally normative-masculine clothing and sings in his rich baritone on songs like "Was It Something That I Said." In the song's brief spoken introduction, The Two Tons O' Fun (Martha Wash and Izora Rhodes, later known as The Weather Girls) offer the following evasive exchange: "Izora: Child, have you heard the latest? / Martha: Uh-oh. What's going on now? / Izora: About Sylvester breaking up! / Martha: He done broke up with, umm…"

Wash noticeably avoids naming Sylvester's love interest, allowing the line to swing both ways. On *Living Proof* (1979), Sylvester dedicated the ballad "Sharing Something Beautiful between Us" to his "lover, who is here tonight, who I love very much."

David Bowie (1947–2016) made headlines when he declared himself gay in a 22 January 1972 *Melody Maker* interview; he later self-identified as bisexual in a 1976 interview with *Playboy*, though he reneged both statements in the 1980s, saying it was "the biggest mistake I ever made" and that he was "always a closet heterosexual." See David Sinclair, "Station to Station," *Rolling Stone*, 10 June 1993, reprinted in Sean Hagan, ed., *Bowie on Bowie: Interviews and Encounters with David Bowie* (Chicago: Chicago Review Press, 2015), 231–48. In *Melody Maker*, 22 January 1972, Bowie told journalists Michael Watts, "I'm gay, and always have been." In the *Playboy* interview, Bowie admitted to Cameron Crowe that "I can't keep track of everything I say. I don't give a shit. I can't even remember how much I believe and how much I don't believe. The point is to grow into the person you grow into. I haven't a clue where I'm gonna be in a year. A raving nut, a flower child, or a dictator, some kind of reverend—I don't know. That's what keeps me from getting bored." Whatever Bowie's private identity/identities, his public comments made queerness visible in important ways.

Elton John initially came out as bisexual in 1976. In 1992, he self-identified as gay in a *Rolling Stone* interview. Freddie Mercury (1946–1991) never publicly self-identified as gay, though he did reveal that he was dying of AIDS on 23 November 1991 in a public statement released about twenty-four hours before he succumbed to AIDS-related illness. George Michael (1963–2016) only came out publicly after his 1998 arrest in a Los Angeles men's room. Barry Manilow, the singer to whom Michael was most often

An undated home video recorded by Elliot Linwood McAdoo, Joel Jason's boyfriend at the time, captures Michael contemplating his musical growth and development.[20] The video appears to be an exercise designed to open Callen up to audiences by looking at them directly as he performs. Capturing his musical habits on camera enabled Michael to examine himself objectively and to strategize ways to boost his on-stage charisma. Frustratingly, Michael found that he could not escape the influence of his favorite singers whose gestures and vocal inflections he had so carefully scrutinized that he had internalized them. While performing, he "tried to make faces, [but he] would make Streisand [or Midler] faces, not *Michael* faces," and sometimes he saw himself as just a gay imitation of Streisand's "awkward, gawky, actor-style singing."[21] Some of this stemmed from youth and lack of experience. Most performers need a lot of "gray hair" before they can successfully concoct the alchemy of stardom from an amalgam of talent, technique, and time. However, the video shows that Michael was taking his musical development seriously at the time.

Now that he had found his artistic focus, Michael set extraordinarily high standards for himself. "I want to be funny like Midler. I want to be moving like Midler. I want to be as deep and profound and energetic as Springsteen. I want to be as intellectually penetrating as Joni Mitchell. I want to be as remote as Laura Nyro," he tells the camera. "I'm so very into the words and think that is what is so very important, but I see that some people are able to do it [reach audiences] with sheer volume."[22] From behind the camera, Elliot probes Michael, encouraging him to dig deeper into his artistic psyche. "What is that these

---

compared, may have tickled the ivories at The Continental Baths for The Divine Miss M, but Manilow himself would not publicly come out as gay until 2017.

20 "Mike at Jones St., Early 80s," recorded by Elliot Linwood McAdoo, n.d., home video, RDA.
21 Michael Callen, letter to Clifford and Barbara Callen, 7 November 1979, typewritten original, MCP.
22 "Mike at Jones St." (n.d.)

days that's on your mind [as a performer]?" After pausing to think, Michael states unequivocally, "I have to start writing more up tempo numbers."[23] Obviously taking recent critical reviews of his performances to heart, he notes that:

> All the songs that I have written so far have been very much victim, very much self-pity, very much that the world is basically a horrible place, and if you find happiness, then I don't believe it'll be for the long road [...]. I will always be able to go there, that sort of Joni Mitchell, Laura Nyro moan, how they bay at the moon. But I want to be able also to get in touch with some joy and some happiness and do some song that isn't profound [where] every word isn't critical. What's happening is that the material I write has nothing to do with the stage. It has to do with how I feel walking around my apartment.[24]

Fragments of lyrics written during this time confirm that Michael's compositions remained primarily in the confessional lyric ballad style, and his lyrics were replete with torchy images of empty beds, tousled sheets, broken hearts, and lonely mornings:

> Morning comes in a stranger's bed.
> Stains on the sheets,
> Pain in my head.
> And I can't remember
> If anything was said,
> And I don't even know your name.
> Trading numbers we'll both throw away.
> Seems there isn't much to say, but,
> "Keep in touch, o.k.?"
> "O.k."
> And it looks like another lonely day.[25]

23 Ibid.
24 Ibid.
25 Michael Callen, "And It Looks Like Another Lonely Day," song fragment, 1980, typewritten original, MCP. There are perhaps a dozen fragments of

While some of Michael's songs were based on lived personal experience, he also drew inspiration from real-world events in gay culture, politics, and history. One unfinished song seems to be about the 1978 murder of San Francisco city supervisor Harvey Milk (1930–1978):

> The years pass
> Sentences, not justice, get served.
> They only get what they deserved,
> And as everyone from the bars to the street queens knowns
> "toujours la meme chose."
> […]
> It's easy to let the lies
> Of the passing of time
> Sentimentalize and soften the pain,
> And in the end,
> All this loss and this gain
> And candle-lit marches
> In the cold November rain.
> A man lived.
> A man died.
> A man was tried.
> A wife stands by her husband's side.
> A lover cried in the night.
> […]
> Cop cars burning
> Tear gas and broken glass
> Lighting up the night white with rage
> Street fighting
> We cannot let some things pass
> A movement must come of age
> Rage! Rage!
> Against the light of this dying
> Rattle the cage
> And fight! Keep trying to

songs that explore similarly maudlin topics in the MCP.

End all this pain and this lying
And the crying out for the
Right to love free.[26]

Written in 1981 with his friend Bobby Butler, "Innocence Dying" was inspired by a deadly fire at The Everard Baths (28 W 28th St.).[27] At around 7am on 25 May 1977, the same spring Michael moved to New York City, "scores of men, some clad only in towels or robes fled their rented cubicles and the dormitory" scrambled to escape as nearly two-hundred first responders fought to rescue patrons. Men leapt from second floor windows to the sidewalk on 28th St. as the second-story roof collapsed, killing nine patrons.[28] According to firemen interviewed at the scene, the nine were so badly scorched by the flames that "you couldn't even tell they were bodies."[29] Eventually, all nine men were identified, many by gay friends or lovers because their biological families refused to come forward.

"Innocence Dying" brings together Michael's penchant for piano ballads and his interest in telling gay stories. In the song, a "fragile child" with "porcelain hands and Barbie© doll hair" moves along the currents of gay migration, "out of the south and into the bars" of New Orleans before arriving in New York. Along the way, he befriends "older queens" who guide him through this new milieu, yet he still bears the "scars of a redneck father who never bothered to love him." Possessed by a profound loneliness, he finds himself in "places where young boys go, down on their luck with no place to go, giving head in

---

26 Michael Callen, "Untitled Fragment," n.d., typewritten original, MCP.
27 A fragment in the MCP titled "Song for Robert" contains the first verse and chorus with slightly different lyrics. It ends with this stanza, "Dum da da. Etc. / Go to policeman meeting in bar / Lives crossing paths / flames / you know: happy shit."
28 Laurie Johnston, "9 Killed in Fire Identified by Friends," *The New York Times,* 27 May 1977.
29 Ibid. A comprehensive history of the Everard, including photographs and news footage of the fire, is provided in "Fire in the Everard Baths," *StevenWarRan,* 15 July 2014, https://stevenwarran.blogspot.com/2014/07/fire-in-everard-baths.html.

Fig. 4. Michael Callen headshot proof sheet (1979). Photos by Kenn Duncan. Richard Dworkin Private Archive.

some stranger's bed just hoping he'll buy you breakfast." With a few dollars earned from sex work, the young man rents a cubicle in The Everard Baths, where he smokes a joint, pops a Quaalude, and resolves to "settle for sleep [and] worry about love tomorrow." However, tragedy soon strikes. "Trapped in [his] gay prison cell," the young man perishes in his sleep as "fire, like some lover, runs its fingers though [his] hair."

The autobiographical connections are fairly transparent. Like Michael, the song's protagonist made his way from a rural hometown to an intermediate city, and finally to New York, where he turned to sex work as a solution to starvation. However, the song is not merely a confessional account of Michael's journey, for he introduces a surprising twist. Throughout the first and second verses the narrator speaks in a third-person omniscient voice, recounting the action but not as a participant himself. In the final verse, however, the voice shifts to first-person, and the narrator reveals himself to be the John who could not be bothered to show compassion and kindness to a hungry, lonely "blonde kid from down south" whose face stares back at him from among those who perished in the Everard fire. Decades later, in October 1993, Michael received a letter from his former boyfriend, George Harvey, purporting to reveal the identity of one of victims of the fire as Robert Alexander Richards; however, Richards is not listed among the dead in contemporary media coverage of the story. Although the song remains unreleased, Michael did record it for his final album in 1993.

- Innocence Dying (1981)*[30]
- Let Me Down Easy (also with Mark Howansky, 1981)*
- Old Maids (1981)*
- On the Other Side (1981)**

— Songs written with Robert Butler

---

30 *unreleased; ** released on *Purple Heart* (1988).

- I Know (1981)*
- I Love You Now (for Norma Ettori and David Sandgrund on Their Marriage, with Love, 1981)*
- Nobody's Fool (1982)**
- Just Know I Love You (for George D. Harvey on His Birthday, 1981)*
- Strangers (1981)*
- Street Singer (1981)*
- But There's No One Here (1981)*

— Songs written by Michael Callen

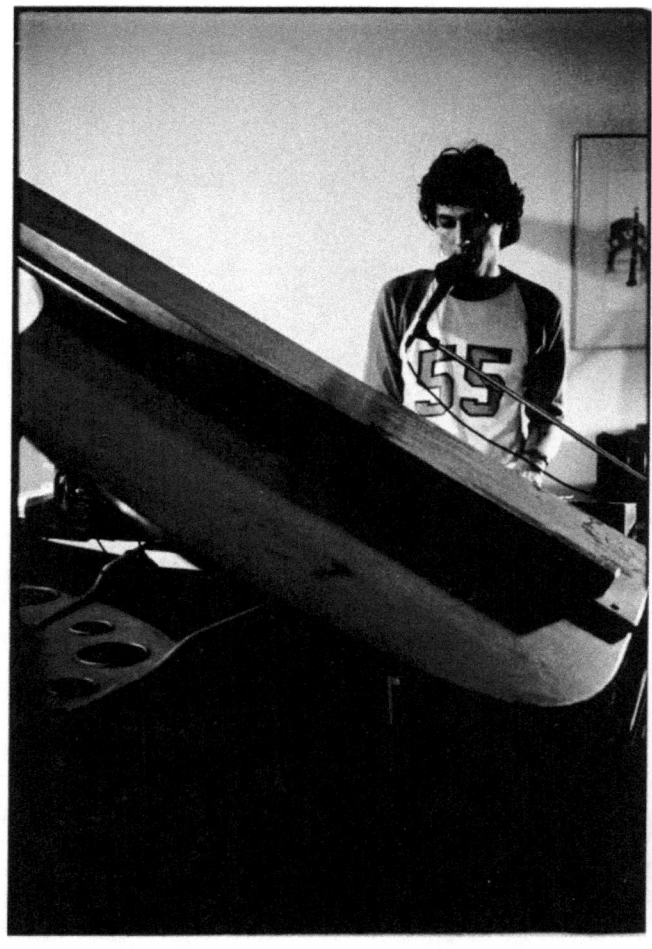

Fig. 1. Michael Callen at the piano, 129 Duane St. (c. 1985). Photo by Richard Dworkin.

7

Living in Wartime

> *Conspiracy of silence*
> *The enemy within*
> *Complacency and arrogance*
> *make us think we cannot win*
> *make us think that the battle has been won*
> *But the thunder in the distance*
> *says it's only just begun*
> — Michael Callen

Across the twentieth century, Americans were on the move. The Great Migration (c. 1916–1970) brought more than 6 million African Americans out of the Jim Crow South and into Northern, Midwestern, and West Coast cities where they hoped to "drink of new and cool rains, bend in strange winds, respond to the warmth of other suns, and, perhaps, to bloom."[1] By the end of World War II there were an unprecedented 8.3 million active duty US soldiers, most away from their homes and families for the first time, many from small towns and rural America. Ironically, the military's rigorous homosocial environment allowed many closeted gay men and women to explore their same-sex attractions for the first time. After the war, rather than going to back to cities, small towns, and rural areas across the country,

---

1 Richard Wright, *Black Boy: American Hunger,* restored edn. (New York: HarperCollins, 1998).

they settled in the port cities where they returned: New York, San Diego, San Francisco, Los Angeles, and elsewhere. Likewise, LGBTQ+ Americans joined their own Great Gay Migration. Gay enclaves flourished, sometimes in the immediate neighborhoods surrounding the ports, and with them, opportunities for gay sex in cruisy parks, tearooms, bathhouses, and bars multiplied.

Sexual mores were also loosening, in part, because of these demographic shifts, but also due to advances in science and changes in the law. More Americans were having more sex and, as a result, more STIs. During World War II, rates of syphilis and gonorrhea were so high that the US military mounted aggressive public awareness campaigns (replete with misogyny, racism, and xenophobia), and across the mid-twentieth century, STI rates increased steadily.[2] However, the discovery of antibiotics in the 1950s meant that bacterial infections, including common STIs like chlamydia, gonorrhea, and syphilis, could now be readily treated. The widespread availability of legal and effective birth control after 1960 gave women an unprecedented degree of agency over their reproductive destinies, and the 1973 *Roe v. Wade* ruling ensured the right to a safe and legal abortion. New STIs, including the human papillomavirus (HPV), were discovered in the 1950s, then linked to cervical, anal, and other cancers in the 1980s. The Tuskegee Syphilis Experiment was an especially egregious and racist study that began in 1932 and ended in scandal in 1972 but left a legacy of distrust in Black American communities that influenced the response to the AIDS epidemic and continues to overshadow public health efforts today. Over four decades, more than six hundred Black men, many with wives and children, were deceived into an observational study of untreated syphilis. The disease ravaged their bodies, families, and communities and was only halted after an Associated Press exposé resulted in public outcry. The Tuskegee Syphilis Experiment exacerbated distrust between minority communities and

---

2   See Sevgi Aral, Kevin Fenton, and King Holmes, "Sexually Transmitted Diseases in the USA: Temporal Trends," *Sexually Transmitted Infections* 83, no. 4 (2007): 257–66.

medical and public health authorities, and these tensions persist into the present.³

Sex has long been operationalized in US American politics, from laws prohibiting sodomy (a catchall category that, at times, included anal and oral sex as well as bestiality) and restrictions on the sexual agency of women, people with disabilities, and people of color to the fight for marriage equality and the #MeToo movement. In the 1950s, homophile activists began a fight for legal rights of LGBTQ+ Americans, though these early activists sought to minimize overt discussions of sex and sexuality.⁴ After the Stonewall uprising in 1969, Gay Liberation activists foregrounded these once taboo aspects of gay life.

"Although the lesbian and gay political agenda was much broader than sex," Michael "was only interested in the part that dealt with pleasure. One strain of seventies gay liberationist rhetoric proclaimed that sex was inherently liberating; by a curiously naïve calculus, it seemed to follow that more sex was more liberating. I should consider myself more liberated if I'd five thousand partners than if I'd had five hundred. Some of us believed we could change the world through sexual liberation."⁵ Furthermore, Michael believed that gay men were "promiscuous by nature," and he enthusiastically participated in New York's gay sexual subculture.⁶

While his general health had never been terrific — he had endured a number of serious childhood and adolescent illnesses — Michael, like many gay men of his generation, gave almost no thought to his *sexual* health. During his first year at Boston

---

3   For a timeline of the Tuskegee Experiment, see the CDC's page, https://www.cdc.gov/tuskegee/index.html. James Jones's *Bad Blood: The Tuskegee Syphilis Experiment* (New York: The Free Press, 1993) is a classic account of the experiment's history. Fred Gray's *The Tuskegee Syphilis Study: An Insider's Account of the Shocking Medical Experiment Conducted by the Government against African American Men* (Montgomery: New South Books, 2002) was written by one of the lawyers who represented plaintiffs in the lawsuits.
4   For more, see Eric Cervini, *The Deviant's War: The Homosexual vs. The United States of America* (New York: Farrar, Straus, and Giroux, 2020).
5   Michael Callen, *Surviving AIDS* (New York: Harper Perennial, 1993), 4.
6   Ibid., 3.

University, he had contracted his first case of gonorrhea. In New York, the frequency with which Michael had sex increased as did his number of different sexual partners; so, too, did the frequency with which he was diagnosed with STIs. At this point, he reasoned, he'd only slept with a few hundred men — what was the worst that could happen? Things began to snowball quickly:

> First came hepatitis in 1976. Then more gonorrhea and NUS [*sic*, NSU, or Non-specific urethritis]. In 1977, amoebas and Hepatitis B. More [NSU] and gonorrhea. 1978: more amoebas. And my first case of shigella. And of course more VD. Then in 1979, hepatitis yet a third time: this time, non-A, non-B. More amoebas, adding giardia this time. And an anal fissure. And my first case of syphallis [*sic*]. And of course more gonnorhea [*sic*]. In 1980: the usual gonnorhea, shygella [*sic*] twice/more amoebas.[7]

By age twenty-seven, Michael could count more than three thousand different sexual partners, a figure he arrived at by means of simple arithmetic. As he explained,

> I have been having gay sex in tearooms, bathhouses, bookstores, backrooms, and movie houses since I came out at 17. I estimate, conservatively, that I have had sex with over 3,000 different partners. I arrived at this figure by taking a long, hard look at the patterns of my sexual activity. I estimated that I went to the baths at least once a week, sometimes twice, and that each time I went in I had a minimum of 4 partners and a maximum of… well, let's just use 4. And let's not count this last year because I have stopped promiscuity entirely. So, that's 9 years of active promiscuity. 52 weeks in a year, times 4

---

[7] Michael Callen, "The Luck Factor," unpublished speech, c. 1983, typewritten original, in the Michael Callen Papers at The LGBT Community Center National History Archive (henceforth, MCP).

people a week, is 208 different partners a year. Times 9 years is 1,872. And that's just the baths.[8]

To that figure he added another thousand or so men he met in assorted bookstores, sex clubs, orgies, cruisy theaters, and parks around the city. Although he felt three thousand was probably a *conservative* estimate, Michael believed that his experience typified the sex lives of many men on the urban gay circuit.

Michael had been inspired by the rhetoric of gay leaders, including writer Edmund White, who encouraged gay men "to wear their sexually transmitted infections like red badges of courage in a war against a sex-negative America.[9] Michael saw himself as a frontline soldier in the war against sex negativity. "Every time I got the clap," he reasoned, "I was striking a blow for the sexual revolution!"[10] However, "by 1981, [he] got some combination of venereal diseases EACH AND EVERY TIME [he] had sex and [he] finally contracted herpes."[11] As a result, Michael was beginning to doubt his commitment to sexual warfare. He signed up for a class at The New School called "From Gay Ghetto to Gay Community," anxious to hear his hero, Ed White, speak about gay liberation and sexual politics. As White called for gay men to proudly display their "badges" won on the battlefield of sex, Michael sat in the audience, a moist herpes lesion oozing pus down his lip. Frustrated and, frankly, grossed out by the fetid blister, Michael felt the stirrings of discontent. Leaving the lecture, he fantasized about scooping a wad of pus

---

8   Callen, "The Luck Factor." CDC figures from the same period suggested that gay men had an average of 1,160 partners, which Michael calls an underestimate. He reiterated a similar sexual inventory in numerous articles, speeches, and interviews across the next decade, and his friends and former lovers lovingly confirm his status as the biggest of bottoms.
9   Jeffrey Escoffier and Michael Callen, "My Rise from Complete Obscurity," in *In My Time: Essays and Sex, Science, and AIDS by Michael Callen*, ed. Jeffrey Escoffier, unpublished manuscript, 1993, Richard Dworkin Private Archive (henceforth, RDA).
10 Michael Callen, *Surviving AIDS* (New York: Harper Perennial, 1990), 4.
11 Michael Callen, "The Luck Factor," MCP. Allcaps in original.

from his lip, hurling it at Ed White, and yelling out, "Here, Ed! Have some medals!"[12]

Michael began hearing whispered rumors of a new deadly "gay plague" and a killer "gay cancer" among New York's gay residents. It was initially labeled "GRID," an acronym for Gay-Related Immune Deficiency, because the first cases reported were among gay men.[13] At first, he shrugged off the rumors as hysteria and paranoia. How could a cancer target just gay men, anyway? Even doctors played down the rising concern among the city's gay community. In the *New York Native,* a gay weekly newspaper, Dr. Lawrence Mass attempted to alleviate anxieties among New York's gay population, writing that "there were rumors that an exotic new disease had hit the gay community in New York. Here are the facts [...] the rumors are, *for the most part,* unfounded."[14] The curious qualifier "for the most part" worried some readers, who watched friends, lovers, and former tricks waste away and die in the prime of their lives. They were certainly worried. Others, however, put their trust in Mass and those like him; after all, they were doctors.

Just a few weeks later, in June of 1981, the CDC reported five sexually-related cases of *Pneumocystis* pneumonia (PCP) among "active homosexuals" in Los Angeles in its *Morbidity and Mortality Weekly Report* (MMWR), a professional newsletter that cir-

---

12 Richard Berkowitz, interview with author, 8 June 2020.
13 Initial cases were diagnosed among white gay men in urban areas who had access to healthcare. Cindy Patton identifies cases of PCP pneumonia among intravenous drug users in the 1970s, though because drug users are usually afraid to interface with healthcare over fear of arrest, these deaths were largely overlooked. See Patton, *Inventing AIDS* (New York: Routledge, 1990), 128. Almost immediately, "GRID" was also diagnosed among straight women who inject drugs or were the sexual partners of men who injected drugs as well as among the children of women who inject drugs, though women would not become part of the official epidemiological picture of the epidemic until many years later. For an excellent overview, see Gene Corea, *The Invisible Epidemic: The Story of Women and AIDS* (New York: Harper Collins, 1992).
14 Lawrence Mass, "Disease Rumors Largely Unfounded," *The New York Native,* 18 May 1981. Emphasis added.

culates among research scientists and healthcare professionals, not the general public.[15] July brought more ominous news:

> During the past 30 months, Kaposi's sarcoma [KS], an uncommonly reported malignancy in the United States, has been diagnosed in 26 homosexual men (20 in New York City; 6 in California). Eight of these patients died within 24 months.[16]

With each passing week, more young gay men in New York, San Francisco, Los Angeles, and other gay meccas succumbed to unusual cancers and pneumonias. A pattern was forming, and Michael recognized himself in the emerging epidemiological picture. Deep down, he later wrote, "there was no doubt in my mind that I would get GRID."[17]

Later that summer, severely dehydrated and jaundiced, Michael stumbled into the Gay Men's Health Project (GMHP) at Sheridan Square, a volunteer STI clinic founded by gay men's health activists Leonard "Lenny" Ebreo, Marc Rabinowitz, and Perry Brass. GMHP was a safe haven for gay men to avoid homophobic doctors and receive treatment without judgment. Joseph Sonnabend happened to be a volunteer physician on duty at GMHP that day, and although he was "just the first warm body [Michael] found," their serendipitous meeting set into motion a series of events that would alter the destinies of both men and save millions of lives.[18]

---

15 Centers for Disease Control and Prevention, "Pneumocystis Pneumonia — Los Angeles," *Morbidity and Mortality Weekly Report* 30, no. 21, 5 June 1981, 1–3.
16 Centers for Disease Control and Prevention, "Kaposi's Sarcoma and Pneumocystis among Gay Men — New York City and California," *Morbidity and Mortality Weekly Report* 30, no. 24, 4 July 1981, 305–8.
17 Callen, *Surviving AIDS*, 4.
18 Ibid. David France provides a beautifully nuanced history of Sonnabend's career and his role in the early years of AIDS in *How to Survive a Plague: The Inside Story of How Citizens and Science Tamed AIDS* (New York: Knopf, 2016). However, a comprehensive biography of Joseph Sonnabend remains an important project awaiting the right medical historian.

Sonnabend was uniquely qualified to respond to a new epidemic of immune deficiency. Born in South Africa in 1933, he had studied medicine in Johannesburg and Edinburgh before embarking on a promising career at London's National Institute for Medical Research. In 1977, he relocated to New York City with a generous research grant which allowed him to set up his own lab at Mt. Sinai Hospital. There he studied Interferon [a signal protein in the immune system] and moonlighted at the New York City Health Department and the Bureau of Venereal Disease Control where he saw first-hand the explosion of STIs. On Monday nights, he volunteered at GMHP.[19] In 1978, Sonnabend's research grant at Mt. Sinai was unexpectedly not renewed, so he took his experience in venereal diseases and a $25,000 loan and opened a private practice on W 12th St. in Greenwich Village, where his clientele consisted predominantly of gay men among whom "the rates of syphilis and gonorrhea [...] were simply staggering."[20]

Packed into a small apartment and littered with massive piles of scientific research journals and "furniture that wasn't worthy of a low-rent garage sale," Sonnabend's office embodied "everything most people believe competent medical treatment isn't."[21] Patients often waited for long periods, and they "sometimes rearrange[d] the order of seeing based on [their] collective assessment of who needed to see him first or who had other appointments to get to."[22] Michael half-joked to friends that they should bring a copy of *War and Peace* to the doctor's office "because you might finish it in the waiting room before you get seen!"[23] Still, Sonnabend's patients adored their doctor, who would "easily spend an hour examining patients, unconcerned about the impact on his cash flow or the bottleneck it caused in the waiting room."[24] Long delays, they reasoned, "were a small

19 Sean Strub, "The Good Doctor," POZ, July 1998.
20 Ibid.
21 Escoffier and Callen, "My Rise from Complete Obscurity."
22 Strub, "The Good Doctor."
23 Escoffier and Callen, "My Rise from Complete Obscurity."
24 France, *How to Survive a Plague*, 25.

price to pay for his attentiveness, his reassuring telephone reports, his willingness to make house calls, and his heartfelt interest in their journeys through gayness."[25]

What many of those patients, including, at first, Michael, failed to realize was that Joe Sonnabend was more than a primary care physician. He was a world-class virologist, epidemiologist, microbiologist, and researcher, someone whose phone calls would be answered by leading researchers like Stuart Schlossman at Harvard, who co-invented the T-cell test that helped define AIDS; David Purtillo, a leading expert on Epstein–Barr Virus at the University of Nebraska; and wealthy philanthropists, like Mathilde Krim (1926–2018) who was a researcher at the Sloan-Kettering Institute for Cancer Research. Unlike many of the other so-called "clap doctors" in New York, Sonnabend had been a research scientist before opening a private practice. Accordingly, he subscribed to medical journals from around the world, which he read to keep abreast of not only developments in his research fields but in medicine more broadly; thus, the piles of papers in his office. The expense of conducting research on his own dime added another layer to the doctor's indifference to décor and tidiness. "Each dollar that came in went toward spiraling research expenses — FedEx bills for shipping blood samples to Nebraska, lengthy phone calls to Europe," and rent and utility bills for his home and his office (both of which were often past due).[26] There were times when Sonnabend had to borrow money from affluent patients to cover his own grocery bill, as well as Mathilde Krim, who recognized his brilliance and kept Sonnabend financially afloat more than once.

To Sonnabend, healthcare was a basic human right, not a market commodity, and he understood that health was holistic. So, he took time with each client, performing comprehensive evaluations in order to understand their psychological, emotional, financial, and physical situations. As time went on and the epidemic grew, Sonnabend also made visits and telephone

---

25 Ibid.
26 Ibid., 74.

calls to his patients who were in hospitals around the city. Sean Strub (founding editor of POZ magazine, and, later, Sonnabend's patient) described those who saw Sonnabend as some of "the most promiscuous gay men in the city," adding that many men received their healthcare elsewhere in order to avoid the stigma of "being linked with those Village clones."[27] Within a few years, however, these distinctions disappeared, and Sonnabend's clients were simply the "sickest gay men in New York."[28] By the summer of 1981, Sonnabend was working an exhausting and mind-numbing schedule. During the week, he saw "frightened young men with a confounding array of symptoms," often until late in the evening, and on Saturdays he "studied their sera under microscopes in his borrowed NYU Medical Center lab."[29] For gay men in New York, there simply was no other doctor like Joe Sonnabend.

AIDS — as the new syndrome was christened in September 1982 — was uncharted territory for scientists, healthcare professionals, patients, and community and political leaders. No one knew what caused this frightening and deadly syndrome. Causal theories abounded, ranging from the plausible to the ridiculous and the conspiratorial. Was AIDS environmental? Dr. Yehudi Felman of the NYC Bureau of VD Control suggested "it could be the bugs out of the pipes in the bathhouses."[30] Was it caused by exposure to semen, a side effect of medications, or recreational drug use? Was there a genetic link between homosexuality and this new disease? In 1981, no one knew for sure; however, advances in the study of retroviruses and the human immune system in the 1970s gave scientists some traction. Immune suppression was not new. Organ transplant recipients, cancer patients on chemotherapy, and people with certain genetic conditions

---

27 Strub, "The Good Doctor." In a personal correspondence with me in May 2020, Strub added some important context here. "For what it's worth, I wasn't a patient of Sonnabend's until well into the 1990s. […] There was no other AIDS doctor like him or with his success in treating people."
28 Ibid.
29 France, *How to Survive a Plague*, 25.
30 Quoted in ibid., 37.

regularly experienced a suppression of immune function. What was new wasn't the fact of diminished immune function but the ages of these patients — most were between their twenties and forties — and the fact that they were all gay or bisexual men.

With his office a five-minute walk from Christopher St., the center of gay male sexual and social culture in New York at the time, Sonnabend knew what was going on in the bathhouses and sex clubs — some of which he frequented himself. And he saw the results in his office every day. Gay men were abusing their bodies with chronic infections of STIs, Epstein-Barr Virus, and cytomegalovirus (CMV). Sonnabend began to build his own theory based on first-hand knowledge of his patients.

Having worked on studies of Interferon in the 1970s, he hypothesized that its presence in the blood of patients with AIDS might indicate a response to some infectious agent or agents. In a pioneering move, he collected blood samples from twenty of his patients — ten with self-reported histories of promiscuity and ten self-described monogamists — and sent the samples to Dr. David Purtilo at the University of Nebraska, then the only place in the country with the technology to perform a CD4/T-helper cell count. A month later, he received the results. Gay men with self-reported histories of promiscuity evidenced greater signs of immune dysfunction than their monogamous counterparts. Sonnabend's research at NYU had proved that this was true — though it did not tell him the underlying cause of their immune dysfunction — and he published his findings in the *Lancet,* one of the world's foremost medical research journals.[31]

Michael was not surprised when his blood came back in the first group, the severely immunocompromised. Initially, Sonnabend "gave this whole song and dance" about the results, trying to placate Michael by reminding him that doctors were unsure what the irregularities might mean. Eventually, though, the doctor leveled with his patient: "your lifestyle is killing you."[32]

---

31 See J. Wallace et al., "T-Cell Ratios in Homosexuals," *The Lancet* 319, no. 8277 (1982): 908.
32 Escoffier and Callen, "My Rise from Complete Obscurity."

Fig. 1. Richard Berkowitz and Michael Callen, Washington, DC, 1983. Courtesy of Richard Berkowitz.

8

We Know Who We Are

> *This is a test of who we are.*
> *Do we care enough to do what's right?*
> *It's down to me and you.*
> *If not us, who will dare to fight this fight?*
> — Michael Callen

Michael had an inquisitive mind, a knack for rhetorical flourishes, and an insatiable intellectual curiosity. He was also downright nosey, unapologetically so. During one of his lengthy visits to Sonnabend's clinic, Michael found himself waiting more than forty-five minutes in an examination room, literally with his pants down. Unbeknownst to Michael, Sonnabend was on the phone with one of Japan's most eminent epidemiologists. The impatient patient dressed and started snooping around the office, quickly homing in on a piece of paper fastened in the doctor's typewriter. Michael read the first paragraph, and what he saw stopped him in his tracks. He quickly found the doctor's other notes and read the whole document. Because of his experience treating massive numbers of gay men with histories of frequent STIs, Sonnabend hypothesized in this paper that the systemic immune dysfunction characteristic of immune deficiency among sexually active gay men might the result of chronic infection with common viruses and bacteria over time, possibly including a novel virus — a *multifactorial* theory.

A light went off in Michael's head. *He* had a long history of repeated STIs, a high number of sexual partners, and he now had AIDS. Was it possible that his immune system went kaput from all as his time in the trenches of the sexual revolution? When Sonnabend returned, Michael had executed a "complete Jekyll and Mr. Hyde change."[1] No longer an impatient client who wondered why his doctor never attended his cabaret shows, Michael now saw them as allies in a struggle, united by Sonnabend's theory. Excitedly, he told the doctor that the paper should be published for the benefit of gay men's health, although Michael may have stretched the truth with his enthusiasm when he assured Sonnabend that his connections with the city's only gay newspaper would guarantee acceptance in the *New York Native*. Though initially hesitant, Sonnabend conceded after Michael promised to translate the essay's arcane medical-scientific jargon into everyday language appropriate for lay readers. Around the same time, Sonnabend was having similar conversations another patient.

Born in 1955, the same year as Michael, Richard Berkowitz grew up in a Jewish household in Union, New Jersey. Despite differences in geography and family culture, both men spent their formative years "singing, dancing, and shopping but couldn't care less about the obsessions with sports that defined boyhood."[2] Although adults, siblings, and family members "stepped in to tone [him] down and butch [him] up," Richard "couldn't find [his] happiness" in stoic, tough guy masculinity. He just couldn't believe that "a carefree, seven-year-old boy could pose a threat to the social order."[3] Like Michael, Richard was "overcome with guilt and shame" for his same-sex fantasies as an adolescent; the potential for "all that pleasure [was]

---

1 David Schmidt, interview with Michael Callen, 12 November 1987, typescript, the Michael Callen Papers at The LGBT Community Center National History Archive (henceforth, MCP).
2 Richard Berkowitz, *Stayin' Alive: The Invention of Safe Sex* (New York: Basic Books, 2003), 7.
3 Ibid.

instantly drowned by feeling sick and dirty."[4] As a journalism student at Rutgers University, Richard was radicalized and politicized, and he successfully organized the first gay rights protest on campus, in response to an anti-gay effigy displayed on the lawn of Delta Kappa Epsilon fraternity house. These formative experiences shaped Richard, just as similar events formed Michael into the activist he would become.

After graduating from Rutgers, Richard lived with a partner, commuting from New Jersey to New York City to attend NYU graduate film school. When that relationship dissolved, Richard relocated to the city where he discovered that working as a BDSM hustler was the only way he could pay for graduate school. Eventually, he dropped out of film school and supported himself with sex work full-time. In those heady last days of Gay Liberation, New York was the gay Promised Land:

> There were always exciting places in Manhattan to be seen, night-and-day sex at the piers off West St., backroom bars and sex clubs that were packed till dawn. Whatever fantasy you had, you always knew you could satisfy it anytime, night or day, at one of the many sexual playgrounds. And always, everywhere gay men congregated, there was that infectious, pulsing disco beat.[5]

As Richard settled into his identity as a BDSM sex worker, he let "four concerns shape what [he] would and wouldn't do: an obsession with hygiene; an acute fear of STIs; an ingrained cultural belief that the 'passive' or receptive partner in sex was taking the 'degrading,' 'feminine' role; and the fact that there was no way that just any stranger who came along could hand [him] a sum of money and expect [Richard] to fuck him on demand."[6] However, in spite of his efforts to maintain high standards of hygiene and his concern about STIs, Richard contracted hepatitis in the

4   Ibid., 7.
5   Ibid., 68.
6   Ibid., 55.

summer of 1981. He was also "experiencing night sweats, fevers, and an unendurable fatigue. [His] lymph glands were swollen and were visibly protruding from [his] neck."[7] Like Michael, Richard had been "extremely promiscuous and [his] lifestyle and symptoms fit the pattern of most gay men with AIDS."[8] Sitting in a consultation with Sonnabend, Richard noticed that his personal medical file was becoming "disturbingly thick."[9] Sonnabend reviewed Richard's lab results and found some swollen lymph glands below Richard's ear and under his arm during a physical examination. So, he drew blood and sent it away for testing. In December, Sonnabend diagnosed Richard as immune deficient. The doctor's advice: "Stop fucking around."[10]

Joe Sonnabend knew that his two patients should meet, and in the summer of 1982, he arranged it. After consulting with each man independently to protect their confidentiality, he gave Michael's telephone number to Richard. During their first conversation, Richard thought that Michael sounded "so tired and weary, like he had seen it all and seen too much," but he accepted Michael's invitation to a support group meeting for men with AIDS at the St. Marks Health Clinic in August.[11] There, men "talked about how terrifying it was to find medical treatment when even the doctors didn't know what was going on; few had health insurance or money saved to cover a medical catastrophe [...]. No one talked about living; the discussion revolved around how to face death while hiding what it was they were dying from."[12] After the achievements of Gay Liberation in the 1970s, AIDS created a new closet in which gay men had to hide, out of fear of "being fired from their jobs, kicked out

---

7 Richard Berkowitz, "AIDS — One Man's Odyssey," in *The Sourcebook on Lesbian/Gay Healthcare: A Handbook for the First International Lesbian and Gay Health Conferences, 16–19 June 1984* (Washington, DC: National Gay Health Education Foundation, 1984), 23–26.
8 Ibid.
9 Berkowitz, *Stayin' Alive*, 75.
10 Ibid.
11 Ibid., 101.
12 Ibid., 106.

of their apartments, discarded by even their gay male friends who were terrified and abandoned. [It was] a cruel, new verse of the same old song."[13] This all struck Richard as absurd, and as a result, his participation in the meeting did not go well. Cantankerous and outspoken, Richard came across as confrontational and too aggressive for the men who had expected an Alcoholics Anonymous-style discussion of end-of-life issues, and he feared that his arrogance (he was relatively healthy by comparison) offended the men in the group.

After the meeting, Michael and Richard went to a nearby diner. During the walk, Richard assessed his new compatriot as a "total queen, burnt-out looks, too thin, nice hair."[14] Over a meal, however, Michael and Richard found they had much more in common than either would have believed possible. Both keenly intelligent and articulate, they shared an admiration for feminist writers and activists and had each just read Susan Sontag's *Illness as Metaphor*. Because they had each been diagnosed with immune irregularities by Sonnabend, they were also both recent converts to sexual celibacy. Their kinship sparked an urgent desire to get Sonnabend's multifactorial theory out in order to save gay men's lives. "Two major sluts like us," Michael told his new friend, "are just the ones to do it."[15]

Armed with hope and their "cockamamie belief that [they] could change the world,"[16] they set to work on an article. "The basic concept was Michael's idea," Richard explained. "We were going to call it 'We Know Who We Are' and write it in the graphic language of the street, or as Michael said, 'queen to queen, slut to slut.'"[17] They toiled on the article for three months, pushing through excruciating revisions to tweak the language so it would appeal to the sensibilities of Gay Liberation but hold no

---

13 Ibid.
14 Ibid., 107.
15 David France, *How to Survive a Plague: The Story of How Activists and Scientists Tamed AIDS* (New York: Vintage Books, 2017), 50.
16 Berkowitz, *Stayin' Alive*, 116.
17 Ibid., 125.

punches when it came to the realities of sexual illness among gay men in the city. Their opening salvo threw down a gauntlet:

> Those of us who have lived a life of excessive promiscuity on the urban gay circuit of bathhouses, backrooms, balconies, sex clubs, meat racks, and tearooms we know who we are. We could continue to deny overwhelming evidence that the present health crisis is a direct result of the unprecedented promiscuity that has occurred since Stonewall, but such denial is killing us. Denial will continue to kill us until we begin the difficult task of changing the ways in which we have sex [...]
>
> Few have been willing to say it clearly, but the single greatest risk factor for contracting AIDS is a history of multiple sexual contacts with partners who are having multiple sexual contacts — that is, sex on the circuit. *We know who we are.*[18]

With those words, they entered The Promiscuity Debates.

Promiscuity was the buzzword of the day, and the ensuing debates clustered around two poles. Michael and Richard encouraged sexually-active gay men (SAGM) to temper their sexual activities until more information about the health crisis was discovered. Others felt the battles of the 1970s had been too hard and too significant, thus they refused outright any attempt to police gay sexuality or push gay men back into the closet. Tensions mounted and tempers flared in response to "We Know Who We Are," and attacks, often personal, flooded the *New York Native*'s mailbox. Some readers recoiled at the suggestion that gay male promiscuity — one of the hallmarks of Gay Liberation — might play a role in the health crisis. Others felt betrayed by these two self-identified insiders who had dared to expose some of the potentially embarrassing or unseemly facts of urban gay culture.

---

18 Michael Callen, Richard Berkowitz, Joseph Sonnabend, with Richard Dworkin, "We Know Who We Are," *The New York Native* 50, 8–21 November 1982, 23–29. Emphasis added.

In his brief introduction to the special issue in which "We Know Who We Are" appeared, *New York Native* editor Charles Ortleb stated his commitment to presenting many different opinions about the epidemic:

> Confusing? Contradictory? Of course. But then so is much of the discussion surrounding the present health crisis [...]. The implications of the epidemic for public health in this country are too great to worry about causing a little bit of controversy.[19]

In another article in the same issue called "Good Luck, Bad Luck: The Role of Chance in Contracting AIDS," Dr. Peter Seitzman (who was also president of the lesbian and gay New York Physicians for Human Rights) speculated that hepatitis B, another rampant infection among gay men at the time, was spread the same way AIDS was spreading.[20] Over the next few months, other op-ed pieces by Joseph Sonnabend ("Promiscuity is Bad for Your Health") and Charles Jurrist ("In Defense of Promiscuity") appeared in the *New York Native*. For readers and staff of the *New York Native*, the promiscuity debates were more than an ideological squabble; they were central to the definition of urban gay male life. For Michael and Richard, the stakes were equally high: life and death.

As veterans of the urban gay circuit and "politically minded, unapologetic sluts," Michael and Richard were "eager to admit [their] mistakes, face the painful truths about AIDS, adapt, and fight."[21] They interrogated their own life experiences for evidence of the political meaning of sex in the construction of urban gay male identity and evidence of gay men's complacency as well as their possible addiction to the narcotic of promiscuity. "The commercialization of promiscuity and the explosion of estab-

---

19 Charles Ortleb, "Editorial introduction," *New York Native* 50, 8–21 November 1982.
20 Peter Seitzman, "Good Luck, Bad Luck: The Role of Chance in Contracting AIDS," *New York Native* 50, 8–21 November 1982.
21 Berkowitz, *Stayin' Alive*, 117.

lishments such as bathhouses, bookstores, and backrooms is unique in western history," and gay men's participation in this sex culture "has led to the creation of an increasingly disease-polluted pool of sexual partners."[22] Constant exposure to common STIs (including chlamydia, gonorrhea, hepatitis A, B, and C, cytomegalovirus, and herpes), they theorized, may have contributed to the epidemic of AIDS, and they had certainly contributed to what Michael described as "disease settings equivalent to those of poor third-world nations in one of the richest nations on earth."[23] Furthermore, Michael and Richard had the observations of a research scientists to back up their suspicious. "The guys in my practice who have a history of oral and penile STDs have no signs of immune deficiency," Sonnabend confided in Michael and Richard. "But the guys who have a history of anal STDs are getting this new disease. AIDS is primarily a bottom's disease."[24]

Michael and Richard challenged the sexual orthodoxy of SAGM in New York. "If going to the Baths is a game of Russian roulette, then the *advice* must be to *throw the gun away* not merely to play less often."[25] However, they concluded that it was "more important to let people die in pursuit of their own happiness than to limit personal freedom by regulating risk."[26] They were accused of being sexual fascists, but Michael and Richard believed that SAGM had the right to have sex as they wanted — and said so in their article. However, they also believed that SAGM had an ethical obligation to inform others of the risks. Although they had carefully framed their argument within the rhetoric of personal choice and responsibility, most readers overlooked the nuanced argument about the ethics of choice. Michael and Richard were accused of the gravest of all gay sins: sex negativity. Sex negativity was tantamount to a cardinal sin in the urban gay milieu, and any suggestion that gay men modify their sexual habits was denounced as heresy.

22 Callen et al. "We Know Who We Are," 27.
23 Michael Callen, *Surviving AIDS* (New York: Harper Perennial, 1990), 4.
24 Richard Berkowitz, interview with author, 7 June 2020.
25 Callen et al., "We Know Who We Are," 29.
26 Ibid., emphasis added.

Michael, Richard Berkowitz, and Joe Sonnabend were labeled pariahs, "the terrible triumvirate" by the *New York Native,* and branded with their own scarlet letters.

Rather than kowtow to critique, Michael and Richard took the offensive and appeared in print and broadcast media to warn gay men about AIDS and urge them to modify their sexual practices. Queer historian and activist Vito Russo (1946–1990) hosted a public access program called Our Time, which dealt with LGBTQ+ news, politics, and entertainment.[27] During a segment called "Point/Counterpoint," Russo invited arts critic Charles Jurrist (1945–1991) and Michael Callen to comment on the current debate around AIDS. Michael argued for temperance and caution:

> In New York, San Francisco, and Los Angeles, in 1983, walking into the baths and backrooms with the delusion that you can check your personal responsibility at the door with your clothes is an act of personal and culture suicide. Either you do not love life, or you do not know death.
>
> What is over isn't sex, just sex without responsibility.
>
> The Stonewall generation, which has permitted sex to become just one more consumer commodity, which has allowed sex and affection to become so separate, and which has become numb to disease must now begin to formulate a long overdue sexual ethic. The formulation of this ethic will require a change radical in its simplicity: we will have to talk to each other. Yes, even before sex, and maybe even after. And we will have to learn how to listen to each other.
>
> We need to have forums on creative and medically safe ways to have sex. Lovers, condoms, jerk off clubs, and closed circles of fuckbuddies are just a few of the alternatives some gay men are exploring. These men are rediscovering how

---

[27] *Our Time* ran for thirteen episodes on WNYC. Jeffrey Schwarz, the director of the documentary *Vito* (2012).

Fig. 2. Richard Berkowitz and Michael Callen, writing *How to Have Sex in an Epidemic,* 129 Duane St., New York, NY, 1983. Photo by Richard Dworkin. © Richard Dworkin.

nice it is not to have to worry about disease or death during or after sex.[28]

In response, Jurrist opined:

> I know about this disease, and I know it may strike me tomorrow. I am scared. […] but I won't give up the physical expression of intimacy […]. We won't start out with a health quiz, nor will we limit our lovemaking to certain acts. I re-

---

28 Richard Dworkin has uploaded this segment to his YouTube channel in three parts. See BettyByte, "AIDS and promiscuity - (1) point counterpoint - introduction - Vito Russo - 1983," *YouTube,* 19 October 2011, http://www.youtube.com/watch?v=PgZh7Kk8cnI; BettyByte, "AIDS and promiscuity - (2) point - Charles Jurrist - 1983," *YouTube,* 19 October 2011, http://www.youtube.com/watch?v=-ltMm3bMnMY; and BettyByte, "AIDS and promiscuity - (3) counterpoint - Michael Callen - 1983," *YouTube,* 19 October 2011, http://www.youtube.com/watch?v=zVlE7Vk4Ivg.

fuse to treat my partner as a sick person or to present myself as one. That's the trip [conservatives] have tried to lay on us [...]. To act otherwise, to give up sexual communication out of the fear of physical illness and death is really to embrace another kind of death, the death of wholeness, the death of the spirit, the death of the self.[29]

For Michael, promiscuity was a "vague word which means different things to different people. But until we develop a better vocabulary, promiscuity remains the best word we have to describe the historically unique phenomenon of large numbers of urban gay men who have large numbers of different sexual partners in commercialized settings such as bathhouses, backrooms, bookstores, balconies, meat racks, and tea rooms."[30] While some gay leaders' primary concern was gay men's civil rights and saw Michael and Richard's discussion of promiscuity as a threat to those rights, Michael spoke with the pressing urgency of disease and death. The AIDS crisis introduced a deadly new element into urban gay male culture, he continued,

Because now gay men are dying — gay men like you and me. To those who understand the realities of AIDS; to those who wake up every morning and examine their bodies for KS lesions; to those who have watched friends, lovers, and former tricks waste away like victims of Auschwitz, disfigured by disease, urban gay male promiscuity as we know it has no defense. The political issues raised by promiscuity are important, but what civil rights do dead men have?

Ending this health emergency begins with each one of us taking responsibility for his own health, and by so doing, ensuring the health of his partners. As long as we continue to selfishly ask, "Is that man a health risk to me?" without first asking, "Am I a health risk to him?" we will never be free from the tyranny of AIDS.

29 Charles Jurrist, *Our Time*, 1983.
30 Michael Callen, *Our Time*, 1983.

Our challenge is to figure out how to have gay, life-affirming sex, satisfy our emotional needs, and stay alive. Hard questions for hard times. But whatever happened to our great gay imagination?[31]

---

31 Ibid.

Fig. 1. Michael Callen's Rooftop Garden, 129 Duane St. (c. 1984). Photo by Richard Dworkin. © Richard Dworkin.

9

How to Have Sex in an Epidemic

> *How to have sex in an epidemic*
> *Without getting caught up in polemic*
> — Michael Callen

The *New York Native* printed dozens of irate responses to "We Know Who We Are," yet the magazine's editorial staff refused to publish any rebuttals by "the terrible triumvirate." Originally, Michael and Richard had planned a follow-up article, and as Michael told journalist Celia Farber, the second piece

> was the important one. The first one was rhetorical. It simply declared the problem. It said: there's an epidemic and we need to change how we have sex. The second part detailed *how* to change. How to *keep* having sex, only safely. But since the practical second part never followed, it came across as if in the middle of this crisis we were just smacking people, saying "You boys have to stop."[1]

So, Michael and Richard employed their gay imaginations to find a solution to this media blackout.[2]

---

1 Celia Farber, *Serious Adverse Events: An Uncensored History of AIDS* (Hoboken: Melville House Publishing, 2006), 104.
2 In *Moving Politics: Emotion and ACT UP's Fight Against AIDS* (Chicago: University of Chicago Press, 2009), Deborah Gould writes "The *New York Native* was the only lesbian and gay paper in New York City during the early

When he was diagnosed in late 1982, Michael had joined the first support group for PWAs in New York City (run by Dr. Stuart Nichols of Beth Israel Hospital) and met two men: Larry Goldstein (who died in 1988) and Phil Lanzaratta (1942–1986). A "handsome, witty, vivacious" businessowner, Goldstein had been diagnosed with KS in 1979, retrospectively making him one of the first-known PWAs in New York and "one of the longest-surviving [PWAs] in medical literature."[3] Michael lovingly called Lanzaratta "the granddaddy of the PWA movement in New York."[4] For Michael, these men demonstrated that long-term survivorship was possible and their survival made it easier for him to join what he later called "the long-term survivor sweepstakes."[5] Befriending Lanzaratta and Goldstein was one of

> years of AIDS. As a source, it presents some problems. It is useful for exploring early lesbian and gay understandings of the epidemic because, unlike any other lesbian/gay papers, it provided consistent coverage from the very first reports. Because of its persistent coverage, and in light of 'mainstream media silence,' the *Native* becomes the newspaper where lesbians and gay men around the country got most of their information about AIDS in the early years; it is also one of the important places where lesbians and gay men in New York and elsewhere discussed central issues about AIDS.
>
> By 1985, however, the *Native*'s credibility had fallen significantly. Much of the reporting reads like a polemic designed to advance specific theories of the causation of AIDS while demoting others. James Kinsella writes that publisher and editor Charles Ortleb 'grew frantic' as the deaths among his friends mounted. The cover of the August 24, 1987 issue prompted a complete loss of credibility; showing a picture of a jumping dolphin, the headline connected mysterious deaths of dolphins to AIDS and warned people to stay out of the oceans. Two gay men who were living in New York at the time have independently told me that the issue put the nail in the *Native*'s coffin" (446–47).

3 Terry Gross, "Michael Callen on 'Surviving AIDS' Long Term," *Fresh Air*, NPR, 16 November 1990. Also see Michael Callen, *Surviving AIDS* (Harper Perennial, 1990), 66 and 69n3.

4 Michael Callen and Dan Turner, "A History of the PWA Self-Empowerment Movement," *The 1988 Lesbian and Gay Health Education Foundation* Program Booklet and reprinted in Michael Callen., ed, *Surviving and Thriving with AIDS: Volume 2* (People with AIDS Coalition, 1988). It can also be accessed on the Michael Callen homepage here, http://michaelcallen.com/mikes-writing/a-history-of-the-pwa-self-empowerment-movement/.

5 Gross, "Michael Callen on 'Surviving AIDS' Long Term."

the first steps to Michael's awakening as a leader in the AIDS self-empowerment movement.

Later in 1982, Michael and Richard Berkowitz formed Gay Men with AIDS (GMWA) to focus on political activism. However, the men who attended "all had [their] hands full staying alive; it didn't occur to [them] to organize politically."[6] So, GMWA became more of a support group for gay men who wanted to make "the difficult transition from a promiscuous lifestyle to medically safer lifestyles" through an emphasis on personal experiences with AIDS, strength, and hope.[7] However, as friendships among the men in GMWA deepened, Michael and Richard realized that they could politicize this group.

GMWA produced an important early brochure and poster called "A Warning to Gay Men." In nine short paragraphs, each with a brief bibliography of published medical research, it cautioned sexually active gay men (SAGM) and gay men with AIDS to carefully consider chemotherapy for KS, Interferon treatments, and exposure to ultraviolet light (such as in a tanning parlor), for all three were known to be immunosuppressive; and to avoid prednisone and spleen removal (common options for people with low blood platelets) because "published medical case studies indicate that this treatment may kill you."[8] GMWA also encouraged those who were sick to explore plasmapheresis (essentially blood cleansing) and advised those who worried that they might be ill to search for competent medical care. Above all, they suggested that SAGM consider taking a break from the gay circuit and called for the formation of community

---

6 Callen and Turner, "A History of the PWA Self-Empowerment Movement."
7 Ibid. and Michael Callen, "The Luck Factor" (c. 1983), unpublished speech, typewritten original, The Michael Callen Papers at The LGBT Community Center National History Archive (henceforth MCP).
8 Gay Men with AIDS, "A Warning to Gay Men," advertisement, *New York Native*, 22 November–5 December 1982. Richard Berkowitz has uploaded a scan of the original poster as well as other important early safe-sex documents on his homepage. See https://richardberkowitz.com/category/2-my-safe-sex-writing/.

support groups to help men break the cycle of promiscuity, if they choose to do so.

GMWA sent copies of their "Warning" to the *New York Native*. However, the magazine refused to print it after deeming its message "too controversial."[9] The editors wanted to avoid being labeled with the same "sex negative" tag as the terrible triumvirate. Using $240 of money solicited from Sonnabend's more affluent clients, Michael and Richard purchased ad space to publish their "Warning" in the magazine. In other cities, gay magazines like San Francisco's *Bay Area Reporter* ran the "Warning" for free. Unfortunately, the *New York Native* also attacked the campaign as heresy, and the posters and brochures quickly disappeared from gay commercial sex establishments.[10]

Defeated by Ortleb and the *New York Native*, GMWA soon disbanded, and Michael and Richard formed a new group called People with AIDS, New York (PWA-NY), which produced another important, early safe-sex document called "Safer Sex Guidelines: One Approach." This poster was meant to be displayed at bathhouses from Wall St. to Harlem. PWA-NY condensed the verbiage of GMWA's "Warning" into seven short bullet points along with a list of telephone numbers for local, state, and national AIDS information hotlines. While PWA-NY "believe[d] that AIDS develops over a period of time from repeated assaults on the immune system [and] that AIDS cannot result from a single, 'unlucky' contact," the group acknowledged competing theories, including the single-virus theory, without stigmatizing, dismissing, or invalidating them. Rather, they reasoned that those who believed that "AIDS is the result of a new agent" should come to their own conclusion about the guidelines, whether to follow them or to choose between celibacy or masturbation. PWA-NY emphasized that "which ever [*sic*] theory you choose, the evi-

---

9 Berkowitz has compiled images of this poster and most of his AIDS writing on his website, http://www.richardberkowitz.com.

10 Richard Berkowitz, interview with author, 7 June 2020 (henceforth, RB and MJ [2020]).

dence is overwhelming; AIDS cannot be transmitted by casual contact!"[11]

As with the earlier "Warning" campaign, gay community leaders immediately distanced themselves from PWA-NY's poster. Although it had been printed using GMHC monies, Rodger McFarlane (then GMHC's executive director) told the *New York Native* that the poster failed to present a "balanced argument of the various theories of AIDS etiology. It seems more persuasive than emotional […]. GMHC claims no responsibility for [its] content."[12] GMHC even required that PWA-NY include an all caps disclaimer: "THIS POSTER WAS PRINTED THROUGH A GRANT FROM GMHC. THE VIEWS PRESENTED HERE ARE NOT NECESSARILY THOSE OF GMHC." Furthermore, as the *Native* explained, GMHC would soon be producing it sown poster of sex guidelines "which will be met with review by medical authorities."[13] In one underhanded maneuver, the emergent AIDS establishment discredited Michael and Richard while continuing to deny Joe Sonnabend's reputation as a global authority on sexually transmitted infections.

Around the same time, Richard had an epiphany. One evening, a persistent former client rang his doorbell and, despite Richard's protestations, refused to leave. If they couldn't have sex, the man wondered, would Richard just yank on his boots and let them the man worship him? Richard indulged and in doing so had a revelation. From Sonnabend, he had learned about the dangers of exposure to bodily fluids, and now he real-

---

11 Ibid.
12 Quoted in James E. D'Eramo, "Whose Guidelines," *New York Native* 76, 7–20 November 1983. In 2008, Rodger McFarlane sent Richard Berkowitz an email apologizing for his role in impeding their activist work. He wrote, "I know exactly what you and Joe and Michael accomplished — and many thousands, yea millions, of us live on only because of what you gave us. And you did all that with little help from people like me. I have spent many years contemplating my complicity in several of our worst lapses over the years. I tell myself I was a kid, an ignorant hick, too inexperienced to inherit such epic responsibilities — like all of us. That's what I tell myself." Rodger MacFarlane, p.c., 26 February 2008, courtesy of Richard Berkowitz.
13 D'Eramo, "Whose Guidelines."

ized this BDSM scene was *safe* and hot. In fact, most of the scenes that men paid him for didn't require an exchange of bodily fluids. Making a mental list of BDSM practices, Richard realized that promiscuity per se wasn't causing AIDS. Rather, the culprits were certain sexual acts, performed in specific ways. Sex *could* be safe.[14] The instant his client left the apartment, Richard sat down at this typewriter and wrote the phrase "How to Have Sex in an Epidemic." He knew had stumbled upon something important. However, Michael wasn't interested.

With Sonnabend as his medical consultant, Richard continued to work out his theory of lower-risk sex until he had something that persuaded Michael, himself just out of the hospital after a bout mono and therefore in a more receptive mood. Together, they polished Richard's draft into a safe-sex manifesto. With Callen's tax refund, they self-published 5,000 copies of *How to Have Sex in an Epidemic: One Approach* in May of 1983.[15] The book outlined Sonnabend's multifactorial theory and covered an array of intersecting social, sexual, and political topics in plain, straightforward language that gay men could easily understand. Although a cause for AIDS had not yet been discovered, the book promoted Sonnabend's multifactorial theory while allowing enough wiggle room for those who were swayed by other theories, including that of the single virus. By modifying sex with "safe" techniques and avoiding the exchange of bodily fluids known to transmit other viruses and infections, gay men could continue to enjoy sexual liberation while lowering the risk for AIDS, whether or not a new virus was involved.

This could be accomplished in a few ways. First, by using condoms. Although condoms had been known to reduce STI infections in ancient Egypt, human culture had developed what David France calls a "universal amnesia" about this fact.[16] Second, gay men could engage in other forms of sexual contact

---

14 Ibid.
15 Michael Callen, Richard Berkowitz, and Joseph Sonnabend, *How to Have Sex in an Epidemic: One Approach* (New York: News from the Front, 1983).
16 France, *How to Survive a Plague*, 96. For more, see Aine Collier, *The Humble Little Condom: A History* (Buffalo: Prometheus Books, 2007).

that did not carry the risk of exposure to infectious bodily fluids — like mutual masturbation — as well as the sorts of scenes Richard had carried out with his persistent BDSM client a few months earlier. In the booklet, Michael and Richard detailed the perceived and known risks of every sex act two (or more) gay men could perform together, a list that includes fucking, getting fucked, kissing, rimming, watersports, using sex toys, taking drugs during sex, S/M, fisting, going to the baths, frequenting sex workers, and using personal ads to find sexual partners. The authors concluded with a brief meditation on the importance of love between men:

> The goal of gay male liberation must be to find ways in which love becomes possible despite continuing and often overwhelming pressure to compete and adopt adversary relationships with other men.
>
> It has certainly become easier to fuck each other, but has it become any easier to love each other?[17]

Love, they argued, involved an ethos of care for the self and care for the community, which French philosopher Michel Foucault (1926–1984) once called "Friendship as a Way of Life."[18] Rather than thinking of all potential sexual partners as potential death traps and externalizing all responsibility for one's own sexual health, Michael and Richard asked gay men to consider what risks *they* might pose to their partners. "If you love the person you are fucking with — *even for one night* — you will not want to make them sick. Maybe affection is our best protection."[19]

The time for *How to Have Sex in an Epidemic* was right.[20] In May 1983, the country was waking up to the magnitude of

---

17 Callen et al., *How to Have Sex in an Epidemic*, 38–39.
18 Michel Foucault, R. de Ceccaty, J. Danet, and J. Le Bitoux, "Friendship as a Way of Life," trans. John Johnson, *Gai Pied*, April 1981. Foucault died of AIDS-related illness in 1984.
19 Callen et al., *How to Have Sex in an Epidemic*, 39.
20 A *Time* magazine article by Evan Thomas from 23 September 1985 called "The New Untouchables" describes the panic that ensued from fears about

AIDS. Gay men had long "known that sex is not, in an epidemic, or not, limited to penetrative sex. Our promiscuity taught us many things, not only about the pleasures of sex, but about the great multiplicity of those pleasures. It is that psychic preparation, that experimentation, that conscious work on our own sexualities that [would] allow many of us to change our sexual behaviors [...] very quickly and very dramatically."[21] However, misinformation and fear complicated the efforts of proponents of what was becoming known as "safer sex." When Dr. James Oleske suggested that AIDS might be transmitted through routine, social household contact in the *Journal of the American Medical Association* — a hypothesis to which Anthony Fauci, who was at that time leading the government response to the epidemic, gave credence — the story was picked up by the Associated Press and United Press International. Through the din of the resulting panic, few noticed Fauci's rebuttal of the casual contact theory a short time later.[22]

How to Have Sex in an Epidemic was a resounding success, in spite of the fact that GMHC and the New York State AIDS Institute both refused to help distribute it. Michael and Richard received dozens of letters from gay men around the country praising the book. Some included checks for more copies for distribution at gay men's health clinics, support groups, and other organizations. Reviews appeared in the mainstream and gay presses. Gay men shared copies; orders came pouring in. Publications from the *New York Review of Books* to *DungeonMaster* magazine were all on board with the invention of safe sex. *How to Have Sex in an Epidemic* won the authors a Gay Press Association Award for Outstanding Achievement in Community Projects in 1984 and received a glowing review in the *New York Review of Books*, which praised its "sensible restriction of sex among currently

AIDS in the "general population."
21 Douglas Crimp, "How to Have Promiscuity in an Epidemic," reprinted in *Moralism and Melancholia: Essays on AIDS and Queer Politics* (Cambridge: MIT Press, 2009), 43–82.
22 James Kinsella, *Covering the Plague: AIDS and the American Media* (New Brunswick: Rutgers University Press, 1989), 263.

promiscuous homosexual males."[23] Even Edmund White, the author at whom Callen once imagined hurling herpes pus, felt it was "the sanest, most sensible advice [he'd] read about AIDS."[24] Michael and Richard had brought Sonnabend's theory and their safe-sex suggestions to the forefront of AIDS prevention efforts, and they continue to influence sex education and sexual practices today.[25]

The same month that *How to Have Sex in an Epidemic* was rolling off the presses, tenants at the W 12th St. co-op where Sonnabend had his practice moved to evict him. Sonnabend filed a lawsuit in what was one of the first anti-AIDS discrimination cases in the US.[26] Michael and Richard were both plaintiffs in the case. New York Attorney General Robert Abrahams, with support from Lambda Legal Defense and with financial support from Mathilde Krim, fought the case and won, thereby establishing a legal basis for anti-discrimination protections for PWAs. Though the case was used to fight AIDS discrimination, Richard, Michael, and Sonnabend believed that, in truth, most residents were less afraid of AIDS than of losing the value of their apartments because of the stigma of contagion fostered by Anthony Fauci and the straight media.[27]

Michael also turned the central message of *How to Have Sex in an Epidemic* into a song that served as a jingle for the booklet.

---

23 Jonathan Lieberson, "Anatomy of an Epidemic," *The New York Review of Books*, 18 August 1983. https://www.nybooks.com/articles/1983/08/18/anatomy-of-an-epidemic/

24 Reviews are excerpted on Richard Berkowitz's homepage.

25 *How to Have Sex in an Epidemic* is often credited as the first AIDS-related safe sex pamphlet. However, the San Francisco Sisters of Perpetual Indulgence published *Play Fair!*, a pamphlet advocating safe sex, in 1982 and produced a second brochure, "Can We Talk...?" around the same time in 1983. Michael and Richard always acknowledged these important predecessors in interviews. The American Association of Physicians for Human Rights issued an advisory, "AIDS and Healthful Gay Male Sexual Activity" on 19 February 1983.

26 See Philip Shenon, "A Move to Evict AIDS Physician Fought by State," *New York Times*, 1 October 1983 and "The City: AIDS Doctor Gets Stay of Eviction," *New York Times*, 15 October 1983.

27 RB and MJ (2020).

**MEDICAL AND SCIENTIFIC CONSULTANT:
JOSEPH SONNABEND, M.D.**

Chairman, Scientific Committee,
AIDS MEDICAL FOUNDATION

How to Have Sex in an Epidemic: One Approach

Fig. 2. How to Have Sex in an Epidemic (1983), front cover. Courtesy of Richard Berkowitz. This particular image demonstrates a later printing. The original run, with a cover designed by Richard Dworkin, did not feature Sonnabend's medical credentials at the top; this was later added as a response to GMHC's campaign to undermine Sonnabend's credibility and Michael and Richard's activist work.

With campy humor and a dance beat, "How to Have Sex" recounts one young gay man's thwarted attempts to find sexual release in the age of AIDS. In the first verse, the protagonist cruises a "long and lean mean sex machine packed in tight 501 jeans" in hopes of taking him home for the night. However, his dream lover scolds him by saying, "Where you been boy? Ain't you heard the news? I don't kiss, I just reminisce, and I keep it in my pants." After striking out at the bar, the young man finds himself home alone, late at night, "taking matters into [his] own hands, relax, Betamax playing those *Boys in the Sand*."[28] This time, his satisfaction is curtailed by the intrusion of the "politically correct safe-sex and thought police." Sex negative attitudes and AIDS panic have apparently permeated gay male sexual culture so deeply that it is no longer permissible to enjoy a vintage, pre-condom pornographic film in the privacy of one's own home. Anguished, Michael exclaims, "I'm going crazy [...]. When will it end, my friends, can you tell me, who can say when what is safe and what is not changes day by day?" In the final verse, he expresses nostalgia for the 1970s because "things seemed so simple then. So many men, so little time. Ahh, I remember when…" However, all is not gloom and doom, and the song offers a simple solution. In one of his most inspired lines, Michael advises SAGM to "use a rubber, find a lover, in time you will discover it's ok to get laid." He also manages an ingenious rhyme between "epidemic" and "polemic" in the chorus that would have Cole Porter howling.

"How to Have Sex" uses the sounds of '60s rock, New Wave, disco, and soul to create an upbeat musical setting for a song with a deadly serious message; this is the essence of camp, to make fun out of a bad situation. The opening drum roll sets a bouncy bass line into motion, outlining minor chords with a cheeky wiggle every two bars as offbeat synth accents sparkle like glints from a mirror ball. Vocally, Michael incorporates dramatic leaps, grunts, his piercing falsetto, and a multi-tracked

---

28 Wakefield Poole's *Boys in the Sand* (1971) is a classic gay pornographic film starring Casey Donovan (1943–1987), who died of AIDS at the age of 43.

choir of gospel-influenced background vocals that evoke the '80s pop-soul of the Pointer Sisters. Moments of text painting — when a musical effect matches an image in the text exactly — add to the song's campy feel: an organ tremolo accompanies the words "aching, shaking" in the second verse, and a bugle call signals a successful and safe orgasm in the song's orgiastic coda. Camping up a safe sex message by creating a theme song or jingle for *How to Have Sex in an Epidemic* was a clever inspiration. By transforming the title of the booklet into a mantra set to an insistent beat, Michael used music to pound the title of his safe sex booklet into listeners' ears in hopes that hearing it would save lives. Using vernacular language and campy humor, Michael showed that sex can still be funny and pleasurable, and that re-learning how to have sex in an epidemic did not have to be a morose affair.

The Denver Principles

In June 1983, a month after the publication of *How to Have Sex in an Epidemic*, Michael and Richard traveled to Denver, Colorado for the Fifth Annual Lesbian and Gay Health Conference, where they met other PWAs from around the country. The meeting was electrifying. "Once we were in the same room," Michael recalled, "we discovered that we had similar complaints: no one was listening to us or taking us seriously."[29] Together, Michael, Richard, Bobbi Campbell (1952–1984, a San Francisco nurse, Sister of Perpetual Indulgence, and one of the first gay men on the West Coast diagnosed with Kaposi's sarcoma), and a group of other gay men with AIDS drafted "the founding manifesto of the People with AIDS Self-Empowerment Movement."[30] *The Denver Principles* introduced the term "People with AIDS" as an alternative to pejorative and phobic monikers like "AIDS victim" and turned attention away from dying of AIDS to the notion of *living* with HIV/AIDS. The document also demanded that scien-

29 Callen, *Surviving AIDS*, 8.
30 Ibid.

tific, medical, and governmental agencies dealing with HIV/AIDS include PWAs "at every level of decision-making and specifically [allow them to] serve on the boards of directors of provider organizations." Finally, *The Denver Principles* asserted PWAs' rights to love, life, death, and dignity. At the end of the conference, the authors of the manifesto stormed the stage and read *The Denver Principles* aloud to protest "the powerful forces that were trying to dehumanize us."[31]

THE DENVER PRINCIPLES

(Statement from the advisory committee of the People with AIDS)

We condemn attempts to label us as "victims," a term which implies defeat, and we are only occasionally "patients," a term which implies passivity, helplessness, and dependence upon the care of others. We are "People With AIDS."

RECOMMENDATIONS FOR HEALTH CARE PROFESSIONALS

1. Come out, especially to their patients who have AIDS.
2. Always clearly identify and discuss the theory they favor as the cause of AIDS, since this bias affects the treatments and advice they give.
3. Get in touch with their feelings (e.g., fears, anxieties, hopes, etc.) about AIDS and not simply deal with AIDS intellectually.
4. Take a thorough personal inventory and identify and examine their own agendas around AIDS.
5. Treat people with AIDS as a whole people, and address psychological issues as well as biophysical ones.
6. Address the question of sexuality in people with AIDS specifically, sensitively, and with information about gay male

---

31 Ibid.

sexuality in general and the sexuality of people with AIDS in particular.

RECOMMENDATIONS FOR ALL PEOPLE

1. Support & Membership in our struggle against those who would fire us from our jobs, evict us from our homes, refuse to touch us or separate us from our loved ones, our community or our peers, since available evidence does not support the view that AIDS can be spread by casual, social contact.
2. Not scapegoat people with AIDS, blame us for the epidemic or generalize about our lifestyles.

RECOMMENDATIONS FOR PEOPLE WITH AIDS

1. Form caucuses to choose their own representatives, to deal with the media, to choose their own agenda and to plan their own strategies.
2. Be involved at every level of decision-making and specifically serve on the boards of directors of provider organizations.
3. Be included in all AIDS forums with equal credibility as other participants, to share their own experiences and knowledge.
4. Substitute low-risk sexual behaviors for those which could endanger themselves or their partners; we feel people with AIDS have an ethical responsibility to inform their potential sexual partners of their health status.

RIGHTS OF PEOPLE WITH AIDS

1. To as full and satisfying sexual and emotional lives as anyone else.
2. To quality medical treatment and quality social service provision without discrimination of any form including

sexual orientation, gender, diagnosis, economic status or race.
3. To full explanations of all medical procedures and risks, to choose or refuse their treatment modalities, to refuse to participate in research without jeopardizing their treatment and to make informed decisions about their lives.
4. To privacy, to confidentiality of medical records, to human respect and to choose who their significant others are.
5. To die — and to LIVE — in dignity.

People with AIDS Coalition, New York

"Electrified by the righteousness of the cause of PWA self-empowerment," Michael returned to New York where PWAs "began to express growing frustration at attending GMHC forums where those of us with AIDS would sit silently in the audience and hear doctors, nurses, lawyers, insurance experts, and CSWs [certified social workers] tell us what it was like to have AIDS [...]. The 'real experts,' we realized, weren't up there."[32] However, Michael and other PWAs knew that "GMHC was not about to permit a bunch of upstart, radical 'clients' to tell them how to run their operation" in spite of *The Denver Principles*.[33] PWA-NY dissolved before the end of the year, largely as a result of GMHC's efforts to block the organization's work. Although "GMHC succeeded in destroying the first organized incarnation of PWA self-empowerment in New York," Michael and Richard organized the People with AIDS Coalition (PWAC) "from the ashes of the first PWA group," in 1984.[34] Membership in PWAC swelled, and circulation of their monthly *Newsline* newsletter, "a 48-page monthly newsletter containing some of the best writing of, for, and by PWAs," peaked at around 14,000.[35] Michael served as the editor and a

32 Callen and Turner, "A History of the PWA Self-Empowerment Movement."
33 Callen, *Surviving AIDS*, 9. GMHC did not put a publicly identified PWA on their board until 1987.
34 Ibid.
35 Ibid.

regular columnist for the *Newsline* for many years. He was also a co-founder and member of the National Association of People with AIDS, the Community Research Initiative (CRI, which he co-founded with Dr. Sonnabend), and the New York State AIDS Institute. AIDS activism became the central focus of Michael's life, eclipsing even his musical endeavors as he and other PWAs fought for their lives.

The Cause of AIDS

Cluster studies of PWAs increasingly suggested a viral agent as the likely cause of AIDS, and the discovery of HIV in 1984 effectively turned public opinion against Sonnabend's multifactorial theory. Most media outlets, doctors, and scientists supported the "single-virus" theory, and dissenting views were quickly dismissed as quackery by mainstream media and the AIDS establishment.

Michael and Richard were undeterred, however, and they continued to question whether HIV alone was the sole cause of AIDS, in large part as a result of their own survival, which they attributed to Sonnabend's advice: prophylax against PCP; avoid immunosuppressive chemotherapy; don't be a guinea pig for medical experiments like Interferon; treat the infections as they come; and practice safer sex. The most important factor in Michael's long-term survival was a daily dose of Bactrim (trimethoprim/sulfamethoxazole, an inexpensive and proven preventative treatment for PCP, then the leading cause of death for PWAs). While 30,000 gay men with AIDS died of preventable pneumonia, Michael, Richard, and Sonnabend's other patients were protected from getting it.

Ironically, Michael's survival threatened his credibility in the eyes of some of his critics, who accused him of proffering irrational beliefs about the cause of AIDS. Some even suggested that Michael was pretending to have AIDS in order to promote his musical career. One disgruntled man expressed his disgust "at the way [Michael exploited] the health crisis to promote [his] singing career" instead of using his position to lobby or fund-

Fig. 3. The Denver Delegation (1983). Standing (l–r): Dan Turner, Bobby Reynolds, Bill Burke, Matthew Sarner; seated (l–r): Tom Nasrallah, Bob Cecchi, Phil Lanzaratta (rear), Bobbi Campbell, Richard Berkowitz, Artie Felson (shirtless), Michael Callen. Courtesy of Richard Berkowitz.

raise for people with AIDS who cannot afford their expensive treatments. "We need medicine, not another pop star! This is the AIDS Health Crisis, not American Bandstand. You're embarrassing us all with your bad music and shameless self-promotion. PLEASE STOP!"[36] Such bitter complaints were ironic, given the amount of work Michael did with activist organizations and support groups like PWAC-NY and CRI during these years, smuggling experimental AIDS drugs into the country for the PWA Health Group (a buyers club founded by Michael, Thomas Hannen, and Joseph Sonnabend in 1986), promoting preventative measures for common OIs, and serving as a public face of the most stigmatized disease in decades. Anytime anyone needed him, Michael was there. This included hundreds of hours he spent one-on-one, in person or on the phone, with terrified gay

---

36 J. Williams letter to Michael Callen (n.d.), handwritten original, MPC.

men who reached out to him anonymously because they had no one else to turn to.

Sensationalized in media reports and reduced to little more than modern day Typhoid Marys, PWAs were scorned and condemned by political and religious leaders and subjected to everyday insidious traumas, microaggressions, and acts of prejudice. Conservative provocateur William F. Buckley, Jr. suggested that

> Everyone with AIDS should be tattooed in the upper forearm to protect common-needle users, and on the buttocks to prevent the victimization of other homosexuals.[37]

At about the same time, conservative North Carolina Senator Jesse Helms called for a total quarantine on those who tested positive for HIV or were diagnosed with AIDS:

> I may be the most radical person you've talked to about AIDS, but I think somewhere along the line that we're going to have to quarantine if we are really going to contain this disease. We did it back with syphilis […] and nobody even raised a question about it.[38]

In 1987, Helms proposed a controversial amendment that would prohibit the use of federal money to pay for safe sex information that included discussions of gay sex. "We have got to call a spade a spade," he ranted on the Senate floor, "and a perverted human being a perverted human being."[39]

PWAs also risked losing their jobs and homes if their illness was discovered, and many lost connections with their lovers, friends, and biological families who were afraid of AIDS and ig-

---

37 William F. Buckley, Jr. "Crucial Steps in Combating the AIDS Epidemic: Identify all the Carriers," *The New York Times*, 18 March 1986.
38 Helms initially made these comments on an episode of *Face the Nation*, and they were quoted in "Helms Calls for AIDS Quarantine on Positive Tests," *The Chicago Tribune*, 16 June 1987.
39 Edward Koch, "Senator Helm's Callousness Toward AIDS Victims," *The New York Times*, 7 November 1987.

norant of the ways in which HIV could be contracted. During on-stage preparations for an NBC interview, a crewmember refused to touch Michael in order to pin a lapel mic to his jacket, and during one of his many hospitalizations, doctors and nurses refused to enter his hospital room, forcing him to crawl across the floor to retrieve his own food, which they left outside the door. And these were only two incidents, experienced by one PWA at one network and in one hospital.

Throughout the early 1980s, Michael and Richard did appear on national television programs and in print media, and Michael was invited asked to sing at AIDS rallies, gay pride celebrations, and other events. He also served on the New York State AIDS Advisory Council, whose mission was to help shape HIV/AIDS policy. In August 1983, Michael, Roger Lyon of San Francisco, and Anthony Ferrara of Washington, DC, testified before a Congressional subcommittee on behalf of people with AIDS. These "celebrity" PWAs appeared on television, at public events, and in print media, but theirs was hardly glamorous or aggrandizing self-promotion. Early activists faced great personal and professional risks, even as they worked to counter negative stereotypes about PWAs.[40]

Because some people with AIDS, including Michael and Richard, did achieve a degree of celebrity, it is not unreasonable to think that some people may have been jealous; however, they saw only a media spotlight rather than the substantial activist work undertaken by public PWAs and its impact on Michael's private life, including his music. Reflecting on this period, Michael remarked that, "those of us crazy enough to publicly identify as having the most stigmatized disease of the century agreed

---

40 See Sander Gilman, *Disease and Representation: Images of Illness from Madness to AIDS* (Ithaca: Cornell University Press, 1988) and Crimp's "Portraits of People with AIDS" (1987), anthologized in *Melancholia and Moralism: Essays on Queer Politics and AIDS* (Cambridge: MIT Press, 2009). Stuart Marshall's film *Bright Eyes* (1984) explores the problematic ways in which AIDS appears in mainstream media by linking images of AIDS with other troubling scenes from science including nineteenth-century medical texts and Nazi genocide and eugenics.

Fig. 4. Michael Callen, Roger Lyon, and Anthony Ferra being sworn in before a House Governmental Relations subcommittee hearing on AIDS (1983). Richard Dworkin Private Archive.

that it felt strange to be treated like 'celebrities.'"[41] Only in America, he quipped, "would it be necessary to make a career out of being sick in order to compel a more humane and appropriate government response."[42] And, he reasoned with his trademark wit, there were "easier ways to meet Liz Taylor than by pretending to have [AIDS]."[43]

The Committee for Responsible Sexuality

The discovery of HIV gave scientists a new focus in their search for treatments and, hopefully, a cure for AIDS, but it also confirmed the public's fears of a killer STI.[44] In New York, San Fran-

---

41 Callen, *Surviving AIDS*, 8.
42 Ibid.
43 Michael Callen, "Are You Now, or Have You Ever Been," *PWA Coalition Newsline* 40, January 1989, 34–36.
44 In *Disease and Representation*, Gilman discusses the history and issues surrounding the classification of HIV as primarily, or exclusively, an STI. Because sexual illness is highly stigmatized because it appears to reveal something about a person's morality, HIV was freighted with all of the weight of this historical association between morality, sex, and disease.

cisco, and other cities with large gay populations, bathhouses and other commercial sex establishments fell under the scrutiny of public health officials and groups of AIDS activists who were concerned about the spread of this new virus.

Michael had, of course, been trying to warn gay men about the risks of AIDS before the discovery of HIV, and in 1983–1984 he joined the Committee for Sexual Responsibility (CFSR) with Jeff Richardson (who would later become executive director of GMHC), David Nimmons (who later became an author), and others. The CFSR met with bathhouse owners and city public health representatives to try to distribute safer sex materials in bathhouses, backroom bars, and other commercial sex establishments frequented by gay men. CFSR members also arranged surprise visits to make sure these materials were displayed and readily available for patrons. What they discovered was disheartening.

In 1984, Michael visited several gay bathhouses in a sort of "grand tour to expose the utter disregard which [he] believed bathhouse owners had for the health of their patrons."[45] He assembled his observations into a series of notes for an essay that, ultimately, was never written. His notes offer a fascinating glimpse into the reality of New York City bathhouse culture in the early years of AIDS:

> A demoralization and anguish of untold proportions hung in the silence of the halls of the East Side Sauna [227 E 56th St.]. The image that struck me was one of little boys lost — each wandering around aimlessly, looking for mommy or daddy, holding on to his penis for what small comfort might be left in this hostile, frightening world. Each seemed utterly selfish in his despair: two men approaching one another in a hallway would, in an instant, search the face fo the other for some sign that contact, comfort was possible and not finding

---

45 Michael Callen, "Mike Goes to the Baths — Notes for a Piece Never Written," 1984. http://michaelcallen.com/mikes-writing/mike-goes-to-the-baths/.

> it, would pass without a word onto the next candidate. The eyes seem to beg: is it you? Are you the one who will love me?
>
> Perhaps I project. But perhaps not. The expressions haunted me. I had seen them — or expressions quite like them — before. It was only later that I remembered where: in the endless *Life* magazine photos of children of war.[46]

The results of Michael's tour of bathhouses were mixed. At some, he saw men engaging in safer sex, while in others, men continued on as if the party in the 1970s had never ended. At only one could he locate a safe sex pamphlet (and the desk attendant had to search for it among cluttered drawers and piles of boxes).

Having been branded a heretic by GMHC and the AIDS establishment in New York and having seen his attempts to teach gay men how to continue having sex, safely, in the midst of the growing public health crisis thwarted, Michael was disheartened. "I'm sick of being sick," he wrote, "and sick of this whole political nightmare. I want to move to EUROPE!!!! Or California. But Lowlife and love keep me here."[47]

---

46 Ibid.
47 Ibid.

Fig. 1. Mike & the Headsets in Central Park (1980). Richard Dworkin Private Archive.

10

Lowlife

> *It was a small-town depot on the Massachusetts border.*
> *We slipped past the eagle-eye red cap porter,*
> *And it was true love, till we ran out of quarters.*
> *There was a faucet in my back, and the walls was all greasy.*
> *Matter of fact, the only word for it was sleazy,*
> *But who ever told you love would be easy--*
> *So, we did it anyway.*
> — Pamela Brandt

Michael may not have been part of the downtown avant-garde, but he was surrounded by creative gay men and lesbians who shaped his expectations for his own endeavors. Performing as a solo act was emotionally tough for Michael, whose insecurities could be paralyzing, but he enjoyed being part of a musical group. Back in Hamilton, he had been in church choir, school musical theater, and even a short-lived garage band with some Warr Court kids, but never a working band. In 1980, he decided to put together an all-male, gay close-harmony group with friends he made in the New York City Gay Men's Chorus who, like Mike, wanted to sing a more than the standard choral fare. So, Michael, Joel Jason, Bobby Butler, Chris Humble, and Mark Howansky became Mike & the Headsets, an all-male, five-voice a cappella ensemble modeled on 1960s girl groups; they sang pop, rock, rock-and-roll, doo-wop, and of course, the girl group songs. Joel introduced Michael to a lot of music he grew up hearing on New York's eclectic AM radio including Rosie and the Originals' "Angel Baby" (1960), The Five Satins' "In the Still of the Night" (1956), and The Chantels' "Maybe" (1958), and these songs became part of the new group's repertoire.[1]

A single surviving tape captures Mike & the Headsets rehearsing in Michael's apartment. They were rough around the edges, but what the fledging group lacked in professional polish, they more than made up for in moxie. Mike & the Headsets performed benefit concerts for GMHC at Blue Skies (183 W 10th St., at the corner of 10th St. and W 4th St.), Kelly's West Village (46 Bedford St.), and Badlands (388 West St.).[2] Joel recalled two other shows, one at Rawhide (212 8th Ave.) and another at famed punk club CBGB (315 Bowery), though Joel admitted that their "stuff was nothing like what they were doing."[3] The apogee of Mike & The Headsets' short career was a performance on the dais in Central Park during the 1980 Gay Pride festival. The only press mention of their performance was unkind, and Mike & the Headsets "fell apart piece by piece."[4] Although the group didn't last long, Michael learned a great deal from the experience. When he put together a new group, he knew they would need to rehearse more often, a process that could be facilitated by recruiting top-notch musicians.

For his next musical project, Michael dreamed of something radical, a gender-balanced ensemble of two gay men and two lesbian women, singing songs with queer social and political significance in four-part harmony. His queer version of The Mamas and the Papas would bring gay men and lesbians together in an unprecedented way. Michael loved lesbians, lesbian feminist politics, and women's music; however, in the early 1980s, political and cultural divisions between lesbian and gay male

1   Joel Jason, interview with author, 23 May 2020 (henceforth, JJ and MJ [2020]).
2   Michael Callen, undated résumé, n.d., written at 29 Jones St., typewritten original, Michael Callen Papers at The LGBT Community Center National History Archive (henceforth, MCP).
3   JJ and MJ (2020).
4   Ibid.

Fig. 2. Michael's ad in the *New York Native* (1982). Richard Dworkin Private Archive.

communities made this dream difficult to realize. Still, Michael knew that lesbians and gay men would be stronger together and believed that a musical-political partnership was key. He placed an ad for like-minded musicians in the *New York Native* and the *Village Voice* then waited for the telephone to ring. One of the first responses came from Pam Brandt (1947–2015).

Born in New York City and raised in Montclair, NJ, Pamela Robin Brandt attended Mount Holyoke, a prestigious women's college in South Hadley, Massachusetts. Pam's mother encouraged her daughter to pursue her dreams, and Pam's own "dissatisfaction about the traditional role [her] mother had assumed" strengthened her own position as an independent woman.[5] In college, Pam played bass guitar in rock bands until she graduated with a Bachelor of Arts degree in 1969. She co-founded The Deadly Nightshade with guitarist-singers Helen Hooke and Ann Bowen in 1972. The group signed with RCA subsidiary Phantom Records in 1974, securing its place in music history as one of the first all-female rock bands signed to a major label. A self-described "drummerless but very danceable, high-energy female band," The Deadly Nightshade recorded two albums, *The Deadly Nightshade* (1975) and *Funky & Western* (1976).[6] Although music critic Robert Christgau dismissed the band as lit-

---

5　Robert Brandt, brother, quoted in Pamela's *Miami Herald* obituary: Howard Cohen, "Feminist, Rock Musician and Food Writer Pamela Brandt Dies at 68," *Miami Herald*, 4 August 2015, http://www.miamiherald.com/news/local/obituaries/article30104304.html.

6　"We're The Deadly Nightshade Band," *The Deadly Nightshade Homepage*, 2009. https://www.thedeadlynightshade.net/Home.html

tle more than "squeaky-clean folk rock" mixed with "the smug folkie sarcasm that seems to have its roots in junior high school talent shows," their albums each received Grammy nominations, and the band was popular among feminist rock fans.[7] They even scored a Top 100 hit with their disco version of the theme song to *Mary Hartman, Mary Hartman* (1976–1977), which peaked at #67 in 1976; and the band made a memorable performance on *Sesame Street*. In 2012, they released their final album, *Never Gonna Stop*. Sadly, Pam died of a heart attack in 2015.

Although Pam had been "playing with all-women bands for a long time," she was curious about a mixed sex group. "At the beginning, [she] wondered if this was a step forward or a step down."[8] However, the growth of anti-gay and lesbian activism spearheaded by the Moral Majority and its beauty-queen-turned-agitator, Anita Bryant, in the 1970s convinced Pam that gay men and lesbians should "work together, to focus on our similarities and not just our differences."[9] She and Michael arranged to meet at 29 Jones St., where he had recently relocated from his Christopher St. studio, to chat and rehearse. The pair hit it off instantly, and what should have been a "normal forty-five-minute mutual audition where you try to play together and see if you're musically compatible and all that" turned into the first of many all-nighters.[10] Pam got back home around four in the morning. Enthusiastic about the prospects of a new band, Michael continued his search for other musicians.

Drummer Richard Dworkin also spotted Michael's ad. A Chicago native who had lived on a commune in Minnesota before making his way to San Francisco in the late 1960s, where he

---

7 Robert Christgau, "The Deadly Nightshade" album review (1975). Archived on Christgau's homepage, http://www.robertchristgau.com/get_artist.php?name=The+Deadly+Nightshade.
8 Pamela Brandt, interview with JD Doyle, *Queer Music Heritage*, March 2013, http://queermusicheritage.com/mar2013s.html (henceforth, PB and JD [2013]).
9 Kate Walter, "Rock'N'Roll Lowlife with a Gay Conscience," *The Advocate*, 3 October 1984.
10 PB and JD (2013).

would play for bands like Buena Vista (a gay soul trio featured in the groundbreaking 1977 documentary film *Word Is Out*), Richard relocated to New York in November 1980. Soon, he joined eclectic jazz group The Microscopic Septet, an important force in New York's Downtown scene that included founding member, avant-garde composer and saxophonist John Zorn. Intrigued by the idea of performing with an East Coast gay band, Richard left several telephone messages for Michael, all to no avail. In the meantime, he took a gig drumming with a band on a cross-country train trip and was out riding the rails for two weeks. Upon his return to New York, Dworkin made one final call at about 5:30 pm on 14 June 1982. This time, Michael answered. He and Pam were scheduled to rehearse that very night at Michael's apartment, so Richard hopped on his bike and headed over to 29 Jones St.

As Richard mounted the stairs, bicycle in hand, Michael made quick mental notes, "very Jewish looking, high forehead, balding slightly. He had kinky hair cut short. He was wearing chinos and a T-shirt."[11] Although, he was cute, Michael thought, "this little drummer boy put out no gay vibes."[12] Michael also found it incredulous that someone in New York owned, much less rode, a bike. Richard stashed his bike somewhere and made his own assessment of the situation. The tiny studio apartment contained virtually no furniture, "a carpet, two — maybe more — director's chairs, an upright piano, a Yamaha PA mixer, a mic stand, a microphone, must've had a couple of speakers. Maybe a pillow or two."[13] So, the trio sat on the floor, ordered Chinese food, talked about music, and after enjoying a sorbet Mike made for them, gathered around the piano to harmonize on The Dixie Cups' "Chapel of Love" (1964). There was a powerful energy between the three musicians.

---

11 Michael Callen, "Handwritten Biography," 1981–1982, handwritten manuscript, MCP.
12 Ibid.
13 Richard Dworkin, interview with the author, New York, February 2012 (henceforth, RD and MJ [2012]).

Me and Dickie D

Although Michael wasn't sure if Richard was actually gay, Pam sensed that "some of the excitement in the room was vibes passing forth between [them!]"[14] Around 9:30 pm, she said her goodbyes and returned home to her girlfriend, but Richard lingered. Still unsure of his new acquaintance's sexual orientation, Michael started to worry. "How can I get him out of here? What if he's really straight and an ax murderer who answers personal ads?"[15] To solve the riddle of Richard's sexuality and put an end to the awkwardness, Michael pulled out a book called *SINEMA,* "an overview of porno films of the late-60s and early-70s."[16] That was all the encouragement it took. Richard pounced, trying to plant a kiss on Michael's lips, but Mike responded with "total shock."[17] Flattered yet flabbergasted, he pushed Richard away, exclaiming, "Whoa! Wait a minute. You don't understand. I think I have GRID."[18] Although he hadn't yet been officially diagnosed, Michael had all the symptoms of the new "gay cancer."

Richard was unphased. After spending a decade in San Francisco, he had "been there, done that, so that horse was out of the barn," and he didn't believe that sex with Michael would be "anything novel for [him] in terms of disease."[19] So, Richard stayed. That night, they talked, made love, and had their first fight. A diehard, sex-positive Gay Liberationist, Michael doubted whether love between two men was even possible, while Richard's politics had a romantic countercultural streak. He felt

---

14   PB and JD (2013).
15   Callen, "Handwritten Biography."
16   Ibid.
17   Ibid.
18   GRID stands for Gay-Related Immune Deficiency, an early predecessor used to describe what was eventually termed Acquired Immune Deficiency Syndrome (AIDS). Dworkin's and Callen's memories of this night are quite similar, though in his written account Callen says he warned Dworkin that he had "AIDS." This isn't chronologically possible, as the term "AIDS" was introduced in September of 1982, several months after they met. This suggests that Callen wrote this account sometime after the events happened.
19   RD and MJ (2012).

that love between two men was not only possible but necessary. Though, of course, love between men didn't mean monogamy, marriage, and the other accoutrements of heteronormativity, but *love,* that was possible. "I just adored Mike from the moment I met him," Richard remembered in 2012. "He was cute in a goofy Midwestern kind of way. He was smart. He liked to talk; I liked to listen. He liked to sing; I liked to play drums. He liked to write; I liked to edit."[20] Thus began a musical-romantic relationship that would endure for the next decade.

In the morning, the couple awoke early because Michael had to get to his day job as a legal secretary. As his new lover showered, Richard made a cursory pass through the record collection and spotted Al Jarreau's live album, *Look to the Rainbow* (1977). Pulling the vinyl out of the sleeve and placing it on the turntable, he selected "Could You Believe," a beautiful ballad featuring Jarreau's expressive vocals accompanied only by a quavering Fender Rhodes piano. Accustomed to living in a loft in a largely abandoned building downtown, Richard cranked the volume to full blast, filling the apartment with Jarreau's flexible tenor. Exasperated, Michael leapt from the bathroom, shouting, "What are you doing? What are you doing??!!" and turned down the music so as not to disturb his neighbors. It was a lovely moment in their new relationship that encapsulated complementary aspects of their personalities: Richard, the free-spirit, and Michael, the self-described control queen. For Richard, "Could You Believe" had a gay subtext lodged somewhere between Jarreau's vocal performance and the homoerotically suggestive lines, "I spent the night with David; he taught me what to say. I was looking for a smooth stone when I heard him pray." And, as he later told me, "somehow Mike just made me feel that way."[21]

Michael had been mostly unlucky in love. When he moved to New York, he packed the hope of finding love in his suitcase, but until he met Richard, the search had been fruitless. Michael captured the exuberance of new love in "Me and Dickie D," a

20 Ibid.
21 Ibid.

musical paean to his boyfriend. The title is a pun of the Kris Kristofferson song "Me and Bobby McGee," made famous by Janis Joplin on her final album, *Pearl* (1971). But where Kristofferson's song is a wistful ballad about a transient affair, "Dickie D" is a jive talking, Motown-loving, dancing machine who "goes bump bump" and "hump hump hump [...] like a kangaroo" all night on the dance floor. Michael built his rollicking rock-and-roll tune around a bluesy chord progression and a boogie-woogie piano hook. Vocally, he took cues from Little Richard (1932–2020) and Buddy Holly (1936–1959), growling, stuttering, and scatting his way through the melody with an infectious energy. He leaps from chest voice to his piercing soprano over a bass countermelody sung by Dickie D himself. A campy, feel-good queer love song, "Me and Dickie D" demonstrated that Michael could both croon and rock. John Hagen later arranged the song for a recording session that featured guitarist Richard Lloyd, bassist Pamela Brandt, saxophones played by Hagen, and Dickie D himself on drums. On the day of their sessions, the original pianist never showed at the studio, a decision Richard believes may have been motivated by homophobic, last-minute professional jitters about performing on an openly-gay love song. Mindful of the clock (and the cost) of the studio, Richard frantically called musician friends who might know an available pianist. Eventually, Jonathan Hardy arrived and did a "phenomenal job" with the song.[22] "Me and Dickie D" would be released on Callen's debut solo record, *Purple Heart* (1988). Richard also produced the recording, an experience he described as "absolutely mortifying. Imagine having to play on, produce, and edit a song about YOURSELF!"[23] But it was a labor of love.

Making It Official

About a week after meeting Richard, Michael collapsed in his apartment and was admitted to hospital. Although doctors had

22 Ibid.
23 Ibid.

Fig. 3. Richard Dworkin and Michael Callen in Tribeca Park (c. 1983). Richard Dworkin Private Archive.

been unable to determine the cause of his chronic health problems and generally poor health over much of the past year, this time they unmasked the culprit. "With the satisfaction of Miss Marple," a nurse delivered the diagnosis. "'Well, it's GRID. You have cryptosporidiosis. Before GRID, we didn't think it infected humans. It's a disease previously found only in livestock. I'm afraid there is no known treatment [...]. All we can do is try to keep you hydrated and see what happens. Your body will either handle it or…it won't.'"[24] She then smiled "not too optimistically, patted [his] leg, and left [Michael] alone to confront in earnest the very really possibility of [his] imminent death."[25] Now, at least, he knew he had GRID. When the CDC revised its terminology and defined Acquired Immune Deficiency Syndrome on 24 September 1982, Michael became one of the first men in the US

24 Michael Callen, *Surviving AIDS* (New York: Harper Perennial, 1990), 2.
25 Ibid.

to receive an AIDS diagnosis. At the time, doctors knew very little about AIDS, and what they did know was evolving and changing rapidly. However, a few things seemed certain: AIDS was a serious illness, and it appeared to be fatal.

The diagnosis left Michael feeling like "factory seconds or damaged merchandise," and he almost threw in the towel because he "didn't have a lover and [now was] going to die without a lover."[26] Determined to spare Richard the agony of watching him die, Michael "kept trying to push [him] away."[27] Getting involved with a man who had just been diagnosed with a stigmatized, deadly, and mysterious illness, Michael reasoned, was not exactly an auspicious set of conditions for new love or a lasting relationship. However, Richard visited Michael in the hospital, ignoring warnings from friends and disregarding Michael's own protests. "Some people thought it was amazing or strange or weird that I continued to see him," Richard recalled.[28] Richard realized that Michael "was kind of warning [him] of all the horrible things about him; besides that, he had this new killer disease and wouldn't last that long," but he dismissed Michael's protestations, saying, "Love's a crazy thing."[29] Michael would later misremember that Richard had said, "Love don't need a reason."

After Michael recovered, he, Richard, and Pam began to perform as a trio at small venues in the city. These intimate shows were based around Michael's cabaret act, supplementing and expanding the texture of piano and voice with a variety of percussion elements and bass. Working with an ensemble boosted Michael's confidence on stage. He became a stronger and more confident singer, and he took risks with repertoire. Between songs, he made campy stage banter with the audience and performed amusing impressions of TV divas like June Lockhart, the matriarch of *Lost in Space*. Archival recordings show the group's

---

26 David Schmidt, interview with Michael Callen, 12 November 1987, typescript, MCP.
27 RD and MJ (2012).
28 Ibid.
29 Ibid.

growing sophistication and eclecticism.³⁰ In addition to piano-based ballads and original songs by Michael and Pam, their sets included doo-wop, country, rock-and-roll, rock, and pop, original songs by friends and songwriters they admired like Don Yowell (1953–1984), Bobby Blume (1956–1984), and Grant King alongside Billy Joel, Elton John, and even Bruce Springsteen.³¹

Michael's repertoire choices were guided by his identity as a gay man. As he told an audience at SNAFU in 1982:

> I sit down, and I'm a gay man. And for years, I would listen to the radio, mostly female singers, and I would imagine a man singing to a man. And I always imagine songs that do not require a change of pronoun to express my experience as a gay man. And I found one in the work of Bruce Springsteen.³²

The audience giggles, given Springsteen's reputation as an übermacho man, the embodiment of virile heterosexuality. Michael hastens to add that in this case, he's had to do a little tweaking of the lyrics. "I've changed three lines having to do with New Jersey and cars because I cannot relate to New Jersey or cars," he jokes before launching into a performance of "Backstreets," Springsteen's nostalgic rock epic from *Born to Run* (1975).³³

---

30 Some of these archival recordings are housed in the MCP. Richard Dworkin possess his own private collection of unreleased live recordings as well.

31 Don Paul Yowell was an accomplished songwriter whose works were recorded by Aretha Franklin ("There's a Star for Everyone" from her 1981 album *Love All the Hurt Away*); Leah Kunkle, sister of "Mama" Cass Elliot, recorded Yowell's "I Run with Trouble" for her album of the same name in 1980. Desmond Child has been a champion of Yowell's work, recording and performing "A Ray of Hope" for many years. Michael's recording of Yowell's "Small Town Change" appears on his 1988 debut album, *Purple Heart*.

Bobby Blume received a bachelor's degree in music from the Manhattan School of Music, taught music, directed musical theater productions, and performed around New York City. There are two commercially available albums of Blume's music, *Falling for You Was a Trip* (2000), for which Michael recorded Blue's "Fool Heart," and *With Love, Bobby Blume* (2000).

32 Michael Callen, "Mike at SNAFU," n.d., audio recording. Richard Dworkin Private Archive.

33 Ibid.

Fig. 4. Michael Callen at SNAFU (1983). Poster design by Richard Dworkin. The Michael Callen Papers, Box 5/Folder 60, the LGBT Community Center National History Archive.

Michael loved passionate performances and powerful lyrics, two elements of Springsteen's music, and he aspired to emulate these qualities in performances and in his own songs. Joel Jason remembered that they saw Springsteen together during their days as Mike & the Headsets while on vacation in Ft. Lauderdale.[34] Before the concert, Michael spent some time teaching a very handsome and very stoned young stranger the finer points of Barbra Streisand's choreography from the final scene of *On a Clear Day You Can See Forever* (1970), offering him a peck on the cheek once the young man executed the moves to Michael's satisfaction.[35] Michael may have also been drawn to "Backstreets" out of a feeling of nostalgia.[36] His high school best friend was named Terry Tincher, and Springsteen's narrative revolves around the backstreet adventures of two friends, one of whom is named Terry. Singing "Backstreets," Michael channeled Springsteen's passionate urgency, and he handled the rock piano parts with finesse. Vocally, however, he pushed a bit too hard, shouting more than singing, which led to intonation problems in the final iterations of the refrain.

Eventually, Michael, Richard, and Pam found guitarist and songwriter Janet Cleary, and the new foursome brainstormed ideas for band names: The Amoeba Farts (a campy play on a symptom of a serious intestinal parasite that was being diagnosed among gay men with alarming frequency); The Scandells (a playful take on stylized girl group names); and Take Back the Nitrites (a reference to "poppers," a common inhalant vasodilator used on the gay circuit to produce a quick high and to enhance sexual experience). Eventually, they settled on Lowlife, a moniker selected on the assumption that "some people would figure we were lowlifes anyway, just 'cause we're queer."[37]

Lowlife played at gay benefits, queer proms at the Gay and Lesbian Community Center, and even some mainstream, i.e.,

---

34 This was probably Springsteen's concert at Hollywood Stadium in 1981.
35 JJ and MJ (2020).
36 RD and MJ (2012).
37 Walter, "Rock 'N' Roll Lowlife with a Gay Conscience."

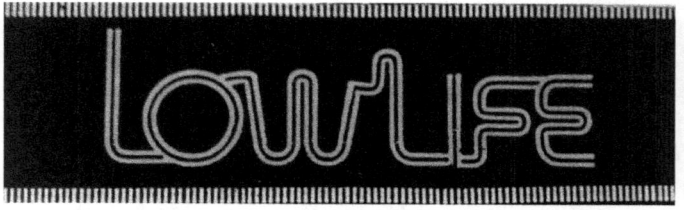

Fig. 5. Lowlife Logo. The Michael Callen Papers, Box 12/ Folder 166. The LGBT Community Center National History Archive.

straight, music clubs. Their sets mixed oldies from the rock-and-roll era, girl-group hits, country, reggae, and rock alongside originals that covered "the gamut from fucked-up love affairs to gays fighting for our rights."[38] In 1984, Michael told the *New York Native* that "all songs are chosen for their queer content. If it's not there, we force it."[39] Lowlife's intersectional political stance made them unique among New York's gay and lesbian musicians, and the balance between gay men and lesbian women in the group brought diverse constituencies together "in a room, having a good time together. This is what the band can do. Maybe the men are watching [Richard] and Michael, and the women are watching Janet and Pam, but inevitably they have to look at the whole band, and at everyone else in the room."[40] *Ms.* magazine praised the group's mixture of "good-time rock with a political bent," and Bruce Eder of *The Village Voice* wrote, "I don't know if the world is ready for Lowlife yet — but I'd like to think there are a few thousand of us, gay and straight, who are."[41]

Although each member of the band took queer politics seriously, they also made room for fun and pleasure — two important political tools — on stage. Michael would yodel, a vocal technique he learned from his mother and something both Pam

38 Kate Walter, "High Spirits," *New York Native*, 26 August 1984.
39 Ibid.
40 Richard Dworkin quoted in Walter, "Rock 'N' Roll Lowlife with a Gay Conscience."
41 Unknown, *Ms.* 13, 10 April 1985 and Bruce Eder, "Lowlife Laughs," *The Village Voice* 29, no. 35, 28 August 1984.

Fig. 6. Michael yodeling and twirling a baton with Lowlife. Pam Brandt, Jan Cleary (1985). Richard Dworkin Private Archive.

and Richard recall that he could "actually [do] really well, really, really, really, really well." He also twirled "one of those electric batons that had light-up ends, so it almost looked like you're twirling flaming batons."[42] Mike's antics were a hit with audiences, who delighted in his unapologetic flamboyance. Eventually, however, Lowlife had to face the music. Unable to play as many gigs as they hoped or to secure a record contract, the group disbanded in 1986. Brandt's only regret was "that we were ahead of our time. I really wish that the time had indeed been right for a band of gay men and gay women working and playing together because I think it was a darn good band. And I wish we had gotten more recognition when we were doing it. I wish it had gone farther."[43]

---

42 PB and JD (2013).
43 Ibid.

Although Lowlife never released an album, the band did raise $5,000 to record several demos at Philip Glass's Living Room Studio in 1985. The resulting tape included two original activist anthems by Michael ("No, No" and "Living in Wartime,"), two songs by Pam ("Uh Oh!" and "Mama,"), and their campy rendition of the 1960 Connie Francis classic, "Where the Boys Are."

Activist Anthems

Michael was determined to use his music to express experiences of PWAs and to use music as a tool for AIDS activism. One of his first activist songs, "Living in Wartime," captures the zeitgeist. It's an angry song, fueled by the righteous indignation of PWAs who were frustrated by the glacial pace of the federal government's response to the crisis. Michael employs military metaphors that were common in 1980s AIDS activist rhetoric, and his wordy text decries the "conspiracy of silence" and the "bigotry and greed" that mire activist efforts, obstacles that can only be surmounted by PWAs and their allies working to overcome their differences and fight together.

Like Joni Mitchell's *Dog Eat Dog* (1985) and Starship's "We Built This City" (1985), "Living in Wartime" harnesses the sounds of '80s synth-pop ironically to buttress the damning social critique in the lyrics. The song commences with an angular, syncopated fanfare on a synth organ over a wailing air raid siren, two musical gestures that signify intensity and danger. In the verses, murky minor-tinged harmonies churn over a low tonic pedal, while Michael calls for action: "This is no time for doubting/ to stop and wonder why / This is a time for shouting: / I don't believe the lies!" The swirl of synthetic sounds and the monotonous, mechanical music suggest alienation and cold indifference, and the contrast between Michael's voice and these synth effects gives his singing a humane poignancy. His is the voice of a PWA crying out against powerful forces that would rather see him, and people like him, ground to dust. The music of the chorus works its way from minor to major with a series of rising melodic sequences. In Western music, the journey from

Fig. 7. Lowlife at *The Late Show Tonight* (c. 1985). Richard Dworkin Private Archive.

minor to major has been interpreted as a narrative trajectory from strife to victory, benediction, or a happy ending (mostly famously, perhaps, in Beethoven's Symphony No. 3, but also in Leslie Gore's "You Don't Own Me," [1963], which uses a shift from minor to major to articulate a stance of feminist empowerment). In "Living in Wartime," Michael employs the minor to major tonal trajectory to mirror his hope that the war against AIDS would soon be over.

Lowlife recorded the song during their sessions at The Living Room in 1985. That year, it was also chosen as the exit music during the original run of Larry Kramer's AIDS activist play, *The Normal Heart*. Testing the Limits (a filmmaking collective formed in 1987 by Gregg Bordowitz, David Meieran, Sandra Elgear, Robyn Hutt, Hilery Joy Kipnis, and Jean Carlomusto as an ACT UP affinity group) used "Living in Wartime" as a "vehicle to organize information and propel the viewer through" their first documentary film, *Testing the Limits*.[44] In the film, Michael's song "functions to organize the dense arrangement of information, shaping it into a work of propaganda."[45] Although Michael's song resonated with other activists, Richard Dworkin mused decades later, "Maybe it was too late for an anthem anyway."[46]

Queering the Cover

Censorship and cultural taboo kept overt references to homosexuality out of movies, television, and popular songs. However, queer culture creators employed complex, multi-layered, and double-voiced techniques to hide queer points of view in plain sight, following the examples of Cole Porter (1891–1964) and Noel Coward (1899–1973) as well as earlier Black American blues queens like Lucille Bogan (1987–1948), Ma Rainey (1886–1939), and Gladys Bentley (1907–1960). But Michael was not content with subtext. Having done the work of coming out to live openly and proudly as a gay man, he craved songs that affirmed and celebrated gay experiences. In his covers, he retained male love-object pronouns in songs originally performed by women (a musical choice for which his father had once slapped him when Michael was a child), and as he had with Mike & the Headsets, Michael changed other lyrics as needed to make them gayer. He also manipulated the pitch, timbre, and inflection of his singing, especially through shifts in the accent or tone of single syllables and carefully placed sibilants, to sing in what many listeners would hear as a stereotypically "gay" voice.

Lowlife's cover of Connie Francis's "Where the Boys Are" exemplifies Michael's campy cover style. Originally the title song of a 1960 movie about college co-eds on spring break, "Where the Boys Are" is a piece of mid-century pop schmaltz and sentimentality. Its lyrics detail the fantasies of many a young, straight

---

44 Gregg Bordowitz, *The AIDS Crisis Is Ridiculous and Other Writings: 1986–2003*, ed. James Meyer (Cambridge: MIT Press, 2004), 31.
45 Ibid., 31.
46 Richard Dworkin, interview with the author, 2 June 2012.

woman who yearns to find her special beau somewhere in the hazy, heteronormative future. Francis's expressive voice swells with longing, but her desire remains G-rated. She's a good girl who waits, patiently, in the holding cell of adolescence, knowing that all it will take is a single look to spot the man of her dreams, then it's off to the bridal shop, next stop, Chapel of Love! "Where the Boys Are" reinforces heteronormativity, yet a masterful performer can queer it by "decoding and recoding the heterosexual or heteronormative meanings already encoded in that culture so that they come to function as vehicles for gay or queer meaning."[47]

Michael transforms this anthem of compulsory heterosexuality into a celebration of the possibilities that await young gay men where the *gay* boys are, namely in cities like New York, San Francisco, and Los Angeles where cruising for sex on public streets was an everyday part of urban gay life. On the recording, he used studio production techniques to camp up the cover. Multi-tracked vocals proclaim the titular refrain with a mock seriousness that also includes a cheesy synth trumpet call that adds to the bombast and silliness. Throughout, he uses shrieks, giggles, cracks, purrs, squeals, and slides to make fun *out of* the sentimental song and changes the lyrics to suit his aesthetic agenda. When Michael sings of throngs of urban denizens on crowed sidewalks, gay listeners know that the smiling face and tender embrace are more likely to be those of a mid-day trick than a lifelong partner. In the original lyrics to the second verse, Connie Francis sings "I'll climb to the highest steeple and tell the world he's mine." Michael queers the text by changing three little words: "I'll climb *right up on* his steeple and tell the world he's mine," adding an orgasmic cry just to drive home the point that this steeple was not erected atop any church.

Arguably the queerest moment in the song occurs on the penultimate note. A lifelong devotee of *La Streisand* and an avid collector of trivia about her, Michael vowed to break his favorite

---

[47] David Halperin, *How to Be Gay* (Cambridge: Harvard University Press, 2012), 12.

diva's record for the longest belted note on a recording. As the song comes to a close, he belts an E4 on the insignificant word "for," holding it for a staggering twenty-three seconds — a feat he had to repeat twice in the studio after the sound engineer erased the first take. Pam remembered that in live performances Michael "would camp it up like crazy when he sang it, of course, and sing really high, much higher than Connie Francis ever sang!"[48] Michael played up the campy humor of his "Streisand" moment by pantomiming funny gestures, making faces, glancing at his wristwatch, or feigning a yawn as he showed off his powerful voice. However, behind the camp façade lurked more serious realities.

- "Where the Boys Are" (Connie Francis, Neil Sedaka & Howard Greenfield, 1960)
- "Maybe" (The Chantels, 1957)
- "Come See About Me" (The Supremes, Holland-Dozier-Holland, 1964)
- "Be My Baby" (The Ronettes, Jeff Barry, Ellie Greenwich, Phil Spector, 1963)
- "Love Potion No. 9" (The Searchers, Jerry Lieber and Mike Stoller, 1959)
- "Little Bitty Pretty One" (Bobby Day, Thurston Harris, 1957)
- "Secret Agent Man" (Johnny Rivers, P. F. Sloan and Steve Barri, 1964)
- "We Did It Anyway" (Pamela Brandt)
- "Vigilante" (Pamela Brandt)
- "Living in Wartime" (Michael Callen)
- "No, No" (Michael Callen)
- "Uh Oh!" (Pamela Brandt)
- "Mama"(Pamela Brandt)
- "If I Could Only Win Your Love" (The Louvin Brothers, 1959)
- "The Locomotion" (Little Eva, Carole King and Gerry Goffin, 1962)

---

48 PB and JD (2013).

- "You Don't Own Me" (Leslie Gore, John Madara and David White, 1963)
- "Great Balls of Fire" (Jerry Lee Lewis, Otis Blackwell and Jack Hammer, 1957)
- "Who Hit Me" (Janet Cleary)

— Lowlife Repertoire List, c. 1985

Fig. 1. Peter Allen, Michael Callen, and Marsha Malamet at the 1986 AIDS Walk debut of "Love Don't Need a Reason" (c. 1987). Richard Dworkin Private Archive.

11

Purple Heart

> *If your heart always did*
> *What a normal heart should do,*
> *If you always play a part*
> *Instead of being who you really are...*
> — Peter Allen, Michael Callen, & Marsha Malamet

Throughout the twentieth century, piano bars and cabarets flourished in New York City.[1] Would-be Broadway babies, show tune aficionados, and pre-karaoke off-key belters crowded around small tables and grand pianos played by men and women with encyclopedic knowledge of the American songbook. In intimate venues with like-minded audiences, Peter Allen, Melissa Manchester, and Manhattan Transfer felt "free to try out-of-the-ordinary things without worrying about pleasing hundreds or thousands of paying customers."[2] Likewise, aspiring young songwriters like Michael could also try out their new material before small, receptive audiences in rooms like Helen's

---

1 Portions of this chapter have been adapted from Matthew J. Jones, "'Luck, Classic Coke, and the Love of a Good Man: The Politics of Hope and AIDS in Two Songs by Michael Callen," *Women & Music: A Journal of Gender and Culture* 27 (2017): 175–98.

2 Don Shewey, "Cabaret!," *The Advocate*, 5 October 1977. http://www.donshewey.com/music_articles/cabaret_1977.html. For more on the history of cabaret in New York, see James Gavin's *Intimate Nights: The Golden Age of New York Cabaret* (New York: Grove Weidenfeld, 1991).

Piano Lounge (196 8th St.), The Five Oaks (Grove St.), Marie's Crisis (59 Grove St.), The Duplex (60 Christopher St.), Don't Tell Mama (343 W 46th St.), Eighty Eights (228 10th St.), and Brandy's (235 E 8th St.), which dotted the cityscape until the triple whammy of rising rents, changing tastes, and HIV/AIDS caused many piano bars to close.

Although he never performed there himself, Michael spent a lot of time listening to songwriters at Reno Sweeney (126 W 13th St.). Founded by Lewis Friedman (who died of AIDS-related illness in 1992) and named after a character in Cole Porter's *Anything Goes,* Reno Sweeney served as "the hub of a cabaret revival" from 1972 until 1979 until it "was finally curtailed by the onslaught of disco."[3] During its heyday, Reno's provided an alternative to the "youth-oriented, T-shirt-clad rock culture, and it quickly became the model for the dozens of clubs that constitute[d] the cabaret circuit. The key word was elegance. Or nostalgia. Or sophistication. Call it escapism — or relief."[4] The club featured the art deco Paradise room filled with potted palms, indirect lighting, and touches of "glamour [and] '30s and '40s flash."[5]

At Reno Sweeney, Michael met fellow songwriter Marsha Malamet, another rising star on the cabaret scene. Born and raised in New York, Marsha was a precocious talent whose musical abilities manifested early. Like Michael, Marsha felt the axis of her world shift when she caught an episode of *The Garry Moore Show* featuring "a strange, intriguing, brilliant woman named Barbra Streisand, who sang a song, and [Marsha] became obsessed."[6] Awestruck by Streisand's "pure, unadulterated emo-

3 Steven Holden, "Reno Sweeney Alumni to Stage AIDS Concert," *The New York Times,* 7 April 1988, https://www.nytimes.com/1988/04/07/arts/reno-sweeney-alumni-to-stage-aids-concerts.html.
4 Shewey, "Cabaret!"
5 Ibid.
6 Geri Jewell, David Zimmerman, and Marsha Malamet, "Lesson to Be Learned," ABILITY, undated but likely 2017 when Gould's debut album, *Dangerous Man* was released. Marsha, who cowrote many songs for the album, was covered in the press often as a result of this collaboration with Gould. Streisand appeared on *The Garry Moore Show* on 20 May 1962 during her

tion" and her "voice [which could] emote lyrics so perfectly,"[7] Marsha endeavored to begin writing songs with the hope that one day Streisand would record one. She even wrote a lullaby called "For Jason," dedicated to Streisand's son, Jason Gould (b. 1966).[8]

In 1964, Marsha met lyricist Jason Bonderoff, and the two enrolled in a theater songwriting class with legendary arranger and musical director George Taros. In turn, Taros introduced Marsha to a young arranger named Lee Holdridge, who negotiated a meeting with Robert Lissauer, a composer, music historian, producer, and author of *Lissauer's Encyclopedia of Popular Music in America: 1888 to the Present*. Lissauer signed Marsha and Bonderoff, and her debut album, *Coney Island Winter*, was released by Decca Records in 1969. "An LP of total sympathy, the fragility and gentle drama of the songs couched in cellos, flutes, oboes, Christmassy bells and chimes [Marsha's] crystalline voice," *Coney Island Winter* sounds very much like the music of fellow New York songwriters Laura Nyro (1947–1997) and Janis Ian.[9] The album sold about 10,000 copies and then faded into obscurity, in part because Marsha's debilitating stage fright made promotional touring impossible.

Over the years, Marsha's songs would be recorded by Barbara Cook, Patti LaBelle, Judy Collins, Diana Ross, Meatloaf, Faith Hill, Jessica Simpson, and Barbara Streisand. In 2017, Malamet collaborated with Jason Gould and producer Quincy Jones for Gould's debut album, *Dangerous Man*. Today, Marsha is still composing new music. She has released several albums and has been working on a jukebox musical based on her life. She also

legendary Broadway debut in Harold Rome and Jerome Weidman's *I Can Get It For You Wholesale*. She performed Harold Arlen and Ted Koehler's "When the Sun Comes Out."
7   Ibid.
8   In 1966, Streisand gave birth to a son, Jason Gould, and Marsha composed a lullaby called "For Jason," which she recorded on a 45 record and sent to Streisand, to no avail.
9   Bob Stanley, "Heart Carny: Marsha Malamet, Coney Island Winter," *Mojo Magazine*, n.d., 128. A scan can be found on Malamet's homepage at http://www.marshamalamet.com/mojo-magazine-review.html.

advocates for people with Lyme disease, which she has been fighting for several years. On 29 May 2018, a benefit show called "Love Don't Need a Reason" at Catalina's Jazz Club in Los Angeles featured performances by Melissa Manchester, Amanda McBroom, Michele Bourman, and many others who turned out to show their deep appreciation of Marsha's talent and music.

Marsha and Michael made the rounds through the close-knit cabaret scene and grew to admire one another as songwriters and friends. One afternoon in 1986, the two bumped into one another in front of Symphony Space (2537 Broadway). Michael was over the moon because he'd recently been asked to compose a song for a possible film adaptation of Larry Kramer's *The Normal Heart,* which was enjoying a successful Off-Broadway run and for which his "Living in Wartime" had been selected to play as patrons exited The Public Theater after each performance. None other than *La Streisand* herself had acquired the film rights to Kramer's AIDS-themed play, and Michael desperately hoped that she would actually sing his song.[10] While Marsha was

10 Kramer's play debuted at The Public Theater in April of 1985 and was revived in 2011 on Broadway. The revival received a Tony Award for Best Revival of a Play as well as two awards for Best Featured Actor (John Benjamin Hickey) and Actress (Ellen Barkin). Barbra Streisand purchased the film rights to the play in the 1986 and lobbied for ten years but could not convince a studio to invest in a gay AIDS film. Kramer and Streisand each tell competing versions of exactly what happened during that ten-year period. Kramer claims that Streisand made changes to the essential elements of the story so that it became a vehicle for her starring role as Dr. Emma Brookner. Kramer write, "She cut Ned [Weeks, the central character and an avatar of Kramer] so much that when she offered the movie to a major star who had played the part on stage, he said, 'I can't play this. The character has no motivation anymore. She subsumed all of the motivations into her part, as the doctor.'" Streisand offers a different spin, telling *Entertainment Weekly* (see Adam Markovitz, "Barbara Streisand and Larry Kramer Trade Blame for Failed 'Normal Heart' Film," *Entertainment Weekly,* 7 May 2011, https://ew.com/article/2011/05/07/streisand-normal-heart/) and *The Hollywood Reporter* (see Gregg Kilday, "Barbara Streisand on 'The Normal Heart': 'I Tried Very Hard to Get It Made,'" *The Hollywood Reporter,* 9 April 2014, https://www.hollywoodreporter.com/news/barbra-streisand-normal-heart-i-694691) that she "tried very hard to get [the film adaptation] made [...]. After 10 years, the rights went back to Larry. But even when I had no contractual involvement,

thrilled that her dear friend would have an opportunity to write a song for their mutual favorite diva, she was floored when Michael proposed that they write it together. "All the good luck fell on me. He could have run into any number of other songwriters that day, but he chose me."[11] She agreed to collaborate on one condition. By coincidence, she was seeing her friend and occasional songwriting partner Peter Allen (1944–1992) in concert that very night at Radio City Music Hall. Allen had included songs he had co-written with Marsha in *Up in One: More Than a Show*, a 1979 one-man revue that introduced him to New York audiences. Based on her experience writing music with Peter, Marsha thought that, together, they three could write an amazing song not only because was Peter Allen was a fiendish talent and bona fide celebrity whose name could lend credence to their effort, but more importantly, he was also gay.

Peter Allen's career began in the 1960s in the Land Down Under, as one half of The Two Shades with his musical partner,

> I still persisted in pressing to get *The Normal Heart* made, purely because I believed in the project. [...] I worked on it for 25 years, without pay. Larry had the rights for the last 15 years and couldn't get it made, either. [...] In 2007, he sent me a note before giving the project to another director, asking me again if I wanted to direct it — but only with his screenplay. As a filmmaker, I couldn't have my hands tied like that. What if I needed changes? Sadly, I turned down his offer and wished him well." Whatever happened between Kramer and Streisand, an HBO miniseries version of *The Normal Heart*, directed by Ryan Murphy, premiered on 25 May 2014.
>
> In an interview on 17 May 2020, Karen Ocamb, journalist and friend of Michael Callen, recalled overhearing a conversation between Kramer and Michael after Michael's move to Los Angeles in the early 1990s. "He called Larry or Larry called him, I don't remember, but they had this very intense conversation about Streisand buying the rights to *The Normal Heart*, and it sounded like she had promised to sing 'Love Don't Need a Reason' to go with the screen version that she would produce and direct. So, they had an extended chat about that because she kept going back and forth, and it wasn't a done deal. Frankly, he just longed to her Streisand sing that song before he died. That was the bottom line. He was begging Larry to make it happen, and Larry couldn't make it happen."

11 Marsha Malamet, interview with author, 14 July 2017 (henceforth MM and MJ [2017]).

Chris Bell. When that group disbanded, Allen and Bell changed their name to The Allen Brothers and achieved national stardom. Frequent guests on Australian variety shows, the duo eventually caught the attention of Judy Garland's then-husband and producer, Mark Herron. In 1964, Allen came to London as the opening act for Judy Garland and Liza Minelli's concerts at the Palladium, and in 1967, he married Garland's eldest daughter. After the Allen Brothers disbanded in 1967, Peter began to write and record as a solo artist. His eponymous 1971 debut album and sophomore record, *Tenterfeld Saddler* (1972), contained a variety of songs in the confessional singer-songwriter mode, including "Six-Thirty Sunday Morning" which Michael Callen sang in a medley with Diana Ross's "Touch Me in the Morning" as part of his live shows with Buddy Barnes. Michael would later record "Six-Thirty Sunday Morning" in a medley with Harold Arlen's "Right as the Rain," which Streisand had included on *The Second Barbra Streisand Album* (1963).

After an amicable divorce from Minnelli in 1974, Allen embraced his sexual attraction to men and, at the same time, achieved superstardom as a nightclub, dinner theater, and cabaret performer. As his stage shows became more elaborate, Allen incorporated high-energy antics at the piano, choreographed dance routines, and a lot of chutzpah. *Continental American* (1974), *Taught By Experts* (1976), and *Bi-Coastal* (1980) highlighted this new style with songs that blended sentimental ballad-writing, including "I Honestly Love You," which was a massive hit for Olivia Newton John in 1974; nostalgic elements of 1920s jazz in "Everything Old is New Again"; and sheer exuberance in the Latin rhythms of "I Go to Rio." Allen also composed "Quiet Please, There's a Lady on Stage" (written about his one-time mother-in-law, Judy Garland), "Don't Cry Out Loud" (a massive hit for Melissa Manchester in 1978), "I'd Rather Leave While I'm in Love" (co-written with Carole Bayer Sager), and cowrote the Academy Award winning "Arthur's Theme (Best That You Can Do)" in 1981 with Sager, Burt Bacharach, and Christopher Cross. He made a memorable appearance at the 1982 Academy Awards, performing a tribute to Irving Berlin with Bernadette Peters, and he performed sold out shows at Radio City Music Hall, where he became the first male dancer to kick-line with The Rockettes.

Having already lost a partner to AIDS in 1984, Peter (who would himself die of AIDS-related complications in 1992) enthusiastically agreed to write a song with Marsha and Michael, whom he had yet to meet. About a week later, they rendezvoused in Allen's lush Upper West Side penthouse. Marsha described their collaborative songwriting process:

> Peter and I are both composers, and we both play piano. So, we're at his house, and of course I defer to Mr. Allen. There was no way I was going to sit at the piano and just sit there and have Peter throw out a note or two. It was Peter Allen! So, he sat, and Michael threw out lyrics […] and then, as the premier gentleman he [was], he got up and said, 'Ok Marsha, you take over.' I sat at the piano and started noodling […]. It was really collaboration. [Peter] did, I would say, sixty-five or seventy percent of the music, and the rest was me. And he collaborated [on the lyrics] with Michael, but it was mostly Michael. That was how we wrote it, and it came very quickly.[12]

Among the archival documents in the Michael Callen Collection at the NYC LGBT Community Center National History Archives is a rehearsal tape marked "Peter Allen, Marsha, and Me May 1986 — VERY IMPT. NEW SONG IDEA." This tape captures the three songwriters at work, sharing ideas, chords, and a pot of tea. According to Malamet, they worked on "Love Don't Need a Reason" for only a few hours before it was done. "I believe in all the woo-woo stuff," she told me, "and this was woo-woo. It was magical."[13] Michael's lyrics were heartfelt, and Marsha found the right chords and a beautiful melody to support them. Later, Allen added a bridge and smoothed out some of the lyrics for the

---

12 Marsha Malamet, interview with JD Doyle, *Queer Music Heritage*, May 2013, http://www.queermusicheritage.com/may2013s.html.
13 MM and MJ (2017).

final version of the song, which he premiered at New York City's first AIDS Walk on 18 May 1986.

"Love Don't Need a Reason" is a schmaltzy ballad with a political ax to grind. On the surface, its lyrics encourage generic sentiments like being true to yourself, rejecting societal mandates, and embracing compromise. However, the lyrics speak in two tongues, and gay men with AIDS could detect a completely different meaning in the song if they listened closely. The opening lines wonder whether doing "what a *normal* heart would do" and "playing a part instead of being who you really are" are worth the sacrifice of being authentic to yourself. The phrase "normal heart," a direct reference to Kramer's *The Normal Heart* (which draws its title from a line by gay poet W.H. Auden), juxtaposes the notion of "normal," that is heterosexual, love and the "abnormal" (by heteronormative standards) affective bonds of queer individuals. Further, rejecting "the madness that we're taught" is an important step in self-realization and self-acceptance for gay men and lesbians who inherit and internalize homophobic ideologies from the surrounding culture. Finally, the song's speaker worries about running out of time, a sentiment that certainly resonated with both Michael's and Peter's personal experience as well as with those of their listeners whose lives were attenuated by AIDS.

"Love Don't Need a Reason" endures as Michael's most well-known and frequently recorded song, and it became the official anthem of AIDS activism in the 1980s. He released the definitive recording of the song on *Purple Heart* (1988). Allen included his version on his final studio album, *Making Every Moment Count* (1990), and Marsha's version appeared on the landmark LGBTQ+ compilation album *A Love Worth Fighting For* (1995). Michael continued to sing the song at conferences, rallies, and on television throughout the rest of his life, and in 1993, he performed a moving rendition at the Gay and Lesbian March on Washington. In addition to versions by all three songwriters, "Love Don't Need a Reason" has been recorded by Broadway legend Barbara Cook, Women's Music icon Holly Near, songwriter Fred Small, and numerous gay men's choruses around the world, and it was included in *The Boy from Oz,* a 1998 biographical musical based on Peter Allen's life, starring Hugh Jackman.

The years from 1981 to 1987 were the most creative and productive of Michael's life. In addition to his voluminous activist writing, Michael composed most of the original music he would ever write. Michael and Marsha continued to write together. Love was a recurring theme in their collaborations "Love Worth Fighting For" and "Just Look in Our Eyes," which they imagined as the theme music for a film adaptation of Patricia Nell Warren's classic gay novel, *The Front Runner* (1974). They also composed their epic ballad "The Healing Power of Love," which they later described as the *unofficial* AIDS anthem of the 1980s. Because Reno Sweeney had been so central to their musical collaboration and their friendship, Michael and Marsha organized an AIDS benefit concert using a roster of famous singers who once performed there. In 1987, Michael, Marsha, Marvin Hamlisch, Barbara Cook, Jimmy Webb, Janis Ian, Phoebe Snow, Peter Allen, Alan Menken, and Howard Ashman performed a four-night concert which was later broadcast around the world on the A&E Network as *Reno's: A Reunion.* The concerts were recorded for an album, yet to be released.

Purple Heart

For years, Michael had dreamed about making his own album, but just as his father had once dreamed of escaping from Ohio to Arizona, only to see his dream evaporate, circumstances often intervened to thwart Michael's efforts. Certainly, his health was a major factor. Often sick, frequently hospitalized, and even when "healthy" still a person living with full-blown AIDS, Michael sometimes wasn't physically up to the task. At times, his "classic gay low self-esteem" got the better of him. He would unfavorably compare his music to that of his favorite artists, despairing that he would never have the budget to record with a full orchestra. So, why bother trying? Convinced that Michael could overcome his self-defeating tendencies and create an intimate yet powerful album, Richard played him *Nina Simone &*

Piano! (1969), an album that features exactly what its title advertises: ten tracks performed by the High Priestess of Soul, by herself, at the piano. At first, Simone's distinctive vocal timbre grated on Michael's nerves, but Richard encouraged him to keep listening. With time, Michael came to appreciate the beauty of Simone's dramatic interpretations, and the album's minimal aesthetic moved him as much as any elaborately orchestrated Streisand release. Michael started to believe that a simpler musical style could still have a huge emotional impact. He endeavored to create works of equal power and beauty on his own album.[14] A serious bout of bacterial pneumonia in 1987 was the catalyst Michael needed. Worried that he might die before leaving a record of his songs, Michael and Richard worked out a plan to get into a studio.

Immediately, they ran into a number of obstacles. First, Michael didn't have a record contract. Although friends and fellow musicians repeatedly assured him that his sound was commercial enough to land a record contract, his commitment to singing gay music was itself a considerable barrier to landing a record deal, as was his status as a prominent PWA. Every label they approached, including Holly Near's own Redwood Records, rejected the project.[15] This led to a second problem: money. Without the backing of a record label, Michael and Richard would have to pay for studio time out of pocket. Once again, Michael's anxiety and insecurity manifested; he "really felt there was no way that anyone would put out his record, between the combination of the subject matter, him having AIDS, and him having a life expectancy shorter than the current issue of *Vogue*."[16] However, Richard engineered an ingenious solution.

Thumbing through a copy of *Mix Magazine*'s Northeast directory of studios, engineers, and recording professionals, he searched for familiar names who might have access to a studio.

---

14 Richard Dworkin, interview with the author, New York, 1 June 2012.
15 Ibid. Holly Near and Michael became close friends, but Redwood specialized in women's music and declined to sponsor the project.
16 Ibid.

Eventually, he found Classic Sound, the home studio of jazz pianist Fred Hersch.[17] Richard had met Hersch in late 1982 or early 1983. Richard was playing drums for a swing band at The Monster (80 Grove St.), and Hersch was making a name for himself as an innovative pianist at Bradley's, an important cabaret on University Place.[18] Hersch offered the couple his studio and an engineer (Denise McGrath) for the astoundingly affordable price (even by 1980s standards) of twenty-five dollars an hour. Working at Classic Sound, they laid down several tracks for about three thousand dollars and added a few Lowlife songs to round out the album, which Michael named *Purple Heart*.

Purple Heart is a loosely autobiographical concept album. It follows the life of a young gay man who arrives in New York ("Where the Boys Are") and finds love ("Me & Dickie D") before getting involved in AIDS activism ("Living in Wartime") and the invention of safe sex ("How to Have Sex," "Take It Easy"). Along the way, he contemplates the significance of romance ("Love Don't Need a Reason"), his journey from a small town to a sometimes alienating metropolis ("Small Town Change," "On the Other Side"), and gay men's often difficult relationships with their fathers ("Nobody's Fool"). The album comes to a close with Michael's cover of Elton John's "Talkin' Old Soldiers," which he transformed into a tribute to his friend and physician, Joe Sonnabend, and an austere *a cappella* arrangement of Bill Russell and Donald Melrose's "Home," which Michael knew from an obscure 1976 album by Janet Hood and Linda Langford recorded under the name Jade & Sarsaparilla.

---

17 Hersch tested positive for HIV in 1986 and began his coming out process. He revealed his HIV status in the early 1990s. The *New York Times* ran a profile of Hersch in 2010. See David Hajdu, "Giant Steps: The Survival of a Great Jazz Pianist," *New York Times*, 28 January 2010. http://www.nytimes.com/2010/01/31/magazine/31Hersch-t.html. Hersch completed a new, AIDS-themed work, *My Coma Dreams*, after waking from an AIDS-related coma in 2008.

18 Hersch discusses his life as a gay musician and a musician with HIV in his memoir, *Good Things Happen Slowly: A Life In and Out of Jazz* (New York: Crown Archetype, 2017).

Fig. 2. Purple Heart cover (1988). Design by Patrick Roques. © Significant Other Records.

"Purple Heart" refers to the military honor given for injury or death in battle, and Michael chose that title because, as he wrote,

> AIDS is about living daily with the very real possibility that tomorrow — or maybe the day after — we may be dead. AIDS is about bed pans and respirators. It's about loss of control […] of one's bowels and bladder, one's arms and legs, one's life. Sometimes the loss is sudden; sometimes tortuously gradual. It's about the anticipation of pain as well as actual pain itself. It's about swelling and horrible disfigurement, the fear of dementia. It is horror.
>
> AIDS is the moment to moment management of uncertainty. It's a roller coaster ride without a seat belt […]. It's like standing in the middle of the New York Stock Exchange at

midday: buzzers and lights flashing, everyone yelling, a million opinions, a momentum.[19]

In other words, AIDS in the 1980s was a lot like living in a war zone, a point made explicit by Vito Russo and Larry Kramer as well as elsewhere in Michael's own speeches and writing and, of course, his song "Living in Wartime."

But for Michael, AIDS was also about hope, determination, self-empowerment, love, and survival. And these themes are just as important to the meaning of *Purple Heart* as the others because, as he put it, "living is the best revenge."[20] With its weathered gold edges and faded patina, Patrick Roques' cover art for the album resembles a precious keepsake from a distant past, a beloved and frequently touched memento of a cherished one. As such, it subtly alludes to a future when the war against AIDS is just a memory.

Unencumbered by the demands of a major label, Michael could indulge his queerest fantasies, and his gay sensibility permeates the project. He toyed with the normative structure of an album by giving each side a non-numerical, non-sequential name. In lieu of standard numeric or alphabetical designations, he called one side "Tops" and the other "Bottoms," leaving it up the individual listener to decide whether the top or the bottom *comes* first. On an LP, the specific sequence of songs is particularly important, especially the point at which a listener must pause to turn over the disc. Regardless of which side a listener plays first, Michael built on a moment to catch a breath or rev up for more. Given that the "Top" side contains all of the rhythmic, uptempo songs while the "Bottom" is made up for ballads, Michael may also have been telling us something about his own ideas about gay sex.

---

19 Michael Callen, "Remarks of Michael Callen: American Public Health Association Annual Meeting," 1986, in *In My Time: Essays and Sex, Science, and AIDS*, ed. Jeffrey Escoffier, unpublished manuscript, 1993, RDA.
20 Michael Callen, *Surviving AIDS* (New York: Harper Perennial, 1990), 227.

Fig. 3. Michael Callen at San Francisco AIDS Walk singing "Love Don't Need a Reason" (1988). Richard Dworkin Private Archive.

Purple Heart was released in 1988 on Michael and Richard's Significant Other Records. It was immediately hailed as an important record by the gay press. *The Bay Area Reporter* described it as "a virtually flawless debut" and "the best new album by a gay male performer." *The Advocate* endorsed it as "the most remarkable gay independent release of the past decade," singling out Michael's penchant for "singing hard and humorous truths about the plague [with] assured vocals and familiar pop idioms [to] make these tough truths accessible." *The Los Angeles Dispatch* called *Purple Heart* a "startling, sophisticated offering," and the *Bay Area Reporter*'s David Lamble lamented, "Why isn't *Purple Heart* his tenth recording instead of his first?" UK-based gay singer/songwriter Tom Robinson hailed Michael Callen as "the unmistakable voice of gay New York in the late 1980s."[21] The positive critical reception of his solo album demonstrated that Michael's music would find receptive audiences.

---

21 Various *Purple Heart* press releases in the MCP.

However, Michael worried that gay men would not buy his record. "It is a source of frustration for me that gays do not support gay men's music in the same way as lesbians support women's music," he said.[22] Most gay men — including Michael himself — were typically fans of female divas in cabaret, pop, opera, musical theater, soul, and disco, yet he remained hopeful that *Purple Heart* would reach its intended audience. The record sold around 10,000 copies, a respectable figure for an essentially DIY project in the pre-Internet era

Between the breakup of Lowlife and the release of *Purple Heart,* Michael had become a full-time AIDS activist and a part-time musician. However, working with Lowlife had boosted Michael's confidence in his ability to integrate his musical and activist selves into a coherent whole. In an ensemble, he found a comfortable space among like-minded musicians and a familial support network, and he was eager to have that dynamic again. *Purple Heart* had taught him about the recording process: the costs, coordinating groups of players, working with studio engineers, and the non-musical aspects of building a career like publicity and touring to build a following. Michael yearned to perform with a group again. As fate would have it, Richard soon found a way to help Michael perform again.

---

22 David Nahmod, "Heart to Heart: Singer/Activist Michael Callen Talks about Politics, AIDS, and Music as Warfare," article in an unknown magazine, 1988, MCP.

Fig. 1. The Flirtations Sextet (c. 1988), l–r: Aurelio Font, Michael Callen, Elliot Pilshaw, Cal Grogan, TJ Myers, Jon Arterton. Courtesy of Jon Arterton.

12

The Flirt Song

> *You can be anybody you want to be.*
> *You can love whomever you will.*
> *You can travel any country where your heart leads*
> *And know I will love you still.*
> *You can live by yourself; you can gather friends around.*
> *You can choose that special one.*
> *And the only measure of your words and your deeds*
> *Will be the love you leave behind when you're gone.*
> — Fred Small

Jon Arterton and Elliot Pilshaw were restless.[1] After touring for two years with Tom Wilson Weinberg's gay and lesbian musical, *Ten Percent Revue* (1985), the two friends were anxious to keep up their momentum and to continue making LGBTQ+ music.[2] Over breakfast one morning in a Brooklyn diner, they had an

---

1 Portions of this chapter have been adapted from Matthew J. Jones, "Something Inside So Strong: The Flirtations, Queer Politics, and *A Cappella*," *Journal of Popular Music Studies* 28, no. 2 (2016): 142–85.

2 Jon Arterton, interview with the author, 2013 (henceforth, JA and MJ [2013]). Jon caught the "theater bug" and enrolled in an acting program at Smith College in 1975. He moved to New York City the following year, where he worked as an actor/singer in several productions, including his only night on Broadway in *The Utter Glory of Morrisey Hall,* Clark Gesner and Nagel Jackson's infamous flop that opened and closed after a single performance on 13 May 1979. After coming out in 1982, at age thirty-six, Jon got involved with the city's gay music and political scenes.

epiphany. As a child in New Jersey, Elliot had fallen in love with the close vocal harmony he heard in choral performances that his family attended at Princeton University.[3] Jon had sung in collegiate *a cappella* groups, mixed choruses, and men's choirs as an undergraduate at the University of North Carolina at Chapel Hill and as a graduate student at The New England Conservatory of Music. Both men also admired the alchemy of close-harmony singing and progressive politics of Sweet Honey in the Rock. "Why not start some kind of gay men's political singing group that would go sing at ACT UP and gay pride events," they reasoned, "to just lend support and inspiration?"[4] A band, with its equipment and rehearsal space, would be too expensive an endeavor, but a vocal ensemble could rehearse and tour with little more than a pocket-size pitch pipe and the clothes on their backs. A gay *a cappella* group! So, they drew up a flier that read "Singers Wanted for Politically Active, Openly Gay, *A Cappella* Men's Singing Group," printed it on lavender paper, of course, and posted copies in gay clubs, bars, and at the Lesbian and Gay Community Center (208 W 13th St., henceforth The Center).

The time was right for their mixture of *a cappella* pop and politics. Much of the country was in the midst of a close harmony and *a cappella* revival. The Manhattan Transfer (founded in 1972) and Rockapella (1986), Toronto's The Nylons (1979), Huntsville's Take 6 (1980), and San Francisco's The Bobs (1982) enjoyed commercial success with doo-wop-influenced close harmony. Established artists like Billy Joel and rising stars like Bobby McFerrin turned nostalgic *a cappella* harmony into chart-topping hits like "The Longest Time" (1983) and "Don't Worry, Be Happy" (1988), and the music of Ladysmith Black Mambazo found its way into mainstream popular culture through Paul Si-

---

3   Elliot Pilshaw released his first album, *Breaking All the Rules,* in 1982. He has released two other albums, *Native Tongue* (1984) and *Feels Like Home* (1986), and he founded the short-lived gay *a cappella* group Sons and Lovers, who released their self-titled album in 1994. Pilshaw spoke at length about his career with JD Doyle in a 2008 interview. See JD Doyle, "Elliot Pilshaw and Friends," *Queer Music Heritage,* July 2008.
4   Ibid.

mon's *Graceland* (1986) and growing interest in what was called World Beat or World Music. Spike Lee captured this resurgence of close-harmony singing in a PBS documentary called *Spike Lee & Co., Do It A Cappella* (1990).

The *a cappella* turn in music was of a piece with a more general fad, as aging baby boomers revisited, and their children discovered, the music and pop culture of the 1950s. Emerging "oldies" radio programming brought the sounds of the 1950s and early-1960s back to the airwaves on stations that were specifically packaged as nostalgic listening, which fueled demand for concert appearances that helped revive the careers of rock-and-roll, doo-wop, Motown, and girl group stars on the nostalgia tour circuit. In 1985, Nickelodeon created a correlate "oldies" television program called *Nick at Nite* on which the network aired reruns *The Many Loves of Dobie Gillis* (1959–1963), *The Patty Duke Show* (1963–1966), *My Three Sons* (1958–1972), and *The Donna Reed Show* (1958–1966) while contemporary shows aimed at younger audiences like *Saved by the Bell* (1989–1993) included icons of the 1950s: malt shops, burger joints, juke boxes, poodle skirts, and rock-and-roll. Disney even got into the retro act with MMC, a stylized reboot of *The Mickey Mouse Club* (1989–1996) that featured sketch comedy, kid-friendly celebrity news, and of course, lots of close-harmony singing, including numerous covers of 1950s and 1960s classics.

Politically, socially, and economically, this cultural glance to the past may have relieved some of the hard realities of the 1980s. To many, the assassination of John Lennon on 8 December 1980 signaled the end of the counterculture era of which he had been a leading artistic, musical, and political figure. The inauguration of Ronald Reagan ushered in a new era of conservative social policies and neoliberal economics that would define the "yuppie" decade. Unrest was the norm around the world: the bombing of the US Embassy in Beirut; lingering Cold War tensions between the US and Russia; and the devastating Ethiopian famine; while in the US, there were two recessions; the national trauma of the *Challenger* explosion; and the exacerbation of gang activity and the crack epidemic by inner-city poverty, high unemployment rates, and Regan-era defunding of social assistance programs and trickle-down economics. In 1981, the first deaths associated with what would become the global AIDS pandemic quietly signaled an existential threat for humankind.

Turning to 1950s in popular culture provided a convenient fiction, an image of American innocence (or, perhaps ignorance) fueled by post-war prosperity. With money in their pockets, new suburban homes, and college educations, middle-class and mostly white Americans in the 1950s could believe that things would only get better. As the 1980s slogged onward, many Americans sought solace in media myths of that supposedly simpler time.

One afternoon, Richard spotted Jon and Elliot's lavender flier at The Center and thought it would be an ideal opportunity for Michael, who had been kind of rudderless since the breakup of Lowlife and the recording of *Purple Heart*. So, he brought home a copy of the flier and encouraged his lover to audition. Michael was intrigued.

On a wintery day in 1987, Michael swept into the audition room at The Center, his performance résumé and a copy of his newly minted LP in hand and joined a few dozen other hopefuls. With a queenly grandeur that masked his feelings of insecurity, Michael introduced himself and announced his intention to join the group, without actually offering to audition. After some conversation, he did sing, impressing Jon and Elliot with his flexible tenor and his extraordinary falsetto and securing a spot as a founding member of "the world's most famous, openly-gay, all-male, politically active, multicultural, *a cappella* singing doo-wop group," the faaaaabulous Flirtations.[5]

On 8 January 1988, baritones Jon Arterton, Elliot Pilshaw, and Cal Grogan; and tenors Michael Callen, TJ Myers, and Aurelio Font held their first rehearsal at The Center. As he entered the room, Michael spied Aurelio, who he knew from the New

5 Variations of this description appear in numerous publicity materials located in the Michael Callen Papers at The LGBT Community Center National History Archive (henceforth, MCP).

York City Gay Men's Chorus, and greeted him with campy consternation. "Miss Font!," he announced. "I might have known you would be in this group."[6] But the new group quickly got down to musical business. Like Mike & the Headsets and Lowlife, The Flirtations would perform an eclectic repertoire that included American oldies from rock-and-roll, pop, and doo-wop, American Songbook standards, folk music from different cultures, Women's Music, and even a few original compositions.

Their first performance took place in the heart gay New York, at the corner of Christopher St. and Seventh Avenue, where they literally passed a hat to collect pocket change from onlookers. A home video captures the original sextet performing The Angels' "My Boyfriend's Back" (1963) at an ACT UP rally in New York in 1988. Bundled in coats and scarves against the bitter winter wind, the six singers huddle together around three handheld microphones, trading solos, punctuating their singing with rhythmic handclaps, and camping it up for an appreciative crowd, happy to hear a queer version of this classic pop tune.[7] Notions of propriety for an AIDS protest varied widely, and some participants felt that The Flirtations' cheeky humor was inappropriate for an ACT UP event. Jon recalled a performance at an early ACT UP rally near Columbia University in 1988 when protesters tried to drown out their singing with shouts of, "People are dying! Stop singing!"

---

6   Aurelio Font, interview with author, 9 March 2016 (henceforth, AF and MJ [2016]). In our interview, Aurelio recalled a brush with fame when he got to meet Stephen Sondheim. "He created a medley of his pieces for the New York City Gay Men's Chorus, and the director at the time needed some soloists and called me up. I had to sight read ["Not While I'm Around" from *Sweeney Todd*] with Sondheim in the room! You could tell by the state of my armpits how much I was enjoying it!" But during the audition, the composer put down his pen, leaned forward, and listened to Aurelio sing. He got the solo, and Sondheim gave Aurelio a copy of the arrangement inscribed with a note: "To Aurelio Font, Thanks for the Voice." Still beaming with pride over this accomplishment decades later, Aurelio laughed, "I clutched my pearls! And I still have that score!"
7   BettyByte, "The Flirtations sing 'My Boyfriend's Back' at a demo ca. 1988," *YouTube*, 10 October, 2010, https://www.youtube.com/watch?v=1xE5I5hSSWM.

Fig. 2. The Flirtations classic quintet (c. 1989), l–r: Michael Callen, Cliff Townsend, TJ Myers, Aurelio Font, Jon Arterton. Courtesy of Jon Arterton.

The Flirts, as they were affectionately known, were an instant hit. As their reputation grew, they graduated from street corners to venues like The Center and Don't Tell Mama (343 W 46th St.). Faced with the possibility of actually making it as performers, the group reevaluated their sound and determined that an ensemble of three baritones and three tenors had balance issues. Because he was considered by all to be the weakest singer, Cal Grogan was asked to leave, a decision that Jon Arterton admits "created some ill will."[8] Shortly after Grogan's ouster, Elliot Pilshaw quit because he was not ready to make a full-time commitment to a fledgling group, having just started a new job and a new love affair. The loss of two baritones left room for one true bass whose voice would balance the ensemble. Aurelio recalled an acquaintance with whom he once sang in a gospel choir in

---

8   Jon Arterton, interview with author, 17 October 2013 (henceforth JA and MJ [2013]).

Chelsea. A military veteran, literate musician, skilled sight-reader, arranger, and composer who had studied oboe performance and composition at Indiana University, Cliff Townsend perfectly suited the group's musical needs. That he was Black also helped balance the number of white and POC singers, an important factor for the diversity-conscious ensemble. The addition of Townsend solidified the "classic quintet" lineup.[9]

The Flirtations polished their vocal craft in live shows until they were ready to cut a record. As had been the case with *Purple Heart,* the album was a DIY affair. Working on a shoestring budget with Richard Dworkin acting as producer, they released the eponymous album on Michael and Richard's Significant Other Records in 1990. *The Flirtations* captures their eclectic mixture of doo-wop, classic rock-and-roll, folk, and contemporary song, and it was uniformly hailed a classic in the gay press. *The Bay Area Reporter* heralded the arrival of "the hottest new *a cappella* doo-wop quintet out of the Big Apple." Susan Spence of *The Orlando Center Fold* gushed that The Flirts, "simply sang their way into [her] heart and soul [...] on an emotional journey through the triumphs and struggles of the human spirit." The music critic for *7 Days* (Vermont's independent newspaper) praised them for having "the elegance of Take 6, the earthiness of Sweet Honey in the Rock, and the winking humor of *La Cage aux Folles*" as well as for their "courage to be who they are," adding that although "at present their audience looks to be limited to a particular persuasion, it's only because the rest of the music biz hasn't yet caught up."[10] Accolades and adulation piled up, and The Flirtations were on their way.

---

9 Cliff also assumed the role of group historian and librarian, keeping track of their repertoire, performances, and changing personnel in several thick scrapbooks which he shared with me in 2013.
10 Various undated reviews collection in Cliff Townsend's scrapbooks.

The Queer Politics of *A Cappella*

Aside from a few contemporaries like Romanovsky and Phillips, Sylvester (1947–1988), or Jimmy Sommerville, The Flirtations had few models they could turn to in order to craft a career as openly gay male singers. Inspired by these men as well as by the diverse roster of lesbian and feminist artists on Olivia Records, The Flirtations made a conscious decision to perform as openly gay men. To queer up their music, The Flirtations utilized many of the same strategies Michael had used with Mike & the Headsets, Lowlife, and in his solo music: singing love songs directed to men, changing lyrics to make them gayer, adapting easily identifiable queer gestures and language, and campy humor. Jon handled most of the arrangements, making full use of his training in choral music, with occasional input from other members. In rehearsals, they would "sit down and say, 'here's the arrangement,' and sing through it and ask ourselves, 'What is it that we are trying to say in this song? What is its purpose? Is it the camp element? To relay a message? Some were quite apparent, and some were not. Every song that we did, we had a specific reason for doing it. It wasn't just for entertainment."[11] According to Arterton, the group won over the audience "with doo-wop and fun songs from the '50s that [were] given a particular gay slant [...] and once we've got them squealing, then we can launch into some songs that have more of a message to them."[12]

Lyrics were of the utmost importance to The Flirtations, and they would not perform a song whose message did not fit, or could not be adapted to fit, their progressive political convictions. According to Jon, "the words pop out at you; they aren't hidden" in an *a cappella* format; accordingly, listeners pay more attention to the text.[13] Knowing that audiences were listening closely to what they sang and that many of their nostalgic clas-

---

11 AF and MJ (2016).
12 Quoted in "The Flirtations: Out There and Outrageous in the Age of AIDS," a promotional essay in the MCP. The essay was produced to raise funds for a documentary about The Flirtations; the film was never finished.
13 JA and MJ (2013).

sic rock-and-roll and Broadway songs were well-known to their fans, The Flirts could play with listeners' expectations and familiarity with the material. Classic rock-and-roll, Motown, and girl group songs had been the soundtrack of their childhoods, and by performing them *as gay men,* The Flirts offered a glimpse of what it might have been like to feel the first flush of teenage romance and hear a man singing to very own "Jonny Angel."

Their arrangement of The Beach Boys' "Surfin' USA" (1963) offers a lesson in queer history and geography. By namechecking famous gay vacation spots like Provincetown, Fire Island, Key West, and West Hollywood, they drew a musical map of queer America that would make Rand McNally proud. By adding a well-placed and suggestive sigh, TJ Myers turned the innocuous phrase "waxing up our surf boards" into a naughty double-entendre. Likewise, The Flirtations may have sung the word "surfin,'" but they were really singing about "cruising," the gay male subcultural practice of seeking out sex in public, and sometimes, engaging in public sex. In the final verse, TJ even added a flirty emphasis to the line "We'll *cruise* Venice [Beach] all day. Tell our boyfriends we were surfin' USA," just to drive home the point.

While camp was an important weapon in their political arsenal, The Flirtations were well-read intersectional feminists, fluent in the multicultural political topics and theories of the day, and committed to the idea of music as political liberation. They were also serious musicians. Thus, they sang songs that reflected the experiences of other marginalized communities including Sweet Honey in the Rock's "Oughta Be a Woman" (1981, based on a text by bisexual, Jamacian American poet June Jordan [1936-2002]) and "Breaths" (1988), Peter Gabriel's "Biko" (1980) and "Wallflower" (1982). Singing these songs not only linked the struggles of gay men and PWAs to global antisexist, antiracist, and other progressive political movements but also gave these songs a new meaning when they were sung by gay men and gay men with AIDS.

Songs of Conscience and Concern

Two songs became signature pieces for The Flirtations. Fred Small, a unitarian minister, singer-songwriter, and lawyer, has written music about racism, feminist issues, homophobia, environmentalism, and disability rights. "Everything Possible" (from which this chapter's epigram was borrowed) first appeared on his album *No Limit* (1985). It is a lullaby about embracing the full spectrum of gender and sexual identities and being strong in the face of adversity. The austere partwriting of Jon's arragement reveals his training in choral music and the importance that the group placed on declamation of text. Flowing contrapuntal sections alternate with moments of homophony and monophony, text painting, and a variety of techniques borrowed from collegiate and barbershop singing such as "bell chords" and the "blossom."[14] The arrangement ends with a brief but poignant solo, sung by TJ on *The Flirtations*. As he completes the phrase "Oh, the love you leave behind when you're gone," the rest of the group responds with hushed chromatic harmonies that gently fall to the tonic chord with a sweetly dissonant major second, a piquant sound that perhaps signifies the bittersweet memories of departed loved ones or the often belated realization that love is truly the only thing that matters.

"Something Inside So Strong" was composed by British musician Labi Siffre to critique South African apartheid in 1987. Images of prisons, barriers, walls, and fences signify injustice and oppression, but for Black South Africans, there were also literal barriers that divided their country along racial lines. Siffre

---

14 Gage Averill, *Four Parts, No Waiting: A Social History of Barbershop* (Oxford: Oxford University Press, 2010), 205. Averill defines "bell chords" as "four voices enter[ing] in succession to create a chord, each voice ringing like a bell" (205) and the "blossom" as a technique by which four voices begin in unison and expand to a four-part chord in contrary motion" (205). There are two blossoms in this arrangement. The first occurs at the words "Some grow in their own space and time" (1:57 in the 1990 studio recording) and "They will give the same back to you" (2:51 in the 1990 studio recording).

acknowledges the difficulty of overcoming these literal and metaphorical obstacles but insists "I know that I can make it though you're doing me wrong. You thought that my pride was gone, but there's something inside so strong." That something is a persistent yearning for justice, and it resonated with The Flirtations, who were fighting anti-gay discrimination and the AIDS crisis in the US. In his arrangement, Jon again utilized different musical textures to accentuate the sentiment of the lyrics, including persistent percussive rhythms that animate the song and signify the long historical march toward freedom for all oppressed groups.

The Flirtations closed almost all of their live concerts with both songs, and they recorded both songs on all of their albums. In live shows, Michael often introduced "Everything Possible" by asking the audience to imagine "how different you might be and how different the world might be if more parents would sing lullabies like this to their children," and audiences responded with thunderous applause as the final chord rings out in the theater.

One of the most moving moments of their shows was a recitation of the spoken-word piece "One of Us," a version of which appears in the liner notes for their debut album. Each line begins with the phrase "One of us…" as members of the group exchange sometimes humorous, sometimes heartfelt pieces of information about each other

"One of Us" (1990)

One of us has had the same lover for eight years
One of us is from a family in which the gays outnumber the straights
One of us was in the closet until he was 37
One of us took his boyfriend to the high school prom
One of us coached high school wrestling
One of us wants to carry a child to term
One of us helped start Hispanos Unidos Gays y Lesbianas
One of us has never seen a porno film
One of us was an MP in the US Army

> One of us was entrapped, arrested, handcuffed, and beaten by the police
> One of us has smuggled AIDS drugs into the country
> One of us has been arrested for civil disobedience
> One of us was fag-bashed with a two-by-four
> And two of us have AIDS[15]

HIV/AIDS was an important aspect of their musical activism because two men in the group were living with AIDS: Michael, and more quietly, TJ Myers. By the time he received an AIDS diagnosis, TJ was already quite ill, yet for a time, he kept it a secret while he "worked out his relationship to AIDS" in public view.[16] TJ pushed himself, sometimes to the point of exhaustion, during rehearsals and live shows with The Flirtations. Eventually, TJ confided his diagnosis to Michael, but it made things "really weird" for the two PWAs.[17] Because TJ was "getting very bad medical care at the beginning" of his diagnosis, Michael wanted to advise him about his healthcare options.[18] However, Michael's motherly instinct created some tension, and the two friends just "circled each other as far as what [TJ] should and shouldn't do" instead of having a serious conversation about TJ's health.[19] Likewise, the other Flirtations wanted to protect him. They knew that singing and dancing gave TJ "something to live for. If he wasn't performing, he was doing other stuff, but most of what he did had something to do with this group."[20]

Michael believed that "TJ choked on the cosmic injustice of the fact that he got sick [...]. He was a dancer. His body was at the peak of physical fitness. He was the cute one and a can-

---

15 This version comes from the liner notes of *The Flirtations* (1990). However, the text remained open and changed over the years.
16 Michael Callen, *Flirts Post-TJ 1990*, 1990, archival video, Richard Dworkin Private Archive.
17 Ibid.
18 Ibid.
19 Ibid.
20 Ibid.

Fig. 3. The Flirtations: Jon Arterton, Michael Callen, Jimmy Rutland, Cliff Townsend, Aurelio Font. Photo by Andrew Scalini. Courtesy of Jon Arterton.

do person."[21] TJ continued to throw himself into performance with gusto, but as his health declined, his body started to betray him. During a performance at the Judson Memorial Church (55 Washington Sq. S), Jon watched in horror as TJ's legs buckled under him as he executed a dance move. "His body wasn't reacting the way he expected it to. It was really heartbreaking."[22]

In August of 1990, TJ moved to San Francisco to be with his partner, Michael Weiss. Tragically, TJ died on 28 August 1990, a few days after he moved. The Flirts announced TJ's passing in a card mailed to fans, noting that "TJ would expect one thing from us: that we carry on. So carry on we shall, but his boundless energy and spirit will be greatly missed."[23] Michael insisted that TJ should be remembered not for his illness but for the life he lived. He was "the young one, the pretty one, the one who moved well, the one who would take charge on stage if there

21 Ibid.
22 Ibid.
23 Ibid.

was a slow moment. TJ viewed The Flirtations as a collection of strengths and weaknesses and was always trying to lead with his strong suit," and he encouraged the others to do the same.[24]

With a new album and a tour booked, The Flirtations needed a singer to replace TJ. At Jon's insistence, Georgia transplant Jimmy Rutland joined the group, although the other singers felt that he had a weak voice, was a poor sight reader, had difficulty learning his parts. The Flirts rallied, however, making tapes of all his parts so he could learn them by listening and singing along before rehearsals. Jimmy also had the unpleasant task of touring in support of an album upon which neither his image nor his voice appeared, a situation that laid the seeds for tensions that would erupt later and eventually tear the group apart. But for now they hit the road, because the show had to go on.

---

24 Ibid.

THE FLIRT SONG

Singers	Year	Group Combinations	Albums
Jon Arterton	1987	Michael Aurelio TJ Cal Jon Elliot	
Michael Callen		Michael Aurelio TJ Jon Elliot	
Aurelio Font		Aurelio TJ Jon Cliff	
Cal Grogan		Michael Aurelio TJ Jon Cliff	*The Flirtations* (1990)
Jay Guevara	1990	Michael Aurelio Jon Cliff	
Steve Langley		Michael Aurelio Jimmy Jon Cliff	*Live: Out on the Road* (1992)
Thomas Lucas	1993	Aurelio Jimmy Jon Cliff	
Bill McKinley		Bill Aurelio Jimmy Jon Cliff	
TJ Myers		Jay Aurelio Jimmy Jon Cliff	
Elliot Pilshaw		Aurelio Steve Jimmy Jon	
Jimmy Rutland		Aurelio Steve/Thomas Jimmy Jon	
Suede		Aurelio Suede Jimmy Jon	
Cliff Townsend	1995	Suede Steve Jimmy Jon	
	1997	Suede Jimmy Jon	*Three* (1996)

Table 1. Flirtations personnel, compiled by Cliff Townsend

Fig. 1. Michael Callen and Tim Miller (c. 1992). Courtesy of Karen Ocamb.

13

One More Lullaby

> *Can't I just sit one more hour on my rock by the sea?*
> *I'll just pick one more flower from my favorite lilac tree,*
> *And I'll just sing one more lullaby to the evening sun.*
> — Dennis Green & Marsha Malamet

By the end of the "AIDies," as he often called the decade, Michael was tired. Illnesses and hospitalizations seemed to increase with each passing year as did his disappointment when the latest, inevitably ineffective drugs failed to produce effective results. He had been preaching the gospel of prophylaxis against PCP for years (which CRI had shown to be effective in one of its first major victories), only to discover another area of the country where doctors were not routinely prescribing this easy and effective preventative measure. Michael proselytized safe sex, a necessary practice, albeit one he personally loathed but one which, he knew, had saved millions of lives. Now, infighting among different groups of AIDS activists in New York threatened to tear the city's AIDS community apart.

Once Michael's utopia, New York was now a graveyard, a place he associated with his illness, the deaths of too many friends, and the increasingly toxic world of AIDS activism. Michael's friend, the queer performance artist Tim Miller, remembers the late-1980s as a terrible time, "and there were lots of people who'd been terrible to Mike. Of course, he could be quite acerbic and suffered fools *very* poorly. But a lot of AIDS politics was devouring everybody."[1] Ideological and political fault lines formed or widened among and within groups like PWAC, CRI, and GMHC. Although their memberships overlapped, each organization's respective leadership and executive boards grew increasingly dogmatic and contentious. By 1989, even the upstart, militant ACT UP was splintering into competing factions, its various agendas split between radical and reformist priorities, the centrality of scientific research and political power, the role of minorities, women, and even the purpose of ACT UP as an organization.[2] It was exhausting, and it was time to bid farewell to all of it. As Michael explained to NPR's Terry Gross in 1990,

> I've done two tours of duty. It's time for the next generation, and it's time for me to take my own advice. AIDS activism is quite brutal. It's a life or death struggle. And people hold their opinions passionately, and there are many enemies and lots of suffering. I'm a musician, and I would like to have a life beyond AIDS, and I feel that I've done my bit. I've spoken and written […], and it isn't necessary anymore for me to be traveling a hundred and eighty-thousand air miles traveling from one end of the earth to the other, preaching the same gospel.[3]

---

1 Tim Miller, interview with the author, 5 July 2017.
2 David France's documentary, *How to Survive a Plague* (2012) and Jim Hubbard's *United in Anger: A History of ACT UP* (2012) capture these tensions using archival footage and interviews with members of ACT UP. In the late 1980s and early '90s, other ACT UP chapters around the country began to fracture. See Benita Roth's *The Life and Death of ACT UP/LA: Anti-AIDS Activism in Los Angeles from the 1980s to the 2000s* (Cambridge: Cambridge University Press, 2017), Deborah Gould's *Moving Politics: Emotion and ACT UP's Fight against AIDS* (Chicago: University of Chicago Press, 2008), and Susan Chambré's *Fighting for Our Lives: New York's AIDS Community and the Politics of Disease* (New Brunswick: Rutgers University Press, 2006) for more.
3 Michael Callen, interview with Terry Gross, *Fresh Air*, NPR, 16 November 1990.

Personal attacks, too, took their toll. Michael had begun to "feel like the Prometheus of the gay movement. I brought fire back to my community, the ability to have sex and not die as a result, and my reward was to be strapped to a rock and have a vulture eat my liver."[4] Because of his public profile, Michael faced brutal criticism, often from other gay men and from segments of the AIDS community. Irate letters flooded the PWAC's mailbox with accusations that he was exploiting the epidemic for his own financial and professional gain. Michael kept exceptionally mean-spirited, hateful, or just kooky correspondence in a file labeled "Especially Crazy Letters." Among them is an undated missive from "J. Williams," who wrote to express his frustrations at what he saw as Callen's selfish exploitation of the AIDS crisis:

> Michael,
> It's disgusting the way you are using the health crisis to promote your singing career. Seeing you on the stage with Joel Grey and [NYC Mayor Ed] Koch yesterday made the whole event look like a bad nightclub act instead of the political demonstration for our lives that it should have been.
>
> Why don't you use your influence to raise money to buy AL721 [an experimental egg lipid compound thought to be (possibly) effective in treating AIDS] and Dextran Sulfate for PWA's [sic] like me who can't afford it? Isn't that what the [PWA] Coalition was supposed to do originally?[5]

Michael usually took such criticisms with a healthy pinch of salt. After all, he was one of the first and most visible PWAs in the country, and he knew that other PWAs felt invisible or like pariahs. He also knew that many PWAs were responding to the

---

4   Jeffrey Escoffier and Michael Callen, "My Rise from Complete Obscurity," in *In My Time: Essays on Sex, Science, and AIDS*, ed. Jeffrey Escoffier, unpublished manuscript, 1993, Richard Dworkin Private Archive.
5   J. Williams, letter to Michael Callen, n.d., typed original, Michael Callen Papers at The LGBT Community Center National History Archive (henceforth, MCP). It is possible this letter arrived after the 1987 AIDS Walk event at Lincoln Center, which featured Callen, Koch, and a number of celebrities.

noxious mixture of societal homophobia and AIDS panic while confronting their own concerns, fears, and frustrations about the health of their communities, their loved ones, and themselves. One role of a leader is to serve as a punching bag.

Michael also knew that his own record of activism told a different story. He had co-founded the PWA Self-Empowerment movement and the community-based research movement for AIDS clinical trials. He had smuggled drugs into the country and made AL721 available to PWAs through a buyers club. He even starred in a Julia Child-style promotional video in which he explained how to turn the liquid egg product into a supplement using everyday objects found in most kitchens, and the recipe was published in *Surviving and Thriving with AIDS: Hints for the Newly Diagnosed*. He had also used his music, as a solo artist and with Lowlife and The Flirtations, as a platform to address AIDS, homophobia, and other relevant issues directly. He had opened hearts and minds through song; he had touched people; and he had helped foster compassion for PWAs. Michael had been a frontline soldier in the war against AIDS, and he had the battle scars to prove it. So much for those bitter complaints.

Michel also wasn't rich. He had never been in great financial shape, and if the mountain of medical bills, travel receipts, and credit card statements made anything else clear, it was that he would die in debt for the quintessentially American sin of being sick. While he was in high demand as a speaker and singer, Michael paid out-of-pocket for much of his travel. He had begun to insist that organizers pay for airfare and lodging when he was invited to speak and perform. Sometimes his efforts were successful, but Michael was often given an elaborate runaround as he chased down a reimbursement check. Modest income from The Flirtations helped keep him afloat, but Michael earned those wages with his health. Life on the road for a PWA in the 1980s was not easy. And although he was recognized as a prominent AIDS activist and musician, he thought it absurd that this constituted fame in any conventional sense. "Only in America," he mused, "would it be necessary to make a career out of being sick in order to compel a more human and appropriate government response."[6]

In private and in print, Michael sarcastically referred to his public role as The Dancing PWA Bear Act: submissive, sick, and repentant. "As long as I am the dancing PWA bear, producing tears on cue so that the hat can be passed, no one questions my right to represent myself as a PWA," he wrote. "But when I take controversial positions — when I assert that AZT doesn't work; when I argue that HIV may not be the cause of AIDS; when I argue that the gay community should take some action against bathhouses — then enemies […] attempt to knock me out of the debate by undermining my credibility. It's called fighting dirty."[7] Outspoken, articulate, and knowledgeable about the complex social, political, and biomedical aspects of the AIDS crisis, Michael usually refused to play the proper PWA.

The most hurtful and alarming accusations came from those who said that Michael did not actually have AIDS. "From the beginning of my 'career' as a publicly identified PWA," he wrote in 1989, "the rumor has dogged me that I don't 'really' have AIDS — that I am an AIDS 'carpetbagger,' in it for the 'glory.'"[8] As best as he could figure, this smear campaign arose "in direct proportion to the controversial positions [he] assert[ed]" or because he wasn't dead.[9] His very survival, a miracle in the era before effective treatments for HIV, was weaponized against him, and yet "proving you had AIDS is not unlike proving you're gay. Short of publishing photos of yourself *in flagrante delicto* with a person of the same sex, we tend to take on faith the assertion that someone is gay or lesbian precisely because we cannot imagine anyone suffering the sigma for kicks."[10]

Michael was not alone in facing such criticism and skepticism. "The general reception afforded some long-term survivors

6   Michael Callen, *Surviving AIDS* (New York: Harper Perennial, 1990), 8.
7   Michael Callen, "Are You Now, Or Have You Ever Been," *PWAC Newsline* 40 (1989), 34–46.
8   Ibid., 34.
9   Ibid.
10 Ibid.

has been far from supportive," he complained.¹¹ "At times, holding a newspaper in [his] hand or hearing a newscaster blithely deny that [he] and others like [him] had survived," Michael had to pinch himself "just to make sure I'm still alive."¹² PWAs like Michael who refused to "fulfill the 'unstated' expectations [of medical science] by giving up and dying on cue [were] patronized, handed Kübler-Ross, sent into therapy, or [charged with] having AIDS dementia."¹³ He began to gather stories of long-term survival for a new book project, and he heard from one survivor who

> received death threats from the lover of someone who had died of the particular opportunistic disease that he had survived. Another was evicted from his apartment by a grief-stricken landlord whose lover had died of the disease that he [the tenant and survivor] continues to survive.¹⁴

Michael reasoned that his own

> high profile as a long-term AIDS survivor has also led to some mean-spirited responses that reveal how deeply ingrained is the fatalism that surrounds AIDS. My first AIDS-defining opportunistic infection was cryptosporidiosis. [...] [S]ome have suggested that because I didn't die, and because I wasn't initially diagnosed with KS or PCP, I shouldn't really count as a long-term survivor.
>
> It's interesting to examine their message. If I had died from crypto in the summer of '82, no one would have questioned my "right" to an AIDS diagnosis. It is the fact that *I refused to die* that makes me suspect; and the fact of my survival apparently threatens some people's image of AIDS as invariably fatal.¹⁵

11 Ibid.
12 Callen, *Surviving AIDS*, 22.
13 Ibid., 68.
14 Ibid.
15 Ibid.

"Someone would have to be *really* fucked up to pretend to have AIDS as a path to notoriety," Michael reasoned, but to put the rumors to rest, he spelled out his medical history in plain language in the pages of the *Newsline*. "Once and for all, I have AIDS. By whatever definition you want to propose. I wake up every morning to face the real possibility of my own death. At night, before retiring, my lover checks my body for new lesions or rashes. Although I do not believe HIV has been proven to be at all pathogenic, I am apparently an HIV factory."[16] Michael went one step further by including images of his pathology report from the NYU Medical Center's Dermatopathology Section, which confirmed a diagnosis of plaque-stage Kaposi's sarcoma, a photocopy of slides containing the biopsied lung tissue, and a note from Joseph Sonnabend (still his primary-care physician). For those still unconvinced, "private viewings of [his] lesions can be arranged."[17] However, even this did not silence his most vociferous critics.

In February 1988, Michael was hospitalized with a bleeding ulcer after which he fell into a deep depression, agonized by "the sheer drain of knowing that for the rest of [his life], one way or another, [he would] always be dealing with this maddening disease."[18] He asked fellow PWAs and readers of the *Newsline* for their "kind indulgence [with] helping to fight this god-awful war," pleading for their patience as he convalesced.[19] "When you are perceived as a 'leader,'" he wrote, "there will be those who will disagree with you. There will even be those who hate you [...]. It comes with the territory." Although Michael understood the perils of leadership and the necessity of criticism, he insisted that "those of us who have rolled up our sleeves and tried to make a difference deserve the respect of a clean fight."[20] Clean or dirty, the fight drained Michael emotionally and physically, and

16 Callen, "Are You Now," 34.
17 Ibid., 35. Michael's KS lesions were located on his hip and legs.
18 Michael Callen, "Crashing," *PWAC Newsline* 32, March 1988, 35–37.
19 Ibid., 37.
20 Callen, "Are You Now," 36.

he "just couldn't see a way out [or] of being a different person and living in New York."[21]

Michael was also tired of sidelining his music, so he gradually unplugged from his activist and community responsibilities throughout 1989. Midway through the year, he stepped down from the board of the People with AIDS Coalition after so many "brutal, soul-sucking years of AIDS activism" and began the process of retiring.[22] In September, he resigned from the editorship of the *Newsline*, having left the position once before only to resume editorial duties after the death of Max Navarre in June 1988.[23] He remained in high demand as a speaker and performer, and his phone rarely stopped ringing. Even in semi-retirement, Michael was still "the best little boy in the world" who "couldn't say no to these things."[24] To escape his identity as an AIDS poster boy, he needed "to get out of AIDS Central."[25]

At this same time, legal issues with the landlord at Michael and Richard's Duane Street loft added another layer of stress and complications. The building had been sold, and the couple had been locked out and told to vacate immediately. Though they regained access to the apartment, Michael and Richard had to enter into a lengthy and expensive battle in the courts, which they settled with the landlord for a relocation fee of sixty-thousand dollars, one-third of which went to their lawyer. Even with this money in hand, a new apartment in the city's booming real estate market was prohibitively expensive. When they found a two-story, twelve-hundred square foot place at 15 Eighth Avenue

---

21 Richard Dworkin, interview with author, September 2017 (henceforth, RD and MJ [2017]).

22 Michael Callen, "Farewell to Smarm," 25 April 1991. This essay is marked "intended for publication in the *Yale Journal of Law and Liberation*, though it is not included in any of the journal's three issues. YJLL was created "to present both the failures of law and the possibility of using that same law for progressive ends" ("Introducing Law and Liberation," *Yale Journal of Law and Liberation* 1, no. 1 [1989], art. 1).

23 Michael Callen, "Farewell," *PWAC Newsline* 47, September 1989, 2, MCP. Navarre was also the vice president of PWAC.

24 RD and MJ (2017).

25 Ibid.

Fig. 2. Patrick Kelly (c. 1990). Photo by Richard Dworkin. © Richard Dworkin.

between Twelfth and Jane Streets, the $1,800 a month rent was still too high. Even with the relocation nest egg, it would be necessary to split the cost by renting out a room. Fortunately, the apartment's two-story layout meant that their future roommate could have their own private den and bedroom on the second floor. The only problem was finding someone to live with them who would be stable, responsible, and comfortable living with a couple, one of whom was a famous PWA and AIDS activist. Fate intervened when Richard met Patrick Kelly.

My Lover's Name Is Richard; His Lover's Name Is Pat

A native of Portland, Patrick earned a degree in nursing from Oregon Health Services University and worked as a psychiatric intake nurse. The flexible hours — twelve- or sixteen-hour shifts, three or four evenings each week — afforded him time and money to follow his real passion: dance. Before moving to New York, Patrick danced in the *corps de ballet* in companies in Portland, San Francisco, and Cleveland. In New York, he performed as Doris Videnya in the all-male dance troupe Les Ballets Trockadero de Monte Carlo. He later began a master's degree in dance studies at NYU and wrote occasional dance criticism for the *New York Native* and *Dance*. Richard fell for Patrick instantly, and their new relationship seemed to balance the tumultuous energy that had been building between him and Michael. In many ways, Patrick was "the anti-Mike," a terrific counterpoint to Michael's linear and rational thinking, for he was "extremely intuitive, nonverbal; very smart that way, a whole different kind of intelligence."[26] Like Michael and Richard, Patrick was also HIV-positive. From Richard's perspective, Michael and Patrick formed two halves of a perfect partner, and while they functioned as two completely separate romantic and sexual relationships, together they "were everything [Richard] could ever have imagined."[27]

This was not Michael and Richard's first experiment with polyamory. For a variety of reasons, some personal, some political, some pragmatic, their relationship had never been entirely monogamous. Following his initial GRID diagnosis, Michael had sworn off sex to do a lot of soul searching. Not long after his AIDS diagnosis, he described himself as a "hardened old queen [who had been] penetrated by more than three-thousand people but had only 'slept' with six people, and only four of those more than once […] and he had never loved anyone."[28] He concluded that he had engaged in a lot of his past sexual activity not out of actual desire but out of boredom and habit. He had gone to the baths, cruised the streets, and dropped into tearooms when he didn't actually feel like it. Before finding his purpose through activism and music, Michael just hadn't known what else to do. So, he filled his hours with sex, which, ironically, made him doubt his self-worth. Then, he met Richard.

26 Ibid.
27 Ibid.
28 Michael Callen and Richard Dworkin, interview with Quentin Scobel (1960–1996) and Randy "Rand" Snyder (1960–1996), n.d., archival video, MCP (henceforth, MC/RD and QS/RS [n.d.]).

Still, Michael's health complicated things. Chronic anal fissures, gastrointestinal infections and parasites, medicinal side effects, and being generally unwell often meant that, for Michael, sex could be painful, unpleasantly messy, or just uninteresting. He also worried about infections, from the common cold to STIs like hepatitis, any of which might kill someone as severely immunocompromised as Michael. Trauma, too, shaped his feelings about sex. Witnessing the deaths of so many friends to AIDS left him with a sex–death connection that was hard to shake. Nevertheless, Michael and Richard realized that, "for better or worse, we'll love each other for as long as we live."[29] But by 1987, things just weren't happening between them sexually, and truthfully, they hadn't been happening for years.

Early in their relationship, Richard's sexual needs quickly outpaced Michael's. The couple would lay in bed, kissing and touching, but at "the moment where love and affection would become sexual, [Michael] would pull back. [Richard] would get frustrated and angry, and [they] would have a fight. It was a nightly pattern."[30] As demand increased for his public appearances, Michael simply wasn't around; he was "too busy; he was out of town; he was too tired; he was too sick; it was all of these things. And there was just a point where [Richard] had to do something."[31] Michael affirmed his lover's need for sex and encouraged him to explore, but for Richard, it wasn't so simple. For him, intimacy and friendship heightened his sexual experiences, making cruising or bathhouses less desirable options than sex with Michael, a friend, or, perhaps, another lover.

At The Center's annual Garden Party in 1988, Richard reunited with Carl Valentino, a New York City schoolteacher he had met briefly before in 1982. The long-haired son of an Italian American grocer in Brooklyn, Carl was later known around town as the "gay husband" of avant-garde performance artist

29 Callen, *Surviving AIDS*, 77.
30 MC/RD and QS/RS (n.d.).
31 Quoted in Martin Duberman, *Hold Tight Gently: Michael Callen, Essex Hemphill, and the Battleground of AIDS* (New York: The New Press, 2014), 247.

Fig. 3. Carl Valentino (1993). Photo by Patrick Kelly. Richard Dworkin Private Archive.

Diamanda Galás, and his words inspired her song "Last Man Down" (*The Sporting Life*, 1994). Carl could "turn words into sulfuric acid" by walking into a room and saying, "I'm a hateful homosexual and I have AIDS and you can kiss my fucking ass."[32] He also "got his skinny butt out there for many a gay rights demo" and was "instrumental in organizing the 1987 AIDS Walk New York." He was also very funny. He would enter a restaurant, and "if music was playing, like a pop hit from another era, he would start singing really loudly, and [the restaurant management] would want to kick him out, and he'd say 'Why do you want to kick me out? I'm just part of your pop…?'"[33] Carl also volunteered for The Holiday Project, "a do-gooder group [that

---

32 Diamanda Galás, quoted in Susan DeMuth, "Indy/Life," *The Independent*, 27 October 1994.
33 Diamanda Galás, quoted in Rowan Savage, "Diamanda Galás: The Singing Serpent Talks," *Tiny Mix Tapes*, 28 March 2018, https://www.tinymixtapes.com/features/diamanda-galas.

visited] People with AIDS wards in city hospitals."[34] A radical teacher who covertly taught his elementary students about the realities of the AIDS crisis, Carl was also living with HIV. When he later grew quite sick from AIDS-related complications, Carl kept a cot in his school office so that he could sleep during lunch just to make it through the day.[35]

After the Garden Party, Richard and Carl spent the night together, but in the morning, Carl announced that he was leaving New York for the summer. Richard was disappointed, but the two men resumed their relationship in the fall and continued to see one another for the next eighteen months. When Richard introduced his two lovers, they became friendly. Carl volunteered at CRI and eventually joined its executive board. Publicly, Michael proclaimed that he was happy that Richard "was getting laid regularly — it took the pressure off him, he said, and [their own] relationship seemed more relaxed."[36] Privately, however, he confided to friends that he "felt like a failure as a partner and as a person."[37] He may have also been victim to that most destructive of human feelings: jealousy.

As Michael's priorities shifted away from promiscuity to living with AIDS and related activism, his feelings about relationships grew more conventional. By the mid-1980s, he considered himself "basically a one-woman man."[38] Consequently, Richard's experiences of intimacy and sex with another person wounded him in unexpected ways. Likewise, the barbs of heteronormativity caught deep in Carl, who had decided that he wanted a partner that was his alone. He fell in love with Richard, and this development destabilized the whole situation. Richard, Michael, and Carl discussed the complex dynamic of friendship regularly. On Valentine's Day 1989, Richard left Michael alone in their

---

34 theaidsmemorial, *Instagram* post, 13 June 2020, https://www.instagram.com/p/CBZMNPZJMxx/
35 Diamanda Galás, "Conversations I," *The Living Jarobe*, 24 March 2014, https://www.thelivingjarboe.com/2014/03/24/diamanda-galas/
36 Ibid.
37 Ibid.
38 MC/RD and QS/RS (n.d.).

apartment to go visit Carl. He purchased flowers and a box of chocolates, but when he arrived, Carl was brooding and unhappy. Faced with yet another argument about monogamy, Richard broke off the relationship. While still "lost and hurting and pretty ripped up and on the rebound" from the breakup with Carl, Richard met Patrick. As fate would have it, Carl briefly came back into the picture to ask for a reconciliation. Knowing that things were too complicated with Carl and that his need for an exclusive relationship would resurface, Richard bid a painful farewell to a man he had loved dearly then settled into a new relationship with Patrick.

Despite their differences in personality and temperament, Patrick and Michael grew quite close. They bonded over similar senses of humor, their interest in the arts, and their mutual love for Richard. Their friendship would later prove to be the glue that held together their chosen family. Inspired by Michael, Patrick even became a community organizer with the Village Dive Club, an LGBTQ+ scuba social group, and Diving for Life, which hosts the annual International Gay and Lesbian Scuba Jamboree and continues to raise money for LGBTQ+ health organizations.

Sex and a new lover still did not solve Michael and Richard's housing dilemma; however, an opportunity soon presented itself. Patrick's Cornelia Street apartment building was going co-op, and he had an opportunity to purchase his unit at a discounted insider price for current tenants. He missed the deadline for the first offer because he didn't have money for the down payment, but when the second-round offer was still enticing, he took the bait. By pooling Richard and Michael's relocation payment, Michael's $10,000 advance for his book *Surviving AIDS*, and Patrick's savings, they bought the apartment and flipped it for a profit which Patrick and Michael split. However, Patrick now had no place to live, and Mike and Richard still had their expensive new lease — but they also had an empty bedroom.

In spite of the vociferous warnings, dire predictions, and protests of all their friends, Patrick moved in with Michael and Richard at 15 Eighth Ave. on 1 January 1990. At first, three busy men living in one apartment while maintaining two separate intimate relationships seemed ideal. Patrick's schedule kept him at St. Vincent's many nights, and dance rehearsals occupied his other evenings. Michael was busy with the CRI, PWAC, the PWA Health Group, and The Flirtations while Richard was touring, playing more than a hundred gigs a year. Their hectic schedules meant that all three men were seldom even in the apartment simultaneously. It seemed as though things would work out; however, the situation soon deteriorated.

Just as his father had once dreamed of moving out west, Michael had toyed with the notion of moving to California. New York "was not a pleasant place, and the whole downtown thing that people are entranced with now, grittiness and all that, it wasn't appealing to [him]," nor was the brutal cold.[39] Southern California had "sunshine, and people were nice. People weren't crazy, swearing all the time."[40] When Michael decided to move to Los Angeles, where he could "take up a healthier and more gaily-spiritual life," he begged Richard to come with him.[41] Having done his time in San Francisco, Richard had no interest in returning to the West Coast, but he did offer to ask Patrick to move out of their apartment if only Michael would consider staying in New York. But it was too late. Richard knew Michael's stubbornness could not be budged. Michael had made up his mind to relocate, and Richard felt "tricked and trapped" in a situation that, ironically, he had designed.[42]

In the last week of August of 1990, Richard left for a European tour with Bobby Radcliff and Earl King that took him to Lugano, an idyllic Italian-speaking city nestled on Lake Lugano and surrounded by rolling mountains in southern Switzerland. While Richard was in Europe, Michael packed up a car and drove to California, "and he did so without his longtime lover, without

---

39 RD and MJ (2017).
40 Ibid.
41 Douglas Sadownick, "Doug Sadownick's Response to Karen O. (Section 2)," *Gay Psyche Politics*, 24 April 2010 http://gaypsychepolitics.blogspot.com/2010/04/douglas-sadownicks-response-to-karen.html.
42 RD and MJ (2017).

Fig. 4. Michael Callen and Patrick Kelly at the Guitar Asylum (c. 1991). Photo by Richard Dworkin. © Richard Dworkin.

much, if any, support at all."[43] Michael's bullheaded decision to leave while his lover was out of the country struck Richard as an act of cowardice, one that hurt him deeply. Upon his return to the US, Richard felt lost, devastated, and angry. Had Michael orchestrated the living situation with Patrick to facilitate his own departure, making sure that Richard had a companion while he slipped out the back door? Had he stopped caring after all these years? Had Richard let his sexual appetite overshadow Michael's emotional needs? Was any of this fair to Patrick, who stood to lose a friend and a lover? Michael and Richard exchanged angry letters and telephone calls about the situation, warring across the continent, while each privately hoping that this was a temporary obstacle in an ongoing and unfinished romance.

---

43 Sadownick, "Doug Sadownick's Response to Karen O."

Fig. 1. Michael Callen, Genie White (Ryan White's mother), Larry Kramer, Phil Donahue at *The Geraldo Rivera Show* "10 Years of AIDS" (1991). Richard Dworkin Private Archive.

14

Take It Easy

> *Twentieth Century Pretense,*
> *They find you guilty when you're feeling' blue*
> *I got too tired of playing defense*
> *My lifelong love affair with sex is through*
> — Joel Forrester

On the West Coast, Michael enjoyed a much-needed period of rest and relaxation. He moved into a "dilapidated HUD apartment in the run-down Hollywood of the time" in The Montecito (6650 Franklin Ave., Hollywood), an Art Deco structure built in 1936 that had once been home to James Cagney (1899–1986), Montgomery Cliff (1920–1966), and ironically, future President and PWA nemesis Ronald Reagan (1911–2004), that had been converted into subsidized housing in 1985.[1] Los Angeles represented an opportunity to begin anew, "to learn who he was; to breathe better air."[2] Michael adopted some of the laid-back attitude of Southern California, taking his own advice, listening to his body, and slowing the pace of his life. He even let telephone messages, correspondences, and more than a few bills go unanswered or unpaid for weeks. He "wrote dozens of letters a

1 Doug Sadownick, "Surviving Life: An Interview with AIDS Diva Michael Callen," *Frontiers*, ca. 1994, Cliff Townsend's Flirtations scrapbooks. This article was written after Michael's death and probably appeared in print in 1994.
2 Ibid.

day, read countless books [...] and worked to figure out why he was suffering from so much endemic psychological pain" while sleeping on a mattress on the floor.[3] Michael voraciously read everything he could get his hands on from the pile of "about a hundred books calling out to [him] to be read, and a hundred more to be re-read: books that profoundly changed [his] life and that [he] want[ed] to revisit, like an old friend."[4]

Books were not the only old friends Michael encountered in Los Angeles. He reconnected with his New York City pal, performance artist and activist Tim Miller and Miller's boyfriend, the journalist, author, and later, psychologist, Doug Sadownick. A Whittier, California native, Miller moved to New York at nineteen to study dance with Merce Cunningham. In 1980, he co-founded P.S. 122 (150 1st Ave.), a performance art space housed in a former New York public school building. Tim mined his personal life for material in his shows, foregrounding gay male experience, LGBTQ+ activism, and HIV/AIDS politics as he became more involved with ACT UP. With his boyfriend, innovative choreography and dancer John Bernd (who died of AIDS-related illness in 1988), Miller helped shape the city's avant-garde performance scene. In 1987, Tim left New York to return to California, where he co-founded Highways (1651 18th St.), a performance space in Santa Monica.

Tim marveled at the transformation in his old friend. "It was kind of an amazing thing for him to leave politics behind and stop being a political person and reclaim his identity as a sexual person and an artist."[5] Tim felt that the move to the West Coast was Michael's "'I'm Still Here' moment," a reference to Stephen Sondheim's anthem to perseverance from the 1971 musical *Follies*.[6] After years of grueling activist work and sidelining his music, Michael now allowed himself to dream of recording a "mainstream pop album with at least four planned hit singles"

3 Ibid.
4 Michael Callen, "Dinosaur's Diary: In My Time of Dying," *QW*, 30 August 1992, 46–47.
5 Tim Miller, interview with author, 5 July 2017.
6 Ibid.

with a kind of falsetto supergroup featuring Jimmy Sommerville, Lou Christie, David Lasley, and Michael; and an album of standards "written by gay composers [and] traditionally sung by females."[7] The two friends planned to create art together, and they were thrilled when their application for a Rockefeller Foundation Grant won them the prestigious award. The award boosted Michael's confidence in himself as an artist in his own right, and he planned to write a play based on his life as a gay man with AIDS that would include material gathered from his parents and siblings through long-form interviews. In the end, however, Michael would compose no new musical material during his West Coast tenure, nor did his play ever materialize. However, he did finish some older compositions including "Redefine the Family (The Census Song)" and "Now."

Michael also continued to sing with The Flirtations as often as his health allowed. The group was planning an international tour and an accompanying live album, and Michael wanted to be part of both. Even when Michael could travel with the group, life on the road for a PWA was anything but easy. Footage from Eric Lewis' unreleased documentary about The Flirtations captures Michael unpacking a suitcase filled with syringes, IV bags, alcohol prep pads, and dozens of bottles of medication. As he pulled out the specific items he needed for an infusion, Michael dryly observed that this is "life on the road in the age of AIDS. […] To most people, *this* is outrageous. And it is outrageous. But it's what I have to do to stay alive."[8]

By this time, The Flirtations had become a chosen family and an important source of artistic expression for one another. Within this family, each man played a specific role. Michael likened them to a gay sitcom in which

---

7 Michael Callen, "Michael Callen's Projected Album Projects," 3 April 1991, typed copy, The Michael Callen Papers at The LGBT Community Center National History Archive (henceforth MCP).
8 Eric Lewis, unreleased Flirtations documentary, n.d., Richard Dworkin Private Archive (henceforth, RDA).

Fig. 2. Lenny Bloom (executive director, AIDS Project Los Angeles), Michael Callen, and David Drake (1993). Courtesy of Karen Ocamb.

> the role of the father-who-knows-best is played by Jon [...]. Cliff, a.k.a. "Ms. Cliff," stars as the eldest son [...]. Aurelio, a.k.a. "The Fontessa," is as popular as his older brother, but offstage he's something of a loner [...]. Precocious Jimmy, a.k.a. "Little Jeemy," is definitely the baby of the family [...]. Finally, I'm the Mommy, a.k.a. "The Diva." I'm the Queen of Process.[9]

The Flirtations rallied around their beloved Mommy Dearest "silently, without explicit 'who's gonna do what?'"[10] When Michael pulled out his Hickman catheter more than an inch while trying to lift his own luggage, Jimmy began carrying his bags to prevent further injury. Jon made sure that Michael's stage clothes were pressed and ready to give The Diva time to nap before a performance. When he later grew too sick to tour, Michael was sustained in his soul and his pocketbook. The Flirta-

---

9   Michael Callen, "Redesigning the Family," liner notes to *The Flirtations: Live Out on the Road* (1992).
10 Lewis, unreleased documentary.

tions continued paying his salary even as they toured without him. Like any family, their complicated love endured.

Michael also grew close to Doug Sadownick, the other half of his favorite gay couple in Los Angeles. Their relationship intensified as Michael began his journey in gay-affirmative therapy with Richard Levin at AIDS Project Los Angeles (APLA). In therapy, Michael revisited traumas that he had explored years earlier in New York, concurring with Doug's observation that gay people's "main oppressors are the people who raise us. [...] Such suffering either kills you or ennobles you. [...] Any gay person who survives the combination of contempt and invisibility long enough to create himself is, to me, just breathtaking."[11]

Michael also became quite the man about town in Los Angeles. A lover of gourmet foods, he savored delicious meals, including a "quintessential Minestrone" at West Hollywood's Café Benvenuto (8512 California Route 2).[12] People often bumped into him at the West Hollywood Pavilion market, "extolling the virtues of California tomatoes" or "suffering, post-yoga," in the sauna at Sports Connection, where he would "eye the old Jewish men, sad he'd never make it to their frisky seniority or [raise] his eyebrows when a naked god walked in whose 'gifts' deserved no uncertain praise."[13] A kind of spirituality even crept into the self-declared atheist's life as he found contemplative repose and mindfulness among the flora at The Huntington Library Gardens, his favorite spot in the region.

O-Boy!

Much to his surprise, Michael's sex drive returned when he connected with The O-Boys!, a sex-positive group organized by Allan Gassman (Allan O-Boy) and Randy Marshall (Marshall O-Boy). The O-Boys! advocated a second sexual revolution based on a safe return to pleasure, sensuality, and group sex (thus the

---

11 Sadownick, "Surviving Life."
12 Callen, "Dinosaur's Diary," 46–47.
13 Sadownick, "Surviving Life."

O, which stood for "orgy"). Living out Douglas Crimp's vision of a "theory and practice of sex [which] made it possible to meet the epidemic's most urgent requirement: the development of safe sex practices," the O-Boys! celebrated the very safe-sex techniques that Michael had cultivated and popularized in the early 1980s and, for a brief time, became media spokespeople for the second, safer-sex revolution on daytime talk shows and news broadcasts.[14] The O-Boys! canonized Michael as a guru and representative of "the old guard, [since] so few from that period were still alive," and they took Michael's survival as proof that AIDS did not have to mean the end of gay sex.[15]

The O-Boys! tried to strike a middle ground between two less-than-desirable options: totally anonymous sex and total monogamy. As Allan O-Boy told the audience at the National Gay and Lesbian Task Force's Fifth Annual Creating Change conference in 1992,

> Our major *point* is that, while certainly fun and somewhat liberating, completely anonymous sex is ultimately degrading to me. [...] On the other hand, an obligatory declaration of undying monogamy between lovers tends to develop into a series of petty jealousies, minor infidelities, major lies, and debilitating breakups. It's just plain selfish, rude, and stupid

---

14 Douglas Crimp, "How to Have Promiscuity in an Epidemic," reprinted in *Moralism and Melancholia: Essays on AIDS and Queer Politics* (Cambridge: MIT Press, 2009), 43–82. Crimp also writes that "gay people invented safe sex. We know that the alternatives — monogamy and abstinence — were *unsafe* in the latter case because people do not abstain from sex, and if you only tell them 'just say no,' they will have unsafe sex. We were able to invent safe sex because we have always known that sex is not, in an epidemic or not, limited to penetrative sex. Our promiscuity taught us many things, not only about the pleasures of sex, but about the great multiplicity of those pleasures. It is that psychic preparation, that experimentation, that conscious work on our own sexualities that has allowed many of us to change our sexual behaviors [...] very quickly and very dramatically" (252–53).

15 Douglas Sadownick, *Sex between Men* (San Francisco: Harper San Francisco, 1996), 187.

to expect one person to fulfill all of our sexual and emotional needs.[16]

While The O-Boys! espoused a radical stance against monogamy, they were accused of holding some rather conventional beliefs in other areas. Participants in their group sex parties tended to be young, in good physical shape, and attractive. At the same Creating Change conference, Marshall O-Boy tried to explain to the audience that he saw a link "between body image, persona, and self-esteem, [but] audience members accused him of sexual apartheid."[17] Marshall responded to the push back, saying "It's easy to create a group of your own. If you don't like how we do it, make your own rules."[18]

Michael was in the audience in Los Angeles for the Creating Change event, and he spoke up in defense of The O-Boys!:

> There is an aristocracy of beauty: get over it…I am not prepared for the alternative, which is to create a politically correct "I must find everybody equally sexually attractive" [environment]. I would like to declare our sexuality to be the last natural preserve where we are not required to justify in any sort of public way why we are sexually attracted to somebody and not to somebody else.
>
> […]
>
> I am a person with AIDS. I don't expect everyone to be willing to have sex with me. I don't judge them harshly. I will talk to them about why and maybe if there's some education there and some movement that can happen, that's fine. I'm not prepared to define the central politically correct act as having sex with me. That would be nice. But not likely to happen anytime soon.[19]

---

16 Ibid., 207.
17 Ibid., 208.
18 Ibid.
19 Ibid.

While The O-Boys were not especially progressive in their embrace of diverse body types and ages, their willingness to include PWAs like Michael and to insist on safe sex were pretty radical positions in the early 1990s. At their sex parties, condoms were required; water-based lubricant and condoms were freely available; and posters lined the walls announcing their five safe sex rules: 1) No fucking without a condom; 2) Don't cum in his mouth; 3) Be clear about where you draw the other lines, and respect his; 4) Assume that everybody is HIV positive; and 5) Be friendly.[20] In addition to their regular sex parties, The O-Boys! produced a number of adult films including *"O" is for Orgy* (1998), *O is for Orgy: The Sequel* (1999), and *The O-Boys: Parties, Porn, and Politics* (1999). Michael made cameo appearances in these films as a "safe sexpert," popping up on screen to hand out condoms and demonstrate their proper use — forever the safe sex guru.

The O-Boys! renewed Michael's self-confidence and connection with gay men. "I've never had, I don't know what word to use except maybe the *jolt* that I get at an O-Boys! party, whether I get fucked or not," he explained in a 1992 home video. "It's like boys rubbing sticks together. It's $1 + 1 = 5$."[21] Although Michael had never been entirely comfortable with accolades, he received the appreciation and attention from The O-Boys! with gratitude and even allowed himself to enjoy his new status as a sexual icon and a kind of sex(y) symbol. He even joked with Marshall O-Boy about a plan to leave a sum of one thousand dollars so that the group could hold a memorial orgy with the urn containing his ashes somewhere in the midst of a tangle of bodies engaged in hot, safe sex.

---

20 Ibid., 203. In 1993, Gassman defended their door policies to *Steam: A Quarterly Journal for Men* as "'looksist' and 'attitude-ist,' and somewhat 'ageist,' [but] it's not racist" (qtd. in Jill Nagle, "Skinny, 'White' Chicks and Hung, Buff Boys: Queer Sex Spaces and Their Discontents," in *Looking Queer: Body Image and Identity in Lesbian, Bisexual, Gay, and Transgender Communities,* ed. Dawn Atkins [New York: The Haworth Press, 1998], 445).

21 Michael Callen and The O-Boys!, home video, 1992, RDA.

The Honeymoon Is Over

The novelty of Los Angeles buoyed Michael's spirits for a while; however, within a year, his LA honeymoon period ended. "Like a bicycle tire with a slow leak," his reserves of energy and good health began to fail him.[22] Over the past ten years, Michael had experienced extraordinary lows which were always balanced out by a return, not to good health as defined by an HIV-negative person, but to his body's own AIDS-normal. He rarely felt great, but he had also rarely been gravely ill, though he had had crypto and suffered yearly infections of bacterial pneumonia. Yet Michael had always rebounded and mustered the energy to maintain "a schedule that would kill a healthy person."[23] Something was different now. He was more tired more often, and minor health issues made bigger intrusions into his day-to-day life. Michael felt that his body was slowly turning against him.

Toward the end of 1991, Michael asked Doug and Tim to take power of attorney for him, a decision that put Doug at the helm of a team of people in Los Angeles to care for Michael, what with Richard dividing his time between two coasts and two lovers and Tim spending much of the year traveling to perform. Having worked as a legal secretary earlier in his life, Michael drew on his organizational experience to help Doug navigate the increasingly complicated tasks surrounding his care while "minimizing the burden he would make on [Doug's] life" and the lives of others.[24]

Throughout early 1992, Michael experienced chronic shortness of breath and extraordinary fatigue. In May, he began to cough up blood, and doctors made a grim diagnosis: extensive

---

22 Michael Callen, "Doxil: A New Miracle Drug," n.d., typewritten original, MCP.
23 Michael makes this quip in a number of interviews, letters, and editorial essays across his life, and his friends, family, and fellow musicians repeated the phrase often in my interviews with them.
24 Douglas Sadownick, "Doug Sadownick's Response to Karen O. (Section 2)," *Gay Psyche Politics*, 24 April 2010, http://gaypsychepolitics.blogspot.com/2010/04/douglas-sadownicks-response-to-karen.html.

pulmonary Kaposi's sarcoma. "I am, literally, breathless. I am drowning in my own blood," he wrote in May, shortly after doctors confirmed the KS diagnosis. Michael knew that 90% of PWAs with pulmonary KS died within nine months; he had seen it with his own eyes so often that "90-in-9" became a catchphrase or shorthand. He had personally "never known a PWA who survived KS of the lungs much longer than [eighteen months]."[25]

Galvanized, Michael returned to writing, penning op-eds about AIDS for *Genre* and *QW*. In a regular column called "Dinosaur's Diary," a self-deprecating nod to his status as a long-term survivor, he blended anecdotes and observations about life in the 1990s with trenchant political analysis from the perspective of a self-described last-living dinosaur, a first-hand witness to both the sexual revolution of the '70s and the onset of the AIDS crisis in the '80s.

Veteran lesbian journalist Karen Ocamb "didn't know Michael was famous," "had never heard him sing," and "didn't even know what he looked like," but she "*did* know that he was a damn good writer about the incredibly complex subject of AIDS."[26] Unbeknownst to Ocamb, Michael was an admirer of her writing about the politics and policy of HIV/AIDS. Their mutual friend Torie Osborn introduced them in the fall of 1992 outside a performance of Holly Near's one-woman show *Fire in the Rain... Singer in the Storm* at the Mark Taper Forum in Los Angeles (135 N Grand Ave.). They fell into what Ocamb described as "instant intimacy."[27] They continued to talk regularly on the phone and saw one another on occasion, and Karen became part of Michael's Los Angeles chosen family.

---

25 Michael Callen, "Wading the Deep, Messy Waters of Sex," n.d., MCP.
26 Karen Ocamb, "Remembering Michael Callen," p.c., 11 May 2020. Ocamb originally composed this reminiscence for Martin Duberman as part of his research for *Hold Tight Gently: Michael Callen, Essex Hemphill, and the Battlefield of AIDS* (New York: The New Press, 2014). Since little of her piece was incorporated into Duberman's book, she shared it for this project. We also spoke by phone on 17 May 2020.
27 Ibid.

In spite of his hedonistic flirtation with The O-Boys!, Michael's longing for love and stability soon resurfaced. Loneliness had dogged Michael throughout his life. In adolescence and young adulthood, he wrestled with the pain of loneliness that plagues many queer children. As a child, he feared his father and yet longed for closeness with him. His coming out had forced his family to confront and try to reconcile their differences, but almost two decades later, those conflicts remained unresolved. When a first chance for love presented itself after years of repressed desire and unfulfilled longing, Michael's emotions manifested as a disproportionate attachment to George Harvey, and his relationship with Richard Pillard was marred by the difference in their age, money, and distance.

With Richard Dworkin, however, Michael had experienced a profound, immediate, and equitable connection. Although Michael had initially tried to push him away, Richard persisted and swore that he would stay, no matter the consequences. Now, Michael had been the one to leave. Their abrupt separation had, at first, been heady and liberating, but as the full consequence of his departure became clear, Michael's confidence splintered. Specters of his "classic gay low self-esteem" haunted the corners of his apartment.

Even though he was surrounded by friends, Michael still feared "[d]ying unloved — in the passionate, sexual sense [...]. It feels somehow cosmically unfair: I've fought so hard and so long for our right to love. Where's my payoff?"[28] Michael felt "ripe — no, *overripe* — for love, as if I'm rotting on the vine."[29] He even fantasized about marrying one last time, though he ultimately concluded that his relationship with Richard was the apotheosis of his romantic successes. Still, he admitted, "I miss my ex," and

---

28 Michael Callen, "Dinosaur's Diary: In My Time of Dying," QW, 30 August 1992, 46.
29 Ibid.

> [t]o the extent that I ever thought about my death from AIDS, I always assumed he'd be there to help send me gently into… whatever. And his gruff forcefulness would be so *useful* to me now. *He'd* know what to do, my mind races. He'd sit me down and tell me what my priorities *ought* to be. And then he'd help me accomplish them. But the divorce has been so unusually bitter. Now, I'm very much alone.[30]

Standing in a New York magazine shop across from his 8th Ave. apartment on a Saturday night, Richard read Michael's words and felt his wounds torn open anew. He mailed an angry rebuttal letter to Michael the next day.

Occasionally, Michael returned to New York to visit friends or to receive an honor, such as when he was selected to serve as the Grand Marshal of the 1991 Gay Pride festival. Then, the two former lovers would speak, trade pleasantries, and try to engage in "sort of normalized relations."[31] However, Richard fell into a deep depression exacerbated by Michael's departure and other personal matters in New York.

Richard and Patrick had to take on another roommate to afford their 8th Ave. apartment. While Richard was out of town on tour, Patrick found a straight roommate who stayed for a few months then abruptly disappeared, leaving several months of rent and an expensive long-distance telephone bill unpaid. Around this time, a strung-out crack addict broke into the apartment and held Richard at knifepoint for hours, eventually leaving with Patrick's leather jacket, a bass guitar, and other easily pawnable items in hand. Richard never felt safe in the apartment again. He and Patrick couldn't afford the rent, and Richard felt paralyzed. Eventually, they relocated to a small basement apartment on 12th St., between Greenwich Ave. and Washington Ave. Little did they know that these cramped rooms with

---

30 Ibid. Emphasis original.
31 Richard Dworkin, interview with author, September 2017 (henceforth, RD and MJ [2017]).

depressingly low ceilings into which their belongings barely fit would be Patrick's last home.

Back in California, Michael's condition worsened day by day. For years, Michael had followed the advice of Joe Sonnabend, avoiding chemo, radiation, and, especially, AZT. He remained an impassioned advocate for self-empowerment, encouraging PWAs to arm themselves with as much information about treatments as possible then to "go out into the woods by yourself and sort it out and make your own decision."[32] Now, his doctors began to consider more invasive treatments, including chemo and radiation for KS. Michael wanted to live, so he began a standard regime of Adriamycin-Bleomycin-Vinblastine (ABV) to treat his KS.

Chemotherapy is intensive and invasive, and its side effects include familiar patterns of weight and hair loss, extreme fatigue, anemia, nausea, vomiting, and other gastrointestinal problems. For many patients, the initial side effects tend to be relatively minor, manageable with over-the-counter medications. However, their impact on the body is cumulative, and subsequent treatments usually bring more pronounced side effects in their wake. For PWAs, chemo carried further risks because of its known immunosuppressive effect.

Michael's first infusion was relatively painless; he experienced some mild nausea and headache and optimistically thought he might avoid anything worse. His second treatment, though, was terrifying. He woke in the middle of the night with a raging fever, body aches, drenched in sweat, and disorientated, "a geometric progression of traumatic side effects" that Dr. Sonnabend anticipated would probably only get worse.[33] Chemo, Michael concluded, "is not unlike being run over by a bus. In my case, that translates into fevers of 104.5 for 12 hours, nausea, insomnia, bone pain, neuropathy, and, most devastating, mental fogginess."[34] Yet his sardonic sense of humor and Midwestern

---

32 Terry Gross, interview with Michael Callen, "Michael Callen on Surviving AIDS in the Long Term," *Fresh Air*, 16 November 1990.
33 Quoted in Duberman, *Hold Tight Gently*, 259.
34 Callen, "In My Time of Dying," 46.

pragmatism prevailed. "Unlike being mauled by a bus, chemo requires that I give *consent* — and on a regular basis, no less!"[35]

Ever the activist who agitated "so shamelessly about [his] AIDS drama during the past decade, [he] decided to go out as [he] came in: publicly."[36] As the "physical weariness of [his] poor, war-torn body" blurred into "soul weariness," Michael bravely stared down his imminent death.[37] He was neither angry nor caught in the throes of an existential crisis. "Rather, I'm just sad," he wrote. "I shall miss life so."[38] Occasionally, he mused about the things he had missed or even failed to notice:

> Who will be the last person I have sex with? Have I already had my last sex without knowing it was my last time? What will my final solid meal consist of? What will be the last movie I see? I find myself studying the wizened or bloated naked bodies of Yiddish-chattering old men at my gym. I'm embarrassed to admit that I actually experience envy that they've lived so long. I neutrally study their hideously sagging breasts and butts and notice how their testicles all hang so low (The result of a lifetime's gravity?) I've now developed a very clear image of what I would have looked like as an old man. It makes me smile to think of what a *great* old man I'd have made — cantankerous, opinionated, frisky.[39]

Behind his brave public face, Michael was afraid. The thought of losing his bodily integrity, agency, and hair haunted him, and "sometimes [he] found [himself] standing at the kitchen sink, whimpering."[40] Although he had to reduce his daily activities — in a letter to The Flirtations, he bitterly complained that he was accomplishing as little as ten percent of what he could do at full capacity — his schedule remained busy with plans to re-

---

35 Ibid. Emphasis original.
36 Ibid.
37 Ibid.
38 Ibid.
39 Ibid.
40 Ibid.

cord a final album, to tour with The Flirtations when he was able to travel, to appear in Jonathan Demme's *Philadelphia* (1993) and Jonathan Greyson's *Zero Patience* (1993), and to actively plan (as opposed to passively await) his funeral.[41] Michael's preparations for death were inspired by his friend and fellow long-term survivor Max Navarre, who "too had become an AIDS poster boy, machine-gunning messages of hope [...]. But when his time came, and people wouldn't let him 'give up,' he very forcefully refused to be bothered by their needs. 'This is my death,' he snorted, 'and I'll do it my own way, thank you!'"[42] Like Max, Michael intended to die on his terms.

Michael told Doug and Tim that he wished to "be around 'gay people, hot, alive, sexy gay men,' at the last moments of [his] life."[43] And he talked with Richard and Patrick about the possibility of a suicide party. Richard remembered that Michael wanted it to be "very elaborate — somewhere between Socrates drinking the hemlock and Judy Garland, but festive, very, very festive!"[44] However, terminal illness moves at its own pace and its own caprice — a difficult prospect for a self-described control queen. Michael had to admit that "AIDS is, of course, impossible to control [...]. I feel that time is passing so fast, and that I've little to show for it. It seems I'm either doing chemo, recovering from chemo, or dreading chemo. And somewhere in the middle, there is lots of airplane travel and tacky hotels, bad food and wonderful queer audiences."[45] He complained that AIDS was "crowding me out of my home."[46] His apartment looked more and more like a hospital room with "three huge machines to produce oxygen and pills and needles and needle disposals, etc. all around."[47] But what could he do?

41 Michael Callen, letter to The Flirtations, 11 January 1993, typed copy, MCP.
42 Ibid.
43 Sadownick, "Doug Sadownick's Response to Karen O."
44 Richard Dworkin, interview with author, 15 July 2020 (henceforth RD and MJ [2020]).
45 Callen, "In My Time of Dying," 46.
46 Callen, letter to The Flirtations, 11 January 1993.
47 Ibid.

While he was able to spin a joke out of his own tragedy, Michael knew he was inching closer to death. Foremost in his mind was his queer musical family, so he wrote to The Flirtations to candidly explain:

> I'm unwell, obviously. Sicker than you've ever known me. Everyone I talk to seems to be freaked by my attitude. I know I'm dying so I may as well just say it. Of course, I'm still "Living with AIDS" as the propaganda goes, but I've seen enough death to recognize its signs and my body is communicating with me loud and clear. Basically, it feels like somebody turned up the gravity meter and turned down my energy level — an unpleasant combination of side effects.[48]

The sorry state of his health forced Michael to admit that this probably meant the end of his days as a member of the group:

> I think the expectation should be that you'll be doing a lot of four part gigs. I'll coordinate with Jon [Arterton]. Everything depends on my chemo schedule, my reaction to chemo, my lung capacity (it's dangerous to fly if it's under a certain oxygen level), etc. I wish I could be more definitive with you all, but that's the best I can do for now.
>
> I just want to officially thank you all for your many kindnesses — especially your offer to continue my salary for a while. I don't know what I'd do without the income. And I honestly commit to trying to make as many gigs as I can. You've all covered for me and put up with me and endured the pain and uncertainty with me like, well, a family. And I acknowledge and honor that and love you all for it.[49]

Chemotherapy treatments regularly "kicked the SHIT" out of him, and while he thought a new series of sharp pains in his chest were a side effect of the chemo, they were eventually diag-

---

48 Ibid.
49 Ibid.

nosed as KS lesions growing on his heart.[50] Michael's KS failed to respond to either radiation or the ABV regimen, and "fulminant KS [lesions] covered three quarters of both lungs."[51] Each new x-ray proved to be more ominous than the last.

In late 1992, Michael demanded that his doctors level with him. They said he had a "70% chance of being dead in two months."[52] Daily incapacitating panic attacks ensued. Doctors prescribed Imipramine and a "staggering dose of .5mg of Xanax four times a day."[53] The medications relieved Michael's anxiety but caused him to sleep twelve or fourteen hours a day, which wasn't like him at all. As usual, Michael responded to the latest medical crises with campy, macabre humor, writing "I'd rather my heart burst than I drown slowly in my own blood. See? You can put a good spin on anything!"[54]

When friends in New York informed Michael of a couple of new drugs being tested on KS patients who did not respond to other treatments, he called the manufacturer of DaunoXome and "made many frustrating attempts to get access to it; suffice it to say that at no point in [his] search was [he] treated with a SHRED of humanity."[55] His dear friend and champion, Manhattan socialite and philanthropist Judy Peabody (1930–2010), "implored [him] to pursue another experimental chemo drug, Doxil," and his efforts were rewarded.[56] Not only was his experience with Liposome Technologies, Inc. "just the opposite of the people who control [DaunoXome]," but he also worked with Dr. Melody Anderson to coordinate a Los Angeles-based clinical trial at Pacific Oaks Medical Group to ensure that other KS patients could take regular infusions of the "beautiful, Howard-Johnson-esque orange" liquid.[57] While he had "suffered tremen-

---

50 Ibid.
51 Ibid.
52 Ibid.
53 Ibid.
54 Ibid.
55 Callen, "Doxil," 1.
56 Ibid.
57 Ibid.

dously from standard chemotherapy," much to his delight, he had virtually no side effects while on the new drug. He excitedly reported that his "hair has grown back (albeit a slightly different color and texture); [his] lung capacity began to slowly return; and miraculously, [the] external lesions began to literally melt away."[58]

Energized by the apparent efficacy of Doxil, Michael redoubled his efforts to record a new album, a double-disc project he tentatively called *Legacy*. Planning the record gave him a reason to live, a star to pin his hopes to. He made song lists and brainstormed about which of his musical friends and other noteworthy performers he might ask to appear on the album. In December 1992, he turned to Richard. "I really want to make another record now because who knows? I've had KS for six months, but there's a new treatment that makes chemo not as terrible. Maybe I'll get to live a little longer. I want to start right away. Do you want to help me?"[59]

Richard was unsure how to proceed, and he shared his reservations and apprehensions with Patrick, who lovingly intervened:

> Are you kidding? Are you crazy? What do you mean? Of course you're going to do this. It's *Michael*. Even if nothing comes of it, it's a time for you guys to be together. Look, you guys really love each other, and this is a way for you to be together before Mike dies. You may not believe it, but he's gonna die soon, and if you don't do this, you will regret it for the rest of your life. So, yeah, you're gonna do this.[60]

Without Patrick's insistence, Michael's final album might have remained just a fantasy.

---

58 Ibid., 2.
59 RD and MJ (2017).
60 Ibid.

In the first week of 1993, Richard "actually did something that made sense" when he bought a plane ticket to Los Angeles.[61] He and Michael booked a room at Trax Studios just to see what Michael could do, starting with "Better in the Moonlight," a song about sex *al fresco* that the couple co-wrote in the 1980s, and "Love Worth Fighting For," a ballad he co-wrote with Marsha Malamet, who was living in Los Angeles by this time. Michael used his keyboard to produce simple block chord accompaniment, and Richard created a rudimentary track. To the surprise of their sound engineer (who Richard described as "a really sweet straight guy"), the duo arrived carrying an IBM laptop containing the MIDI files for Michael's guide tracks and wheeling a four-foot-high oxygen tank from which Michael ingested oxygen.[62]

Given Michael's pulmonary KS and the effects of chemo, they were not even sure that he would be able to sing. Miraculously, Michael's voice was in extraordinary shape. Although his range had dropped three semitones as a result of KS, he "sang the tits off the songs."[63] Listening to playbacks, Michael could "actually hear the wheezing/swelling in [his] lungs as [he] inhaled. It was creepy. It'll probably end up on the album, but fuck that. That's how I am these days, so there ain't nothin' I can do about it."[64] It seemed possible that *Legacy* was going to be a reality.

---

61 Ibid.
62 Ibid.
63 Callen, letter to The Flirtations, 11 January 1993.
64 Ibid.

Fig. 1. Richard Dworkin and Michael Callen at Chez Panisse (1993). Richard Dworkin Private Archive.

15

They Are Falling All around Me

I will try to sing my song right.
Be sure to let me hear from you.
— Bernice Johnson Reagon

Unfettered from most of his activist commitments and having shown himself that he could still sing, Michael now had to face the biggest obstacle facing *Legacy*: money. Michael's financial situation had never been entirely stable. "You can consider this a failure," he once said to his father, "but you didn't raise any children with any financial sense."[1] The costs of an album could potentially run into thousands, if not tens of thousands, of dollars. By tapping extensive connections in New York and recycling some of Lowlife's studio recordings, Michael and Richard had kept down the costs for *Purple Heart*. But Michael had few connections to the music industry in Los Angeles.

Financing *Legacy* would require creativity, ingenuity, grit, and luck, but Michael was determined to make this album. In early 1993, he participated in an episode HBO's docuseries *America Undercover* with the tantalizing subtitle "Why Am I Gay?" A camera crew followed Michael on tour with The Flirtations, including a performance in Indianapolis, a short drive from his

1 Clifford Callen, interview with Michael Callen, 26 February 1992, audio recording, The Michael Callen Papers at the LGBT Community Center National History Archive (henceforth MCP).

Fig. 2. Barbara, Michael, and Cliff Callen, Indianapolis, 1992. Photo by Andrew Scalini. Richard Dworkin Private Archive.

parents' home in Hamilton. Cliff, Barbara, Barry and his wife, and Linda and her husband all came to the performance and mingled backstage before taking their seats in the audience for the show. Michael expected a bit of a windfall from the network, which he intended to use to help fund *Legacy*. However, legal issues bogged down the process, and the payment was delayed for many months.

In the interim, Patrick came to the rescue with a deceptively simple idea. "People love Mike," he reasoned. Since it was no secret that he was dying, "why not just ask people for money? Let's do a fundraiser!"[2] Patrick drafted a fundraising letter which

2   Richard Dworkin, interview with the author, 5 June 2017 (henceforth, RD and MJ [2017]).

was mailed to hundreds of people, and he designed a cutout donation form which was printed in various gay newspapers, gay magazines, and The Flirtations' newsletter. Several of Michael's famous friends, including Holly Near and Tom Robinson, added their names to the letter as a show of support for the project. With the help of fellow PWA, activist, and (later) founding editor of POZ magazine Sean Strub, who had an impressive background in political fundraising and mail campaigns, Michael undertook a second extensive letter-writing campaign to solicit donations from friends, family, and fans, and he called in favors from people he knew in New York as well as contacts made during his time with The Flirtations.[3] Jon Arterton made a personal loan in the amount of $5,000, and Michael drew up a legal document to assure he would be repaid, even if he died before the album was finished. Clifford and Barbara Callen cashed in an annuity and contributed $4,500. Donations trickled in at first, many accompanied by an effusive letter of support. Those who could afford little sent ten or twenty dollars, apologizing for the meager amount but pledging to buy the album when it came out. Still, every drop in the bucket got it closer to full. Soon, they would amass more than thirty thousand dollars, a handsome budget for an independent record.

Michael also assembled an impressive roster of talented musicians, including Holly Near, Cris Williamson, Marsha Malamet, Fred Hersch, John Bucchino, and The Flirtations, who would offer their time and their talent for little or no money. By this time, Michael had also made some professional contacts among Los Angeles musicians, and he struck musical gold when three of the city's most sought-after backup singers volunteered their voices to the project: Diana Grasselli, Arnold McCuller, and David Lasley. Their voices can be heard on albums by luminaries like Dionne Warwick, James Taylor, Sting, David Bowie, Bonnie

---

[3] Strub founded POZ around the time Michael died, and the magazine eulogized Michael in the first issue in April 1994. Over the years, Michael and Sean worked together on fundraising for People with AIDS Coalition, New York, the Community Research Initiative, and the PWA Health Group.

Raitt, Aretha Franklin, and dozens of other singers as well as their own critically acclaimed solo projects. Their participation on *Legacy* was facilitated by Marsha Malamet, who knew them from her work in the LA music scene. Although Michael and Richard offered them nominal sums for their work, the Mikeettes, as they called themselves, made it clear that their participation was a labor of love, and they worked around hectic touring and paid studio gigs to sing with Michael for free.

Although their relationship was still strained by Michael's painful departure from New York, he and Richard easily fell into a comfortable working rhythm in the studio facilitated by their long history of recording and performing together. In January 1993, Michael completed vocal tracks for several songs: "Love Worth Fighting For" and "The Healing Power of Love," which he co-wrote with Marsha Malamet, and "One More Lullaby" (from *Dreamstuff,* a 1975 musical adaptation of Shakespeare's *The Tempest* with music by Marsha, lyrics by Dennis Green, and book by Howard Ashman).[4] Marsha played keyboard on all three songs. For "One More Lullaby," she used anxious, shifting block chords over a staccato left-hand pedal point to evoke the restlessness of the lyrics: "It's almost time to go. It's almost time to fly, to gather up my memories and kiss this place goodbye." The song perfectly captured Michael's *joie de vivre* and his newfound appreciation for small and fleeting moments: sitting among the natural beauty of the Huntington Library Gardens, relaxing on the beach, or singing one last lullaby. Although the recording studio was equipped with a small electric piano, Richard had in mind a much grander sound for "One More Lullaby." So, he made a MIDI file of Marsha's keyboard track and scoured Los Angeles for a MIDI-capable grand piano. Between hospital visits in the fall of 1993, he located a suitable studio with a nine-foot

---

4 *Dreamstuff* ran for about 40 performances at the WPA Theater in New York's Bowery, a few blocks from the famed club CBGB, which had opened around the same time. It was performed for the first time since 1978 in a 2008 revival directed by Michael Urie at The Hayworth Theater in Los Angeles. A program for this performance can be accessed online at https://linguistics.ucla.edu/people/cschutze/Dreamstuff%20Program.pdf

MIDI Yamaha grand piano and booked a few hours with the instrument. Housed in a massive film studio sound stage, the instrument and room provided just the right grandiose resonance for one of Michael's most expressive vocal performances.

They also finished a song that Michael initially started around the time of the 1990 Census. "Redefine the Family (The Census Song)" articulates a queer vision of family based on *choice* instead of biology.[5] For LGBTQ+ people, coming out often strains biological family bonds, sometimes to their breaking point, and this had certainly been true in Michael's experience. Thus, chosen family emerges as an important alternative, providing love, nurturing, and support as well as sometimes pooling resources for housing, food, and other necessities. Some LGBTQ+ people live in extended chosen families that include lovers, former lovers, friends, biological or adopted children, and even pets. Members of drag communities often form houses with a shared family surname, and in each house, a mother attends to the needs of her children, who become sisters, friends, fellow performers, and staunch allies. "Redefine the Family" is this twin of Michael's earlier song, "Nobody's Fool," which had dealt with the strained relations between a gay son and his father. By contrast, "Redefine the Family" celebrated a queer vision of a supportive, loving family of choice and gave a musical middle finger to heteronormative powers that granted legitimacy on some families while denigrating or ignoring others. It's one of Michael's most political songs, and its reggae rhythms and soulful horns, combined with Michael's campy lyrics, demonstrate his ability to say "fuck you" with a smile on his face.

In the first two verses, Michael confronts a census official who has been granted authority to confer legitimacy on family structures. "A wife and kids! That's a family!" the official exclaims, "The backbone of our democracy, the way the Bible says it should be!" Bemused, Michael rebuffs the census representa-

---

5 Kath Weston, *Families We Choose: Lesbians, Gays, Kinship* (New York: Columbia University Press, 1997).

tive, explaining that "Sir, you're misinformed. Please allow met to clarify:

> We define our family
> We offer no apology
> We celebrate our diversity, you see
> We define our family.
>
> My lover's name is Richard.
> His lover's name is Pat.
> We're one big happy family.
> Is there a box for that?
> We live here with Pam and Lyn;
> They're lesbians and lovers.
> Together, we're raising three great kids,
> Gertrude and her two brothers.

The baffled census representative responds with confusion. As he departs, Michael calls after, reiterating his commitment to "redefine the family so it includes you and me. We must teach respect for diversity. We'll design our own family!"

Musically, "Redefine the Family" is an oddity among Callen's songs because of its strong reggae influence, a stylistic choice that resulted from Michael's fascination with synthesizers. At the piano, he was a competent and expressive player, but his self-taught keyboard skills were limited, especially in terms of rhythmic variety. With a synthesizer's bank of pre-programmed rhythmic tracks, Michael could conjure a variety of grooves with the push of a button and add block chords over them. Richard and Michael purchased their first synthesizers in the 1980s, and these experiments had livened up his songs with the New Wave rock rhythms of "How to Have Sex (in an Epidemic)" and, later, the smooth Latin groove of "My Imagination," also on *Legacy*. "It's a shame he didn't do more of that," Richard later reminisced.[6]

---

6 RD and MJ (2017).

Throughout the winter of 1993, Michael and Richard continued to work on his song selections for *Legacy*. Because he knew this would be his final album, Michael wanted to include a backlog of original songs as well as music by friends and fellow gay songwriters, classics from the American Songbook, and works by Elton John ("Goodbye," "Indian Sunset") and Joni Mitchell ("Down to You"). Since *Purple Heart* had been an experience in frugality, Richard tempered his occasional frustrations to indulge Michael's wildest fantasies; *Legacy* would spare no expense and let no musical whim go unrealized. The song list ballooned to a total of over fifty possible tracks, almost all of which were recorded. Michael's health seemed to decline in inverse proportion to his song lists. The bigger and more grandiose his plans, the sicker he seemed to get. Still, he continued working.

To manage this much music, Michael experimented with different concepts and song groupings. The basic idea was an expanded version of the "tops and bottoms" structure of *Purple Heart,* with two, three, or even four discs. Maybe they could posthumously release one CD at a time over several years, Michael wondered, or a trilogy of albums with similar album art so that fans could buy one album at a time. While he knew he would have to make artistic decisions after Michael's death, Richard let him dream.

In February, Michael flew to New York to record at RPM Studios (now closed, 12 E 12th St. between 5th Ave. and University Place). A massive snowstorm (a precursor to the Storm of the Century that March) hit New York during Michael's visit and threatened to halt his recording sessions. He and Richard called all of the musicians to ensure that they could get to the studio, and in spite of the weather, everyone showed up. As producer for these sessions, Richard had to manage a disparate group of musicians who didn't necessarily know each other and had never worked together before. He also had to prep the studio equipment before recording could commence. Early in the afternoon, he rehearsed with the band in a rented practice space. When everyone arrived at RPM, they discovered that the previous group was still working; their session had run long. Hours passed be-

MIKE'S LIST--Most Recent 8/15/93

DEATH CD

They Are Falling All Around Me
Wish I Had a Dime
See Here
Do Not Turn Away
Mother Mother
One More Lullaby
Goodbyes
If I Love Again
Smile
(AFTER A BIG PAUSE) Nothing Lasts 4-ever

UP, FUNNY, DANCEABLE

Glitter and Be Gay
Grade B Movie
Better in the Moonlight
Hot Stuff Comin Thru
Medley
Victim of Circumstance
Name Names
No No
Redefine the Family
My Imagination
Two Men Dance the Tango

LOVE, PIANO/VOCAL/MY SONGS

All Over
I Know
It's Not Enough
Just Know I Love You
Just Look in Our Eyes
Lucky Day
Overs
Roundabout
The Healing Power of Love
Warm as the Wind
Love Comes
Love Worth Fighting For
Sometimes (Not Often Enough)
Till

GAYNESS, POLITICAL, MISCELLANEOUS

Crazy World
Now
6:30 Sunday Morning/Right as the Rain
Indian Sunset
Innocence Dying
Jockey Man/Lotto
Kerosene Lantern
Strangers
Streetsinger
Street of Dreams
We've Had Enough
Yes, I'll Take My Chances
Sheherezade (Zero Patience)
Sacred
Too Much Input

DROPPED:

Love Don't Need a Reason
Penises from Heaven

Fig. 3a & b. Draft *Legacy* sequences (1993). The Michael Callen Papers, Box 32/Folder 384, the LGBT Community Center National History Archive.

fore the sound engineer could recalibrate all the equipment, a process that took even more time. Michael soothed frustrations by "holding court in the studio lounge [...] getting people to tell everyone about their most embarrassing sexual thing that's ever happened to them."[7] Eventually, the sessions began. Michael and Richard later booked additional dates at Walter Sear's legendary Sear Sound Studios (353 W 48th St.). Known for its incredible collection of vintage equipment and a favorite place to record for luminaries like Steely Dan, Yoko Ono, David Bowie, and Patti Smith. Sear Sound became Michael and Richard's "home away from home in New York. [They] worked there whenever possible."[8]

Recording continued on both coasts as Richard and Michael coordinated by mail, fax, and phone with arrangers Phillip Johnston, Steve Sandberg (who also played piano on several tracks), and Greg Wells, who was introduced to the sprawling *Legacy* family by Marsha Malamet. "The moment Greg appeared, it was clear this was an extraordinary individual," Richard recalled. "We tried to be in his presence as much as possible."[9] Wells arranged and played keyboards on "The Healing Power of Love," "One More Lullaby," "Goodbye," "Sacred," and "Love Worth Fighting For." His work on these songs was "genius. He really [had] a whole conception that goes way beyond [Richard's expertise] in terms of arranging synths and drums."[10] Although he was quite sick and exhausted much of the time, Michael wrote to numerous friends that he was "having the time of his life" working on the "massive and sprawling project. I'm such a PIG!"[11]

Even though he had ostensibly retired from activism, Michael continued to receive invitations to speak at various events around the country throughout the spring, including the 10th

7   Ibid.
8   Ibid.
9   Ibid.
10 Ibid.
11 Michael Callen, letter to Deborah Tannen, 27 May 1993, typed copy, MCP. Callen reiterates this sentence and sentiment in dozens of letters in the spring of 1993.

Anniversary Celebration of Seattle's Northwest AIDS Foundation and *In a New Light,* a two-hour ABC special hosted by Aresenio Hall and Paula Abdul the featured celebrities like Lily Tomlin, John Stamos, Exposé, Elton John, and Patti Austin as well as Michael's moving performance of "Love Don't' Need a Reason." Although he was very ill at this point, Michael agreed to these gigs because each appearance brought in more money for *Legacy*.

On 11 April 1993, Michael celebrated his thirty-eighth birthday and his mother's retirement in Hamilton over the Easter weekend. Michael even sang for his mother at their old church and received a standing ovation from the congregation, much to his surprise and his mother's delight. In a letter sent a few days later, Barry thanked his brother profusely. "I want you to know how much it meant to me (and I'm sure to them) that you volunteered to come to Hamilton, stand up in our old church and sing. Quite a personal sacrifice — like a Jew going back to Dachau and singing in the shower."[12] Afterward, Barbara wrote that she was "truly grateful and appreciative for this celebration."[13] Cliff added a short note himself, writing "I can echo all your mom just said. I often speak of people with what I call 'substance.' I have met very few in my life, but you are one of them."[14] Although Michael's relationship with his parents had remained strained over the years, he was forthright with them about his health. He had told them about his AIDS diagnosis in 1982 and had kept them in the loop about his health over the intervening years. Now, they had to face the grim reality that their gay son was dying.

His mother admired Michael's "great strength and positive attitude throughout [his] painful bout with cancer. [...] You are a great example to many and you have truly MADE

---

12 Barry Callen, letter to Michael Callen, 16 April 1993, typewritten original, MCP.
13 Barbara Callen and Clifford Callen, birthday card to Michael Callen, 11 April 1993, MCP.
14 Ibid.

A DIFFERENCE!!!"[15] She prayed for "another of many miracles — healing of [his] cancer and a long, long life. Hope continues."[16] Barry wrote often to Michael, repeatedly telling his beloved brother that "my heart suffers with you," though he also added levity in the way that close siblings can.[17] He encouraged Michael to "keep making music that touches peoples' hearts [and] keep cheating death the way you always cheated at cards."[18] A few months later, Cliff sent Michael a handwritten note thanking his son for "the pleasure you gave [your mother] by singing at her retirement program. I think I have never seen her so moved as when you sang. I am personally so proud of you and Barry and Linda for making it an occasion none of us will forget for the rest of our lives."[19]

Michael also planned to attend the historic 1993 Gay and Lesbian March on Washington in April, where he would give three farewell performances with The Flirtations and say his goodbyes to public life. Michael wrote to a friend in March that "nothing but death or dire disease could keep me away from the massive love infusion of DC. The '87 March was life-affirming, and I expect this to be extra special for me!"[20]

In DC, Michael would be surrounded by longtime friends, fans, and famous faces, but Richard was not going to be among them. He had joined a group of Knitting Factory musicians, including electronic percussionist Samm Bennett, for twenty-eight gigs over thirty days, traveling south/southwest by bus from New York along the East Coast before trekking to Austin, Los Angeles, San Francisco, Seattle, and Chicago. To Michael's frustration, this also paused the *Legacy* sessions for an entire

---

15 Ibid.
16 Ibid.
17 Barry Wayne Callen, letter to Michael Callen, 29 March 1993, handwritten original, MCP.
18 Ibid.
19 Clifford Callen, letter to Michael Callen, 1 August 1993, handwritten original, MCP.
20 Michael Callen, letter to Karen Stevens, 24 March 1993, typewritten original, MCP.

month. When an attack of appendicitis put Bennett in the hospital and brought the tour to a halt in Chicago, Richard seized the opportunity to fly to DC to be with Michael. Although his Saturday arrival meant that Richard missed Michael's birthday celebration, a huge dinner arranged at his suggestion by Carl Valentino and Patrick Kelly, Michael was surprised and thrilled to see him. They spent Sunday together milling through the crowds on the National Mall.

On Sunday, 25 April 1993, Michael took the stage. From a platform erected in front of the US Capitol, he surveyed the throng: an estimated one million people stretched across the National Mall in the largest public demonstration of queer political solidarity in history. "What a sight," he told the crowd, his earnest Midwestern twang reverberating through loudspeakers. "You're a sight for sore eyes. Being gay is the greatest gift I have ever been given, and I don't care who knows about it."[21] In what would be his final public performance, Callen brought his decade-long fight for gay rights and for the rights of PWAs to an end with his musical family of choice, The Flirtations, who delivered an inspired performance of "Something Inside So Strong" to the adoring and supportive crowd, and Michael's set ended with a gorgeous rendition of "Love Don't Need a Reason," the AIDS anthem he composed with his "major lesbian friend, Marsha Malamet and the late Peter Allen," he told the audience. Michael had just outed Marsha, and it had been broadcast around the world on C-Span. While she had always been out as a lesbian, Marsha had never been "outed in the framework of speaking to that many people. It was funny and wonderful, and it was the most loving thing he ever did for me," Marsha told me in 2017. "That was love. He wanted me to be out in front of three-quarters of a million people, and I was so honored, so thrilled that he did it."[22]

---

21 BettyByte, "March on Washington 1993 - gay wedding - Michael Callen sings," August 23, 2010, https://www.youtube.com/watch?v=Aqawx7_fVYo.
22 Marsha Malamet, interview with the author, 14 July 2017.

Fig. 4. Michael Callen and Richard Dworkin at the 1993 Gay and Lesbian March on Washington. Richard Dworkin Private Archive.

As he ended the final iteration of the titular refrain of "Love Don't Need a Reason" with a trademark falsetto flourish, people stood cheering, crying, and flashing the familiar American Sign Language symbol for "I Love You." For they knew the song's sentiment, its message of having too little time for anything but love, rang true for Michael, whose health forced him to take a hard look at the fact that he was, finally, running out of time.

Fig. 1. Barry Callen, Michael Callen, Richard Dworkin, Andy Dworkin in the studio (1993). Richard Dworkin Private Archive.

16

Sometimes Not Often Enough

> *Sometimes, not often enough,*
> *We reflect upon the good things,*
> *And those thoughts always center*
> *Around those we love.*
> — Henry Mancini & Felice Mancini

Michael had been fortunate to meet so many talented musicians who were willing to donate their time and talent to *Legacy*, but he puzzled over one problem: how to include The Flirtations. He felt strongly that their *a cappella* sound belonged on The Flirtations' records, a separate sonic experience from his own solo records. The Flirtations hemmed and hawed, rejecting Michael's suggestions for repertoire and refusing to commit to a recording date. So, Michael wrote a blunt letter to the group in which he explained, "Hey! I'm dying. Do you want to be on my record or not?"[1] The Flirtations finally agreed, and Michael scheduled a studio at Sear Sound for 16 June 1993.

Initially, Michael and Richard suggested that The Flirtations record an arrangement of Tom Judson's "Two Men Dance the Tango" (*Two Men Dance the Tango*, 1990). Its lyrics deal with the perception of masculine gender in a series of scenarios in which

[1] Michael Callen, letter to *The Flirtations*, 11 January 1993, typed copy, The Michael Callen Papers at The LGBT Community Center National History Archive (henceforth MCP).

male–male intimacy and contact go unnoticed: drinking beer in a bar, working on Wall Street, singing "Home on the Range" on the prairie. Likewise, "when flavors of the Argentine start to issue from the bandstand [...] there is no reason for asking, 'Why?' Don't lose your composure if you should spy two men dance the tango together! Maybe you should, too!" In spite of the campy humor and the political sentiment in the lyrics, which Michael felt would appeal to his chosen musical family, The Flirtations dismissed his choice as somehow too trivial for them.

As a compromise, Michael suggested that they rework Cliff Townsend's arrangement of "Sometimes, Not Often Enough," a song written by conductor and composer Henry Mancini and his daughter, Felice, that had been recorded by The Carpenters on their 1971 self-titled album. The Flirtations agreed to sing the new arrangement.

Although the short, sentimental text encourages listeners to "reflect upon the good things, and [...] those we love" and to remember to tell friends and family "just how much [you] love them," the session itself was anything but meditative or harmonious. Even though the meter was ticking on the studio at the price of one hundred dollars an hour, The Flirtations showed up more than an hour late, and Jon Arterton had brought a semi-professional video camera to film the sessions, much to the chagrin of others in the studio. The sound engineers, too, were confused. Was Jon there to sing — and therefore in need of a mic and sound check — or was his role was that of documentarian? Cliff Townsend refused to learn the new bass part which had been designed to limit doubling with the piano that might muddy the bass end of the final mix. Frustrations reached a breaking point, so Michael corralled the group into the studio lounge for a group therapy session.

While the other men were "honored by [Michael's] extending an invitation to sing backup, and it was a joy to be singing with [him] again, it was an extremely stressful recording — all of us brimming with emotions we couldn't quite name or control."[2] Eventually, they had to face the underlying issue: this musical family was not ready to handle the death of their beloved Mother Diva. The prospect of Michael's death brought back unresolved feelings about the loss of TJ Myers in 1990. Jon felt that the group needed to meet again in order to verbalize "those dark and dirty things that we feel about each other" in a supportive environment and discuss the consequences of those emotions.[3] A few weeks later, they met in Provincetown for a final group therapy session, which they recorded. Jimmy admitted that the group had "major issues" and that he was "pissed off" because Michael would be touring and performing with them less often. However, he knew that the bigger issue was the loss of Michael's nurturing influence, which posed an existential threat to The Flirtations.[4] Jon agreed that "the thought of going on without Michael is terrifying to all of us."[5] However, Cliff remained frustrated over what he perceived as Michael's indecisive flip-flopping. "We agreed to give [Michael] the permission to stay home and rest, but the first chance he had to travel," he joined the group on the road. "What do you want," Cliff demanded, "to stay at home or travel with us?" Michael wanted — *needed* — both.

Do Not Turn Away

Over the weekend of 25–27 June, Michael, Richard, and Patrick traveled to San Francisco where Michael and Richard were scheduled to record with Holly Near, Cris Williamson, John Bucchino, and Arnold McCuller at Hyde Street Studios (245 Hyde St.), the former home of Wally Heider's legendary studio where Grace Slick and The Jefferson Airplane had recorded their album *Volunteers* in 1969. In those historic rooms, Michael

---

2 Jimmy Rutland, announcement in *The Flirtations* newsletter, n.d., Clifford Townsend's scrapbooks.
3 Jon Arterton, Flirtations "Provincetown Therapy" home video, 1993, Richard Dworkin Private Archive (henceforth, RDA).
4 Ibid.
5 Ibid.

recorded his wistful ballad about a street musician, "Street Singer," John Bucchino's "Do Not Turn Away" and Cris Williamson's "Mother, Mother." Together, Michael and his friends worked out a beautiful arrangement of Bernice Johnson Reagon's "They Are Falling All Around Me."

Originally written and released on Bernice Johnson Reagon's *Give Your Hands to Struggle* (1975), "They Are Falling All Around Me" pays homage to "the musicians who lived to make their music and died singing. John Davis, King Curtis, Lee Morgan, Peter LaFarge, Skip James, Fred McDowell, and Mahalia Jackson are names that come to mind. [...] The list grows with each passing day."[6] The text was inspired by Senegalese poet Birago Diop's "Breaths," a text Reagon would later set to music with Sweet Honey in the Rock and that The Flirtations would record. Sung by a long-term survivor of the AIDS epidemic, "They Are Falling All Around Me" becomes what I elsewhere call a "musical plague palimpsest," or a preexisting song with no connection to HIV/AIDS that is given new meaning when filtered through the experiences of PWAs.[7] Michael used the song to pay tribute to those lost in the war against AIDS. In 1990, he wrote:

> I was diagnosed with AIDS before the term AIDS even existed. It's been nearly eight years since a doctor told me I had what was then known as GRID — Gay Related Immune Deficiency.
> According to the best estimate, of the 1,049 Americans diagnosed with AIDS during 1982, twenty-five are still alive.
> I am one of the lucky ones.[8]

---

6 Bernice Johnson Reagon, liner notes for the 1996 reissue of her 1975 album *Give Your Hands to Struggle*, 24–25.

7 Matthew J. Jones, *How to Make Music in an Epidemic: Popular Music-Making During the AIDS Pandemic, 1981–1996* (London: Routledge, forthcoming). I also discuss the uses of extant music in "Anglophone Songs about HIV/AIDS," in *The Oxford Handbook of Music and Queerness*, eds. Sheila Whiteley and Fred Maus (Oxford: Oxford University Press, 2018).

8 Michael Callen, *Surviving AIDS* (New York: Harper Perennial, 1990), 1.

That Michael was still alive in 1993 was more than luck. It was extraordinary, and he wanted to honor his fellow activists and PWAs who had not survivied.

"They Are Falling All Around Me" utilizes a variant of the traditional AAB blues form, adding a third iteration of the A material (thus the form is AAAB). Johnson's recording is in compound duple meter, but Michael and his friends shifted the meter to common time and added a simple organ part, played by John Bucchino. The five singers alternate solo sections, paired duets, and homophony, with each singer adding expressive flourishes and ornaments in individual and idiosyncratic ways. The result is a tapestry of musical personalities, woven by collective effort in the studio. In a sense, the arrangement harkened back to "Home," the final song on *Purple Heart*. But while "Home" had explored austere, almost Medieval polyphony, "They Are Falling All Around Me" is indebted to florid close-harmony traditions with roots in Black gospel.

Michael made subtle alterations to the lyrics of the last stanza, changing Bernice Johnson Reagon's future tense ("I will try to sing my song right. Be sure to let me hear from you") to the present perfect tense ("I *have tried* to sing my song right"). These lines stand as a summative assessment of Michael's activism, and in the context of the AIDS crisis, Michael's rapidly declining health, and his atheism, the final line, "Be sure to let me hear from you," is sweetly ironic. He seemed to be comforting his friends by letting them know that he would be listening to them from beyond the grave.

Archival video footage from the sessions (shot by Quentin Scobel) captures Michael and the other musicians working out details of the arrangement in the studio, singing one line at a time to perfect their individual parts.[9] Between takes, Cris Williamson and Holly Near crack jokes and engage in bits of friendly mischief as Michael sips from his ubiquitous can of Classic Coke. For Holly Near, that day was "full of love but not

---

9 Quentin Scobel, *Legacy* Recording Sessions, 25–27 June 1993, video recording, RDA.

LOVE DON'T NEED A REASON

Fig. 2. Legacy studio session (1993), l–r: Arnold McCuller, Michael Callen, Cris Williamson, Holly Near. Photo by Patrick Kelly. © Significant Other Records.

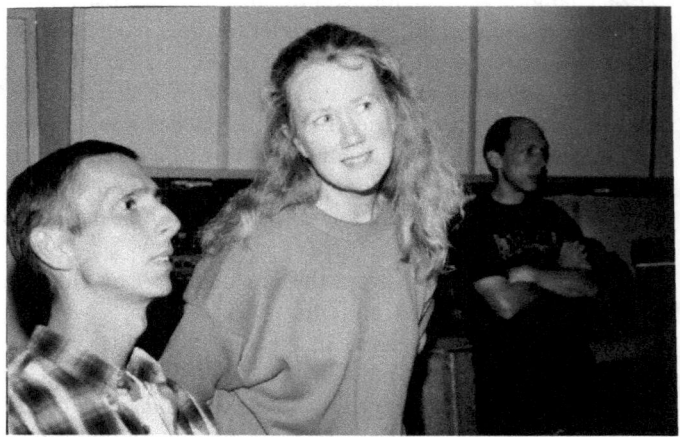

Fig. 3. Michael Callen, Holly Near, Richard Dworkin in the studio control room (1993). Photo by Patrick Kelly. © Significant Other Records.

Fig. 4. Cris Williamson in the studio (1993). Photo by Patrick Kelly.
© Significant Other Records.

lighthearted. Sometimes we made the room for very quiet moments. I was glad that everyone in the room knew how to hold the weight of the situation without falling prey to fear or nervous chatter."[10]

Michael recorded two other covers for these sessions. Originally released on Williamson's *Country Blessed* (1989), an album of country and folk tunes by Williamson and Teresa Trull, "Mother, Mother" is another musical plague palimpsest. The lyrics express intense longing for a maternal figure who will "come into my room at night and hold me in your arms." It is difficult not to hear this song in relation to "Nobody's Fool," Michael's ballad about his strained relationship with his father. In the first verse of "Nobody's Fool," however, Michael portrayed a

10 Holly Near, p.c., 30 October 2012.

sympathetic, though tentative, mother figure, caught between her husband and her child. A biographical reading of "Mother, Mother" continues the family saga. Now, the gay son is dying of AIDS and reaching out for his mother in the final moments of his life. "I was your one true miracle [...]. Keep me safe from harm."

The family theme continues with John Bucchino's touching ballad, "Do Not Turn Away."[11] Bucchino, whose brother died of AIDS-related illness, wrote the song about an experience his mother had at a support group meeting. As the composer explained in a 2009 interview:

> Well, my brother was dying [of AIDS] and my mom had gone to an AIDS support group with his partner, and after this meeting she called me in tears. She said there was this beautiful eighteen-year-old boy who got up and told the group that when he came out to his parents and told them that he had AIDS, they kicked him out of the house and wouldn't have anything to do with them. It just broke her heart; she couldn't imagine how parents could do that to a child. And that's what prompted me to write the song.[12]

Bucchino, who gained initial critical acclaim on the New York Cabaret circuit, has written hundreds of songs, done arrangements for numerous albums, written a musical, and is a longtime collaborator with Holly Near. He described Michael as "one of the realest people I ever met [...] an extraordinary human being, really powerful, really charismatic, and passionate and committed to gay rights and AIDS education... God, what an extraordinary fellow."[13]

Bucchino's lyrics beseech parents who might turn their backs on queer children or family members with AIDS to instead offer love and support. "Death is looming; hope is frail. Do not

---

11 My thanks to John Bucchino for providing me with a copy of the score for "Do Not Turn Away."
12 JD Doyle, interview with John Bucchino, *Queer Music Heritage*, April 2009, http://www.queermusicheritage.com/apr2009s.html.
13 Ibid.

Fig. 5. Chez Panisse, 1993, l–r: Patrick Kelly, John Bucchino, Quentin Scobel, Richard Dworkin, Michael Callen, Tret Fure, Cris Williamson. © Significant Other Records.

turn away." Together, he and Michael recorded an intimate performance of the piece with just piano and vocals, though there was some dispute over the actual performance. John wanted Michael's melodic line to follow in lock-step with the piano, which doubles the tune. However, Michael felt that singing *rubato* (or in and out of time with the accompaniment) heightened the song's impact. Ultimately, Michael's aesthetic sense won, and the version on *Legacy* is sung *molto rubato* to haunting effect.

Whether or not Michael intended "Mother, Mother" and "Do Not Turn Away" as testaments of his personal feelings, or meant to leave them as posthumous salve for wounds that would endure after he was gone, the two songs, along with the other music Michael recorded that day, left the entire crew emotionally spent. Patrick arranged a celebratory dinner at Alice Water's famed farm-to-table restaurant, Chez Panisse. A stretch limo charioted them to the restaurant where they laughed and reminisced over a locally sourced meal, decades before the farm-to-table craze became the norm. The meal capped off what Richard believes may have been "the best day in Michael Callen's life. He got to do what he loved at a very high level: to sing with incredible artists in an amazing studio and eat incredible food with people he cared deeply about."[14] On Sunday, Michael rode in the International Lesbian and Gay Freedom Day Parade alongside the lesbian women of Olivia (the pioneering record label that reformed as a lesbian travel company in 1988) — a fitting end to a fabulously queer weekend.

---

14 Richard Dworkin, interview with the author, 5 June 2017.

Fig. 1. Barry Callen and Michael Callen (c. 1993). Courtesy of Barry Callen.

17

On the Other Side

> *Don't pity me!*
> *I've played this game too long.*
> *Oh, I have loved,*
> *and I have lied.*
> *And I'm just trying to reach you*
> *on the other side.*
> — Michael Callen & Robert Butler

In July 1993, Michael returned to his squalid apartment in Los Angeles and decided he needed a change. He asked Doug to move his "dying bag of bones" into West Hollywood, the gay ghetto of Los Angeles.[1] Patrick flew out to help Michael look for apartments, and the two hatched a plan to finally get Richard to leave New York. If Patrick quit his job and cashed in more of his life insurance, they could afford a place in Los Angeles that was big enough for all three of them. If Michael and Patrick signed the lease, Richard would have to move, and they were right. Richard, who continued to marvel at their loving friendship, would have gone to California to be with them, no questions, no protestations. However, Patrick had to return to New York before they could decide on a suitable apartment. So, Doug

---

1 Douglas Sadownick, "Doug Sadownick's Response to Karen O. (Section 2)," *Gay Psyche Politics*, 24 April 2010 http://gaypsychepolitics.blogspot.com/2010/04/douglas-sadownicks-response-to-karen.html.

orchestrated a herculean move to a beautiful two-bedroom apartment at 1274 N Crescent Heights Boulevard in West Hollywood, just a few blocks from Karen Ocamb. The apartment was covered by Section 8 subsidies for people with disabilities, including HIV/AIDS, in both Los Angeles County and the City of West Hollywood.

From New York, Patrick, who loved bright colors, helped Michael pick a sunny yellow paint for his living room and a dark purple for the bedroom study. Richard remembered the apartment as "very *Death in Venice*. You could look from the balcony and see boys slathered in suntan oil poolside with massive erections stretching the elastic of their speedos. I know that was Mike's reason for moving there!"[2] However, what really caught Richard's attention was the building's manager's sensitivity to the needs of PWAs. Michael was in near constant pain and discomfort. "From his groin down, [Michael] had become covered in leathery purple KS lesions, especially his legs, where hardly an ounce of untainted skin remained, and [his right leg] was rife with edema and necrotic tissue, now in the process of falling off."[3] As a result, he needed a wheelchair most of the time, so the building manager installed a ramp to make the building more accessible. Unfortunately, wall-to-wall carpet inside the apartment made maneuvering a wheelchair impossible, and Michael ended up dragging himself across the floor much of the time. Ever the campy wit, Michael distracted his friends from the horrible things happening to his body and the unexpected discomforts in his new home with gallows humor, likening his foot to a salted Christmas pig.

Richard divided his time between New York and Los Angeles, spending as much time with both Patrick and Michael as each man's condition demanded. Meanwhile, Doug organized a group of gay men and lesbians that included Matt Silverstein,

2 Richard Dworkin, interview with the author, 5 June 2017 (henceforth, RD and MJ [2017]).
3 Douglas Sadownick, "Surviving Life: An Interview with AIDS Diva Michael Callen," *Frontiers*, n.d. (but likely early 1994 after Michael's death), Cliff Townsend scrapbooks.

Karen Ocamb, Shawn Eric Brooks, and nurses Mike Hill, Lisa Marks, and Marisue Davidson. They would care for Michael in shifts, attending to his daily needs at home, running errands, and driving him to appointments. Michael held what he called "huddles" with his caregivers during which he

> would teach [them] how to shop for imported virgin olive oil, how to file like a legal secretary, how to be patient enough with incompetent medical personnel so as to squeeze the deplorable system for enough saline solution to last a week, how to write about the HIV hoax and the 'second sexual revolution,' and how to survive the soul-sucking condemnation from the community for airing its dirty laundry. But the one great lesson that sticks most in [Doug's] mind is Mike's effort to teach [him] how to talk, one gay man to another, about each other, to teach other.[4]

Although this kind of process-talk is a quintessentially "California" thing, such conversations were important to their deepening friendship. Their talks lasted for hours, and when mealtime rolled around, Michael "barked orders at [Doug,] his clumsy sous-chef."[5] From his wheelchair or a reclining position on the floor, Michael used his "Martha Stewart panache at orchestrating elaborate, seven-course Marcella Hazan-influenced 'Italian Kitchen' meals in his [apartment] to feed hungry and depleted gay activists in search of warm, maternal kindness."[6]

Even in such moments when he was surrounded by friends, Michael's old demons resurfaced, and he was occasionally mistrustful of Doug's motives. Propped up in his king-size bed, Michael would cock his head to one side and inquire, "What's a nice, eligible, married, non-monogamous man like yourself doing with a bag of bones on a Saturday night when you could be getting your brains fucked out?" Doug never really came up

---

4   Sadownick, "Doug Sadownick's Response to Karen O."
5   Ibid.
6   Ibid.

with an answer. At times, however, and by his own admission, Doug could be "aggressively bullying to Michael," particularly about his "perpetual mismanagement of funds and his almost-obsessive need to make elaborate meals for everybody, even though eventually he could barely stomach a spoonful without vomiting."[7] Fiercely independent, Michael was bothered by the helplessness that AIDS introduced into his life, and he would sometimes respond with hurt feelings. However, the West Coast way of processing he developed with Doug allowed the friends to weather such storms. "When you tell me that I have to stop cooking," Michael explained, "I get the feeling that you are my father, even though I know you are not. Or when you are late to see me, I get angry and upset, but then I realize that you are as fucked up as I am, and thus you resent me in ways, and then I forgive you. [...] You are the producer. And I'm the diva. And the grand finale is death."[8]

As he prepared for his own grand finale, Michael seemed to become even more outlandish, more thoroughly himself. KS had rendered his right leg useless, but he refused to hide it. Around this time, Holly Near witnessed this first-hand over lunch with Michael at a café. She remembered that "Michael was wearing shorts, his lesions proudly showing. He was ready to walk anyone through a consciousness raiser on the spot," and Holly "loved him for that bravery."[9] In more private moments, Michael yearned for touch and intimacy. He also needed medical, therapeutic massage, so members of his care team would massage his legs to provide relief as well as a sense of loving closeness.

In early July, Michael returned to Hamilton for a reunion with his friends from Warr Court. He spent the weekend reliving old times with friends and family. After the reunion, various members of the Warr Court gang sent letters to Michael. Some were amazed at the transformation in him since high school.

---

7   Ibid.
8   Sadownick, "Surviving Life."
9   Holly Near, p.c., 30 October 2012.

Fig. 2. Warr Court Reunion, 1993. Courtesy of Barry Callen.

He seemed "more self-confident and interesting [...] so free."[10] Others were shocked at Michael's candor about things that happened to him in Hamilton, including the physical abuse he had kept hidden for years. Michael was especially thrilled that another Warr Court kid had come out as a lesbian and was expecting a child with her lover.[11] The majority of the letters Michael received before and after the reunion were full of warm sentiments, friendship, admiration, and well-wishes for his health and recovery. One member of the Warr Court gang, however, condemned Michael. In December, she sent him a Christmas card and a pamphlet from the First Baptist Church of Milford, OH. "I know you think you know more than I do," she wrote.

---

10 Gigi, letter to Michael Callen, n.d., handwritten original, The Michael Callen Papers at The LGBT Community Center National History Archive (henceforth, MCP).
11 Michael Callen, letter to Andrea Ennis-Huff, 24 March 1993, typewritten original, MCP.

"But Mike, your only hope is Christ. I wish you could come to know the Christ of Christmas. He came to love you."[12]

In late August, Michael returned to New York for what would be his final recording sessions. When he arrived in the city, Michael checked into a hotel but had a horrible night. He was sick and uncomfortable, so Patrick came to the rescue, again using some of his viatical payment to book a room at The Plaza. Patrick and Richard made sure Michael was comfortable and left him to sleep for the night. The next day, they moved Michael to the more affordable Marriott Marquis, from where he could also catch a shuttle to the airport for his return to Los Angeles.

Working at Sear Sound over the next few days, Michael recorded several takes of Canadian New Wave band Rough Trade's campy BDSM-themed "Grade B Movie" (1980), obscure singer-songwriter Judy Mayhan's "See Here" (1971), and "Two Men Dance the Tango," the campy same-sex duet rejected by The Flirtations earlier that year. Michael wanted to record it as a duet with Richard, but Richard resisted, insisting that he was not a capable enough singer. Nevertheless, Michael recorded a lead vocal and a soprano harmony, and Richard reluctantly agreed to record a preliminary vocal for the duet, listening to Michael's guide vocal to aid his singing. However, he was sure he could find a better singer and kept searching. Richard also tried to get Michael to finish "Victim of Circumstance," an unfinished song Michael had started in the 1980s and that they jokingly referred to as "Victim of Circumcision." Michael was uninterested in completing the song, which he felt portrayed gay men in a negative, self-hating way. "Fuck this," he said. "I didn't live my life this way."[13]

Michael also recorded two Elton John songs from *Madman across the Water* (1971), "Indian Sunset" and "Goodbye."[14] The

---

12 Karen, letter to Michael Callen, n.d., handwritten original, MCP. This letter was enclosed in a Christmas card, so Karen likely sent it in December.
13 Richard Dworkin, interview with author, 15 July 2020 (henceforth RD and MJ [2020]).
14 "Indian Sunset" remains unreleased, and I am grateful for Richard Dworkin's generosity in sharing the unreleased recording with me.

first, which remains unreleased, had been part of Michael's repertoire in the 1980s, when it was "the showstopper of [his] shows."[15] It's an interesting piece of English Americana in which lyricist Bernie Taupin imagines conflicts between Indigenous and white Americans. Inspired by a visit to a reservation, Taupin's impressionistic lyrics contain a mélange of references to the different cultures and nations that make up the Great Plains Indians, and they play a little fast and loose with historical fact.[16] In the final section, Taupin's protagonist recounts that he "heard from passing renegades [that] Geronimo was dead / He'd been laying down his weapons when they filled him full of lead." In truth, Geronimo (1829–1909) lived into old age and even became something of a celebrity, but the mythopoetic invocation of Geronimo strengthens the resolve of the song's speaker-protagonist-warrior — an apt metaphor for Michael's own relationship to the war against HIV/AIDS. Paul Buckmaster's arrangement on *Madman across the Water* gives the song a cinematic scope and grandiosity, but Michael wanted to create something very different. He retained the original opening a cappella introduction but otherwise kept the rest of the instrumentation sparse, just Richard on talking drum and other percussion and Steve Sandberg on piano. Their minimal approach draws greater attention to the sentiment at the heart of the song: a warrior facing his final battle, knowing it may end in his death. As with his earlier cover of Elton John's "Talkin' Old Soldiers," Michael found a new resonance in a song that pre-dated the AIDS crisis and that used images of combat and warfare. Lines like "Now there seems no reason why I should carry on" and "I think it's time I strung my bow and ceased my senseless running" assume a new poignancy when sung by a veteran of the fight against AIDS, near the end of his life. Michael outdid himself by reaching to the bottom of his KS-covered lungs and belting the final

---

15 Michael Callen, letter to Steve Sandberg, 19 April 1993, typewritten original, MCP.
16 Elizabeth Rosenthal, *His Song: The Musical Journey of Elton John* (New York: Billboard Books, 2001), 34.

note for thirty-two seconds, bringing the performance to a powerful and defiant close.

"Goodbye" had also long been in Michael's repertoire, and he "knew it cold."[17] He quickly laid down several excellent takes from which Richard was sure they could assemble a final version for the album. However, Michael continued to sing it again and again. "Everyone was devastated by the time he was done, but who could tell him no?"[18] His weight had dropped below 130 pounds, so Michael's physical condition echoed the song's closing refrain, "I'll waste away. I'll waste away." Sensing that he would likely die before the end of the year, Michael was singing farewell to his friends, family, fans, and to the life he had lived so fearlessly.

After the sessions wrapped up, Richard and Patrick took Michael back to the Marriott Marquis Hotel to catch an airport shuttle. It was a scorching August day in New York, but Michael, sick and exhausted, sat down on the sidewalk outside the hotel. "He was just like that," Richard remembered. "He would make himself comfortable anywhere."[19] Richard later chastised himself for not arranging a limo or at least hailing calling a cab, because those turned out to be Michael's last moments in New York, sitting on the pavement on a sweltering summer day, waiting for a shuttle.

In September, Michael was admitted to Midway Hospital to have his gallbladder removed, and from that point on, he was in the hospital most of the time. In his West Hollywood apartment, moving boxes were still piled on the floor, unopened. Richard, Patrick, Doug, and other friends decided to unpack Michael's things so that the apartment would be ready for him when, or if, he was released from Midway. Michael needed three phone lines, two for calls and one for a fax, and Doug had contact information for a gay phone man. When the phone technician showed up, in his overalls and work boots with fifty feet of cable

---

17 Richard Dworkin, interview with the author, New York, September 2012.
18 RD and MJ (2017).
19 RD and MJ (2020).

strapped to his tool belt, he proved irresistible to Doug and Matt Silverstein. Richard found them in a state of undress, making out in a bedroom and quietly left them to their erotic explorations, thinking, "At least somebody got laid in that apartment while Michael held the lease!"[20]

As his KS worsened, Michael's doctors considered amputating his leg in order to save him from gangrene or other infections. Knowing that Michael was going to die, possibly before the end of the year, Richard devised a system whereby Michael could effectively mix his own vocals for the album. He brought a portable DAT machine to the hospital and let Michael listen to all the different vocal tracks, rating them, line-by-line. Richard would return to a nearby studio with Michael's notes, create a mix, then bring the results back for Michael to hear. It was a slow process, but it meant that Michael could stamp his seal of approval on as much of the album as possible.

Working on *Legacy* kept Michael focused, though his thoughts sometimes turned to death and dying. Again, he discussed plans for a suicide party with Patrick, arranging a schedule of visitors in his final weeks. Because Patrick was a psychiatric nurse and familiar with the psychological profile of suicidal patients, he took Michael's plans as little more than macabre camp and played along as Michael abstractly planned the party. Unbeknownst to Patrick and Richard, Michael had also discussed plans for an assisted suicide with other friends. One afternoon, Karen Ocamb was driving Michael to or from a medical appointment. From the passenger side of Karen's car, Michael asked, "When it's time, will you help me die?" After some moments, she put her hand on his forearm and said, "Of course."[21] However, Michael had also written to a friend who threatened suicide in February that "I'm dying for real, and I have NO patience for people wanting to prematurely end their

---

20 RD and MJ (2020).
21 Karen Ocamb, interview with the author, 17 May 2020.

lives."²² He had always tried to resist the propaganda of hopelessness, but now that his own life was on the line, Michael was determined to die on his own terms, even if that meant suicide.

Although his own condition was quickly deteriorating, Michael was more concerned about Patrick. In 1992, he had developed KS on his pale Irish skin, mottling his arms and his penis, and throughout the summer of 1993, Patrick developed a persistent cough. Michael recognized it immediately. "Richard, do you not hear that cough, that dry cough? I've heard this before. I've been around AIDS. Patrick either has pneumonia or PCP, or both."²³ During a routine temperature check, the nurse found that Michael's persistent fever had, for the moment, subsided. Patrick asked the nurse to check his temperature, and when she did, it was 101. She just stood there for a moment, looking back and forth at Michael and Patrick. Unsure what to do, she left the room. Soon thereafter, Patrick returned to New York to finalize plans for the scuba Caribbean scuba trip with Diving for Life.

Barbara Callen wrote to her son in October, sending "positive thoughts about [his] physical wellbeing" and expressing her admiration at her son's friends who were "beating a path to [Michael's] door to see [him] and help [him] out if they can. That must be a very rewarding feeling to know that they care so much. You've really earned their love and respect."²⁴ Likewise, Michael's old high school friend Terry Tincher sent his love via Michael's mother, offering to help finance *Legacy* and to express his "concern that none of [Michael's] writing will be lost or destroyed."²⁵

In October, Michael was able to spend a few days at his apartment, where he and Doug had "one of [their] last grand talks [...] on Halloween night."²⁶ The topic was one of Michael's fa-

---

22 Michael Callen, letter to Anthony Roberts, 16 February 1993, typewritten original, MCP.
23 RD and MJ (2020).
24 Barbara Callen, letter to Michael Callen, n.d. (but likely early November), 1993, handwritten original, MCP.
25 Ibid.
26 Sadownick, "Surviving Life."

Fig. 3. Cliff Callen, Michael Callen, Barbara Callen, 1993. Courtesy of Barry Callen.

vorites: gay men and spirituality. Specifically, they discussed the eternal existential question of life after death. "Worms eat you," Michael pronounced, adding that he wanted to be cremated. "I want to fertilize a fruit tree. I was a tart in life, and I want to be a tart in death. Preferably cherry, since I lost mine so many times."[27] As the sun set, Halloween revelers took to the streets, and Michael encouraged Doug and Matt Silverstein to "don elaborate Cher and Streisand drag" and join the festivities, insisting that it would be an exercise in fun and empathy.[28] "You cannot begin to understand oppression if you haven't begun to understand what it's like to be a woman," he explained as he painted their nails and gave them tips on walking in heels.[29] Shooing his friends out of his apartment, Michael called out, "If you have the good fortune to get laid tonight, shoot one for me. You've worked hard enough. There's nothing wrong, my dears,

27 Sadownick, "Surviving Life."
28 Ibid.
29 Ibid.

with feeling good about yourselves."[30] Then he dragged himself across the floor, alone, to bed.

A few days later, Doug found Michael in a deep depression and attempted to lift his spirits "by providing him with some festive drag: a pair of baseball sliding pants and other kinds of body padding. [...] a fluorescent baseball, a pink baseball T-shirt, and a blue Florida Marlins cap. The metaphor worked, at least for [Doug]. This diva was nothing if not a good sport."[31] Unpacking his gifts, Michael "pursed his lips and muttered: 'Baseball. I detest baseball.'"[32] However, the next day, Doug arrived to find Michael modeling his new outfit. A nurse asked, "Isn't he cute?" to which Michael replied, "I've been many things, my dear. Cute is not one of them"[33]

---

30 Ibid.
31 Ibid.
32 Ibid.
33 Ibid.

Fig. 1. Patrick Kelly and Michael Callen at a Night of a Thousand Gowns (1993). Richard Dworkin Private Archive.

18

Goodbye

For I am a mirror.
I can reflect the moon.
I will write songs for you.
I'll be your silver spoon.
I'm sorry I took your time.
I am the poem that doesn't rhyme.
Just turn back the page,
I'll waste away
— Elton John & Bernie Taupin

Richard didn't think he should go to Europe, but Patrick and Michael insisted that the quick tour over Thanksgiving would give him a much needed reprieve. Patrick was feverishly preparing for his AIDS benefit scuba trip in the Caribbean with Diving for Life which he'd organized. He'd even bought a blue diving suit to wear, but he was hospitalized for pneumonia, which threw his plans into chaotic uncertainty. Ultimately, he would not be able to attend. Still, with the blessing of both Michael and Patrick, Richard left for Prague, where he was frustrated to discover that his hotel didn't have phones in the rooms. From the lobby, he called Cabrini Medical Center and spoke with Patrick, who was still despondent about missing the Diving for Life event. To cheer him up, participants promised to send pictures, souvenirs, and other mementos of the trip. Then Richard called Los Angeles. Michael was at home, anemic, unable to walk, and yet entertaining Doug Sadownick and Judy Peabody, who were following his meticulous directions to make gnocchi.

Though his love for Michael gave him "delightful, confirmatory feelings of warmth, affection, and inspiration," Doug had recently started to feel "completely overworked, over-burdened, frightened, lonely" and even a little bored; frankly, he wanted life back.[1] When an opportunity to write a piece on AIDS Project LA arose, he abdicated as much responsibility for Michael's care as possible to the other members of the caregiving team.[2]

Tensions had begun to mount among Michael's caregivers, the result of emotional stress, burnout, and especially ideological differences surrounding Michael's plans to say goodbye to his biological family. To Doug and Tim Miller, Michael had expressed an explicit desire "to die as gay as possible! sans the parents!" However, Karen Ocamb felt that Michael and his biological family yearned for peace, that in spite of the impasse of their complicated, homophobic religious beliefs and the long history of conflict over Michael's sexuality, Cliff and Barbara were grieving his imminent death.

Ever the stage manager and control queen, even on his sickbed, Michael arranged for his family to visit so that "they [c]ould all say their goodbyes when [he] was still relatively strong."[3] He asked Doug to be in the room to bear witness, and Karen was present for some of their visit. Michael "lay in his hospital bed […] as his parents — with masks over their faces as they had been instructed — took his hand and tried to be soothing. But no one knew what to say."[4] Cliff and Barbara defaulted to Midwestern politesse. Gradually, Barbara warmed to Michael's friends, whose loving kindness toward her son touched her deeply. However, Michael's father "remained physically cold,

1 Doug Sadownick, "Doug Sadownick's Response to Karen O. (Section 2)," *Gay Politics 24* April 2010, and Doug Sadownick "Surviving Life: An Interview with Michael Callen," *Frontiers*, n.d. (but likely early 1994 after Michael's death).
2 Sadownick, "Surviving Life."
3 Sadownick, "Doug Sadownick's Response to Karen O."
4 Karen Ocamb, "My Remembrance of Michael Callen," p.c., 2009.

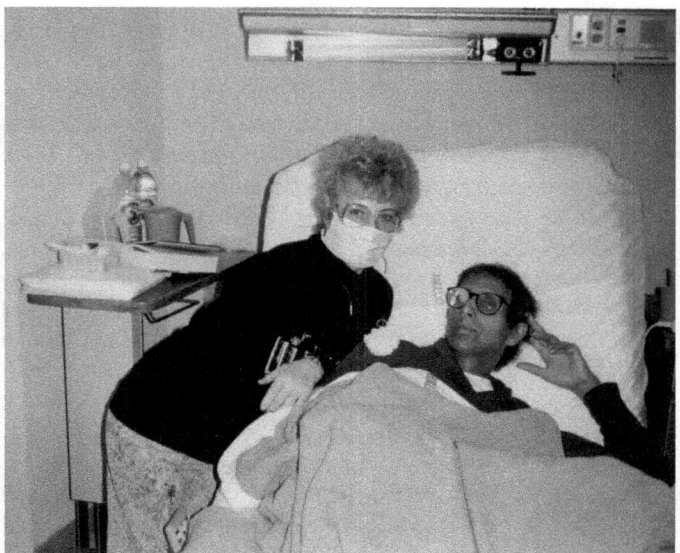

Fig. 2. Barbara Callen and Michael Callen at Midway Hospital (1993). Courtesy of Karen Ocamb.

aloof, and downcast. [...] no doubt in terrible pain to watch his son die, but he tried to hide it. He could not open up enough to accept Michael being a decent human being as a gay man [...]. It appeared like he was fighting back tears a lot."[5] Eventually, Michael gathered his strength and asked his parents a direct question. "Can you love me unconditionally despite the fact that I'm gay?" Barbara answered, "Yes," but Cliff "could only put his head on Michael's sunken-in chest and silently cry."[6] Michael just "patted the man's head and called for peace."[7] Afterward, Doug took the family out to dinner, and the old rigidities remained. Although he found Cliff to be "more human without [Michael] present," it was clear that Cliff was still struggling to

---

5   Sadownick, "Doug Sadownick's Response to Karen O."
6   Ibid.
7   Ibid.

accept his gay son, and now to accept his gay son's death from AIDS.[8] However, as Doug had understood Michael's wishes, this was to be Michael's final goodbye to his family. If his father remained stubborn in his moral opposition to homosexuality, Michael was prepared to die with that tension unresolved. There would be no last-minute deathbed reconciliation.

When Richard returned to New York at the end of November, Patrick's condition had not improved. By 30 November 1993, Patrick couldn't get out of bed, and he was coughing violently around the clock. After spending several hours trying to cheer up his lover by performing goofy tricks with his wheelchair in the hospital room, Richard said goodnight and returned to their apartment to try to sleep. It was too much. Michael and Patrick were both ailing, and he was powerless to do anything about it. He might well lose them both before the end of the year.

Michael, too, was worried about Patrick and about the impact of a double loss on Richard's well-being and emotional health. Richard "doesn't have a lot of friends, and he doesn't make friends easily," Michael knew from their decade together.[9] He worried that his lover would be lonely. Over the phone, Michael assured Richard that he would return to New York to help care for Patrick; "a clear impossibility," Richard knew, "but an accurate gauge of Mike's tendency to worry about others over even himself in extremis."[10] The sentiment moved Richard profoundly.

As November gave way to December, Michael "was taking over seventy pills a day; his skin was orange. He looked like a Buchenwald survivor. He was in true agony, but he wouldn't die."[11] In a moment of desperation, he called Barry to ask his brother to help him commit suicide. "He had planned out how to do it, and in the end, I agreed to help him," Barry told me, "even though it made me feel like a murderer."[12]

8   Ibid.
9   Quoted in Martin Duberman, *Hold Tight Gently: Michael Callen, Essex Hemphill, and the Battlefield of AIDS* (New York: The New Press, 2014), 286.
10 Ibid., 287.
11 Barry Wayne Callen, interview with the author, 21 September 2013.
12 Ibid.

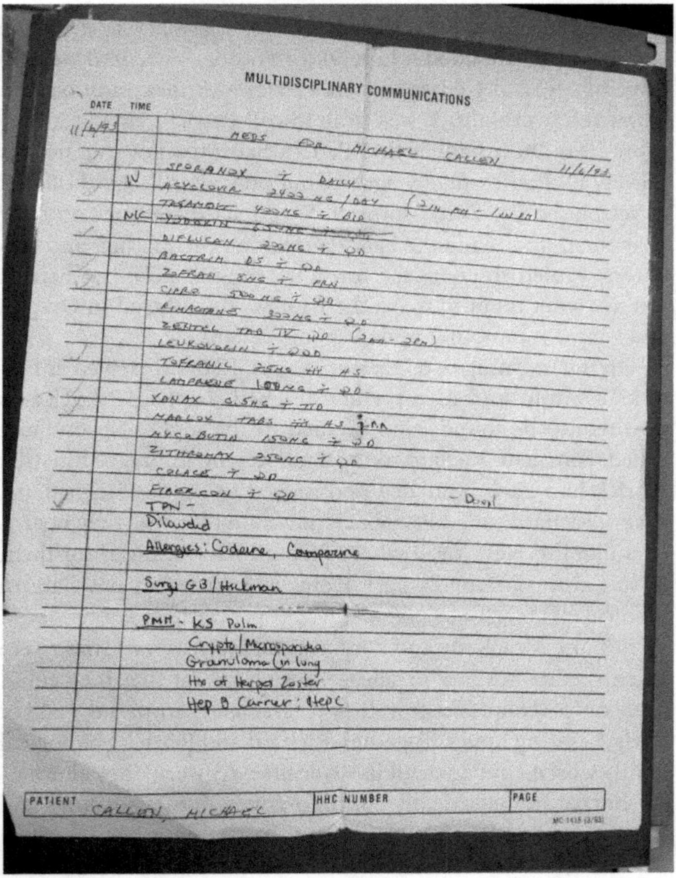

MULTIDISCIPLINARY COMMUNICATIONS

DATE TIME

11/6/93

MEDS FOR MICHAEL CALLEN 11/6/93

SPORANOX DAILY

IV ACYCLOVIR

DIFLUCAN QD

BACTRIM DS QD

ZOFRAN 8MG PRN

CIPRO 500MG QD

ZERITOL TAB IV QD

LEUKOVORIN QOD

TOFRANIL 25MG HS

LAMPRENE 100MG QD

XANAX 0.5MG TID

MAALOX TABS HS PRN

MYCOBUTIN 150MG QD

ZITHROMAX 250MG QD

COLACE QD

TPN -

Dilaudid

Allergies: Codeine, Compazine

Surg: GB/Hickman

PMH - KS Pulm

Crypto/Microsporidia

Granuloma (in lung

Hx of Herpes Zoster

Hep B Carrier; Hep C

PATIENT CALLEN, MICHAEL

HHC NUMBER

PAGE

Fig. 3. Michael's Medication List, November 1993. Richard Dworkin Private Archive.

On 1 December 1993, World AIDS Day, Richard woke in the late morning, attended a funeral for another PWA, and went to Cabrini Medical Center to visit Patrick, whose condition had worsened overnight. It was time to call Patrick's family in Oregon, who knew neither that Patrick had AIDS nor that he was gravely ill. Patrick finally agreed, but only after Richard offered to telephone the Kellys himself. So, Richard returned to their apartment and made the call. Patrick's mother, father, and two sisters wanted to come to New York immediately, but Patrick did not want them to make the trip. So, they stayed in Oregon and waited for another update from Richard.

On the morning of 6 December 1993, Richard arrived at Patrick's room to find it empty and the bed stripped. Patrick was nowhere to be found. Had he died in the night? No one had called. Panicked, Richard found a nurse, who informed him that Patrick had been intubated and moved to the ICU downstairs. Again, Richard called Patrick's family, and this time they boarded a flight to New York, where Richard had arranged for them to stay at the Gramercy Park Hotel, a short walk from Cabrini Medical Center.

Because Mrs. Kelly and her daughters were nurses, they were given special hospital privileges, which meant that they could more or less come and go as they pleased and stay past the end of official visiting hours. Together, Richard and Patrick's biological family worked out a schedule. Over the next week, they alternated shifts at his bedside, the family arriving in the mornings and Richard staying late into the night. They held his hands, talked with him, and administered yoga-style stretches and massages to his legs, which Patrick loved. Richard lovingly joked that because Patrick's legs were well developed from years of dancing and diving, "it was a lot of leg to move around!"[13] Richard had no idea how to communicate with Patrick, who was in a state of semi-consciousness from the sedation administered to insert the ventilator. The Kellys, however, knew to ask yes or no ques-

---

13 Richard Dworkin, interview with author, 15 July 2020 (henceforth, RD and MJ [2020]).

Fig. 4. Patrick Kelly Memorial Bulletin. Courtesy of the New York City National LGBTQ History Archives.

tions so that Patrick could blink once to indicate an affirmative response and twice for a negative response. It was rudimentary, but it was better than not being able to communicate at all.

Richard had medical power of attorney for Patrick, and the Kelly family respected Patrick's wishes, deferring to Richard to speak with doctors about treatment options. On Friday, 10 December 1993, the doctors urged Richard to consider turning off life support. Richard consulted with the Kelly family, and they agreed. Later that day, the nurses unplugged the machines that were keeping Patrick alive. Surrounded by his loving family and partner, Patrick Kelly died, at the age of forty.[14]

Together, Richard and the Kellys sat in a small grief room and spoke with hospital staff. Patrick's body was eventually taken to Redden's Funeral Home (325 W 14th St.). Richard and Joe, Patrick's father who was handling the arrangements at Redden's, decided to bury him in the new scuba suit he had purchased to wear with Diving For Life. Patrick's family shipped his body to Oregon, where they quickly held a funeral service. Richard didn't attend that, but flew to Portland a few days before Christmas for a memorial gathering. He was welcomed warmly and treated "as much as a part of their family as you could possibly imagine."[15] Together, they laughed, cried, looked at family photos, and watched home movies. Joe Kelly took Richard to the cemetery to visit Patrick's gravesite, which still lacked a headstone. "What should we put on it?" he asked Richard. Eventually, they decided on a pair of ballet slippers and something scuba related. Before Richard's departure, the Kellys gave him several mementos of Patrick, and as he left, Patrick's young nephews even called him "Uncle Richard."

On 22 December 1993, Richard flew from Oregon to Los Angeles. Michael had taken a turn for the worse and was again in the hospital. Richard arrived in the late evening, and after sleeping for a few hours, he drove to Midway Hospital the next morning. When he arrived, Michael was oscillating between wanting to stay in the hospital, where he would wait to die, and wanting to return to his apartment. "Maybe we'll have a few good months together," he pleaded to Richard, who could only give in

---

14 "Patrick Kelly, Dancer and Writer, Dies at 40," *New York Times*, 13 December 1993, https://www.nytimes.com/1993/12/13/obituaries/patrick-kelly-dancer-and-writer-dies-at-40.html.

15 RD and MJ (2020).

to whatever Michael thought he needed, even if it shifted moment to moment.[16] In the end, Michael determined to go home.

Checking out of the hospital took several hours. Doctors consulted with Richard about every aspect of Michael's care and ensured that they had all of Michael's necessary medications and medical supplies. Eventually, they arrived at the apartment, and Richard did his best to make Michael comfortable. Michael tossed and turned through the evening, unable to rest or to swallow a few sips of Ensure without vomiting. Around 3 am, he admitted defeat and asked Richard to take him back to Midway. Richard tried to convince him to wait until morning, but Michael was adamant. He was ready to die but wanted to do so comfortably, in the hospital where the nurses who knew him so well could administer Demerol or morphine. Then, he could at least sleep in a quiet ward. So, Richard re-dressed Michael, got him into his wheelchair, and took him down to the car. They returned to Midway but because they had been gone so for many hours, they had to begin the arduous process of checking into the hospital.

On Christmas Eve Day, Michael had stabilized enough to talk though some of his end-of-life plans with Richard. First, he had been working on a new version of his will. Although he had few truly valuable possessions, Michael cared about so many people and wanted to leave them a memento of their friendship. He bequeathed some of his books, porn, and sex toys to various gay friends; gave kitchen odds and ends to people he thought would appreciate them; and appointed Richard as the executor of his will, leaving him in control of Michael's personal papers and his music. As they worked through the list of forty or fifty beneficiaries, Michael's stamina and focus gave out. Exhausted, he could not deal with the minutiae of the task and told Richard to decide how to distribute the rest of his belongings.

Throughout the day, Michael faded in and out of consciousness. Because Michael had been adamant about revising his will, the lawyer advised Richard not to allow the nurses to administer

---

16 Ibid.

narcotic painkillers until the papers were signed. As his pain crested and fell, Michael and Richard had their last real conversations. Michael still wanted Richard to sing the duet vocal on "Two Men Dance the Tango," but Richard deftly dodged doing so by suggesting gay singer Tom Robinson (perhaps best known for "Glad to Be Gay" [1978]) as a suitable alternative. Michael quietly agreed. They reminisced about their eleven year romantic and musical history and talked over Michael's wishes for a funeral service. Did he want a memorial in Los Angeles or New York, or possibly both? Who should speak, who should sing sing, and what other music should be played? And they debated whether who to call and tell that Michael was dying. Before falling into a deep slumber, Michael looked at Richard and said, "No regrets."

A lawyer from AIDS Project Los Angeles arrived around 5 pm to begin the paperwork for Michael's will. Once the document was in order, the lawyer agreed to return the next day to finalize things. Since he could not get a notary on Christmas Day, the lawyer advised Richard to gather as many people as possible to witness Michael's signature.

On Christmas Day, Richard returned to the hospital where groups of "Santa's little AIDS helpers were trying to bring cheer" to patients in the AIDS ward.[17] As friends arrived to witness Michael's will, Richard gently woke Michael, who looked around and acknowledged everyone by name. He then held court from his hospital bed. Leafing through the pages of his notebook, Michael announced, "Andy, I have a date for you!" Richard's heterosexual brother, Andy, had lived in LA for about twenty years and had helped Michael settle into the city when he first arrived. Now, Michael would pay him back by playing yenta one last time. Eventually, he found the contact information for someone he had met at the hospital. "Oh, this woman is so nice, and she's a social worker!" Everyone cracked up because Richard and Andy's mother was a social worker, too, and because Michael was using what he expected and actually hoped to be his last

---

17 RD and MJ (2020).

lucid moments to set Andy up. Michael insisted that Andy call her, and he promised Michael that he would.

Later that afternoon, Richard turned the television in Michael's room to a football game. To his surprise, Michael did not protest. Michael loathed sports and would normally complain until Richard changed the channel. At some point during the day, Karen returned to the hospital, and Richard stepped out to stretch his legs and walk around the building. Upon his return, Richard overheard her talking to Michael about "going toward the light." As Richard had understood his lover's wishes, Michael wanted no religion or spirituality at the end of his life. Richard was disgruntled, but since Michael was too weak to express an opinion either way, he let it go.

The lawyer returned in the early afternoon, and once the papers were signed, Richard asked the nurses to delay giving him the medication until he and the lawyer privately for a few minutes. Richard escorted him out of the room and thanked him profusely for working on Christmas Eve and Christmas Day, a kindness that touched Richard deeply. When he returned to Michael's room, the nurses had already given Michael his first dose of Demerol. From that point on, Michael was "more or less beyond coherent speech."[18]

Throughout the night, Michael slept. With IV fluids keeping him hydrated, doctors could only guess how long he might linger. Richard and Michael's friends could only wait and see what happened.

The day after Christmas, Michael's parents called the hospital for an update. Karen, who had answered their call, told them that Michael had taken a turn for the worse.[19] Barry bought a ticket to LA, determined to see his kid brother once more before he died and to represent Michael's biological family. Karen of-

---

18 Ibid.
19 The chronology here is somewhat unclear. In different interviews, articles, and other conversations, respondents give contradictory dates. Some people recall the confrontation with Karen Ocamb happening on 25 December, two days before Michael died.

fered to put the telephone next to Michael's ear so that his parents could say goodbye. As she explained,

> First, his father told him he loved him and was proud of him. "I love you, son," his father said. And then it was his mother's turn. She talked to him a while, promising to bury his ashes under his favorite apple tree in their backyard. And then she said, "I love you, Michael. I will always love you." Mike said, "I love you, too."[20]

When Richard and Doug returned to the hospital, Karen explained what had transpired. They were furious. Michael had already said his last goodbyes to his parents and wanted no possibility for a last minute, guilt-induced reconciliation. Karen had, in their opinion, blatantly disregarded his expressed wishes, and the terrible argument between Doug and Karen that followed irrevocably changed their relationship.

Throughout the next day, there was a flurry of activity in Michael's room as nurses tried to keep him comfortable. At some point, they had inserted a catheter since Michael could no longer get out of bed, and amidst their coming and going, Richard spied an intravenous bag of clear liquid left behind in the room. Demerol or morphine, he surmised, and wondered if the staff had left it in the room accidentally-on-purpose so that Mike's friends could carry out his suicide plan. Richard called for the nurse to take it away.

One of Michael's dear friends from New York, Jeff Richardson, who was now the executive director of GMHC, had arrived to say a final goodbye to his comrade in the war against AIDS. As the organization's first executive director who was out about his HIV status, Richardson's appointment to the GMHC board was a major victory for PWAs and a point of pride and celebration for

---

20 Karen Ocamb, "Who's History? My Curious Encounter with Radical Faeries," *The Bilerico Project*, 20 February 2009, http://bilerico.lgbtqnation.com/2009/02/whos_history_my_curious_encounter_with_t.php. Ocamb also repeated this story to me in an interview on 17 May 2020.

the two friends. Jeff and Richard sat on either side of Michael's hospital bed and spoke lovingly with him, even though he was unresponsive. Barry was due to land at LAX in a few hours, though he would not make it in time to say goodbye.

With Michael sleeping comfortably with Jeff at his side, Richard decided to go across the street to the Westside Jewish Community Center for a quick swim. When he returned, Michael was again restless. His nurses changed his sheets, cleaned him up, and tucked him into bed. As Michael drifted back into a peaceful sleep, Marsha Malamet suddenly and unexpectedly arrived. Richard ushered her out of the room so as not to disturb Michael. They wandered to the hospital's central courtyard for a snack while Richard caught her up on the events of the last week.

When they returned to Michael's room, the nurses met Richard and Marsha in the hallway to tell them that Michael was gone. Grief-stricken, Jeff told them that Michael had sat up, looked toward the window, and died. At the age of thirty-eight, Michael's long battle with AIDS was over.

Fig. 1. Michael Callen Memorial Program (1994). Photograph by Andrew Scalini. Richard Dworkin Private Archive.

19

The Healing Power of Love

> *Life don't always go the way we planned*
> *Sometimes you have to take a stand*
> *And if I stumble, can I take your hand*
> *And feel the healing power of love*
> — Michael Callen & Marsha Malamet

Memorial services for Michael were held at the Callen family home in Hamilton, Highways Performance Space in Los Angeles, and the New York Society for Ethical Culture in Manhattan. The Callen family invited Karen Ocamb to attend their service. She remembers 66 Warr Court as "cozy, filled with family who didn't know what to say [so] they kept showing me old photos of Michael and told stories about [him]."[1] To ease the tension, she suggested that they make red AIDS ribbons for all the guests. Later, Barry introduced Karen to the mourners gathered in the small living room, whom she felt "really needed to know […] that this boy they knew and loved — this gay boy who had been through so much here growing up, so much they probably never even knew about — had literally saved thousands and thousands of people around the world by telling the truth about himself."[2] The day was raw and cold, and Cliff got on his hands and knees to pound away at the frozen Ohio ground. Together, Barry,

[1] Karen Ocamb, "My Remembrance of Michael Callen," p.c., 2009.
[2] Ibid.

Linda, Cliff, and Barbara, took a portion of Michael's ashes and buried them beneath the apple tree in the backyard.

The winter of 1994 was the snowiest on record in New York since 1960. The brutal cold, wind, and snow started in January and did not relent until April. On 22 March 1994, friends and loved ones braved a bitter snowstorm to pay homage to Michael at the New York Society for Ethical Culture (2 W 64th St.). Richard Dworkin selected eleven of Michael's friends and family to share brief recollections about Michael, including Carl Valentino, Judy Peabody, Celia Farber, Doug Sadownick, and Richard Pillard, though the weather kept Richard Pillard from making the trip from Boston. There were live performances of Duke Ellington's "Come Sunday" by Phillip Johnston and Joe Ruddick, "Sacred" by Steve Sandberg, "Love Don't Need a Reason" by Marsha Malamet, and music by The Flirtations in addition to recordings by David Lasley, Holly Near, and Michael's version of "They Are Falling All Around Me" from *Legacy*. There was also a twenty-minute video presentation of Deborah Wasser's *Legacy*, a documentary-in-progress about Michael, and a short tribute to Michael produced by Mark Chestnut for *In the Life*.

The Flirtations' Final Act

After Michael died, The Flirtations still had many professional obligations to fulfil, so they brought in guest vocalists including gay singer-songwriter Bill McKinley, Thomas Lucas, and Jay Guevara. However, none of these singers could replace Michael. Exacerbated by the lingering trauma of TJ's death three years earlier and, now, Michael's passing, tensions turned toxic. Cliff and Aurelio felt that they were treated as tokens of diversity by the white members of the group. They also perceived a persistent devaluation of their musical contributions and believed that Jimmy was manipulating Jon. By 1995, Aurelio had quit, and Cliff was fired via a telephone call from Jon.

Michael always fantasized that The Flirtations would be a mixed-sex group with a couple of powerful lesbian women singing a cappella with the boys. While his gender-balanced vision never became reality, Michael's longtime friend, lesbian singer Suede, did join the group in 1995. There were still sharp divides between lesbian and gay male politics, even as the AIDS epidemic had brought the two communities closer together. Suede received criticism from some women who felt that she had betrayed lesbian feminists by joining a male group. However, Suede saw this as an opportunity to honor Michael and to push herself musically. "Boy! I have never felt like I've used my voice more," she said of Arterton's arrangements. "It was really fun, challenging; but a lot of fun!"[3]

The Flirtations recruited another Black singer, Steve Langley; however, Langley was fired after a short time, a decision Langley believed was motivated by prejudice. "I was put out 'with love' because my voice did not match their tone. […] In less than a year, The Flirtations, who pride themselves on how they embrace diversity, had excised three men of color and [were] now all White."[4] After Langley was fired, Jon, Jimmy, and Suede reformed as a three-voice ensemble and released a final album in 1996. The aptly titled *Three* featured new three-part arrangements of songs that had been in the group's repertoire for years ("Breaths," "On Children," Mister Sandman," and "Everything Possible"); other songs about politics issues including food politics (Don Dixon, Bland Simpson, and Jim Wann's "Food Chain," from their 1996 musical *King Mackerel & the Blues Are Running*), women's rights (Meg Christian's "Can't Turn Back" [1983]), and HIV/AIDS (John Bucchino's "Do Not Turn Away"); as well as songs that featured their new singer's jazzy style like "Miss Celie's Blues" from the movie *The Color Purple* (1985). Scattered among these are also current pop songs like Cyndi Lauper's "Time After Time" (1983), Bonnie Raitt's "Something to Talk About" (1991), and Carly Simon's "Life is Eternal" (1990). They dedicated the album to "the spirit of Michael Callen."

3 Suede, interview with author, 28 March 2017.
4 Steve Langley, "A Failed Flirtation with Diversity," n.d. This article was cut from a magazine and pasted into Cliff Townsend's scrapbooks with no source information.

However, *Three* sold poorly, and demand for performances of this new iteration of The Flirtations dwindled. In December 1997, Jon announced that the group would disband, bringing a decade of LGBTQ+ music and activism to an end.

Finishing the *Legacy* Album

The double loss of Patrick and Michael within a few short weeks threw Richard into a deep depression. Emotionally exhausted and grieving, he could not bear to listen to Michael's music, so he shelved *Legacy* for a while. In the interim, Richard moved out of the apartment he had shared with Patrick and found a new home in Chelsea, where he still lives. Over the ensuing months, he closed both Patrick's and Michael's estates and resumed his professional life as a drummer in a band with Alex Chilton (1950–2010), who he had met in while working on the Chet Baker tribute album *Medium Cool* (1991). By late October 1994, he felt ready to return to *Legacy*.

At the time of Michael's death, fewer than ten of the fifty tracks had been mixed, and Richard still needed to decide which songs to include then sequence them into a coherent album. Working at Sear Sound and Looking Glass studios, where studio manager Kurt Munkacsi offered Richard free use of the studio when it wasn't otherwise booked, Richard mixed the tracks, sometimes working with Greg Wells on the songs that Wells had arranged and played on. To help narrow the track selection and finalize the sequence, Richard sent out cassettes of songs to trusted friends. n an accompanying letter, Richard wrote:

> Here, for the perusal of you and a select group of other lucky masochists, is a set of tapes representing the current state of this sprawling project. [...] For a variety of reasons which you can probably guess, it's virtually impossible for me to objectively evaluate this material. I desperately need some feedback [...]. If you don't like this way of grouping tunes, please

suggest one!! I look forward to reading your most brutal and cutting critical commentary![5]

Richard's paramour, Carl Valentino, was among Michael's most ardent musical supporters, and his feedback was vital to Richard as he completed *Legacy*. Tragically, Carl also died of AIDS-related illness, just two days before Richard received release-ready copies of the CD in 1996.

With a list of twenty-nine songs, Richard began the arduous process of mastering the album, which was done free of charge at Sterling Sound, one of the city's premier mastering studios. Creating a cohesive sound for an album recorded with so many disparate musicians and in such varied studio settings proved difficult, and the first engineer, who came from the world of dance music, lacked the requisite understanding of Michael's musical milieu. The mastered recordings were not going to work. So, Richard begrudgingly asked for a new engineer and started the mastering process over.

Richard also had to decide on cover art, packaging, and liner notes. Through mutual friends, he met Steven Amsterdam (who would go own to be an acclaimed author). Amsterdam suggested renowned book designer Archie Ferguson, who agreed to take on the project. Together, he and Richard sorted through thousands of photographs of Michael to assemble the booklet and cover art. Eventually, they decided on a beautiful photograph taken by Andrew Scalini, an Indianapolis photographer who had documented a Flirtations concert in the city and whose work also had been used for the cover art for their second album, *Live Out on the Road* (1992). The sepia tinged photograph is quintessential Michael Callen: head cocked to one side, a cool pensive expression with just a suggestion of his wry smile. He could be lost in his own thoughts or he could have just delivered one of his one-liners and paused, stone faced, as his friends broke into laughter.

5 Richard Dworkin, letter, late 1994, typed original, The Michael Callen Papers at The LGBT Community Center National History Archive.

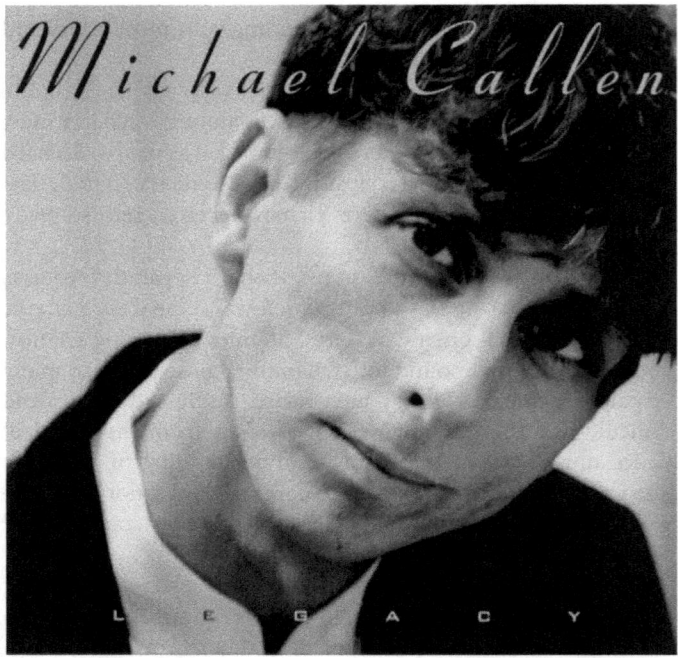

Fig. 2. Legacy album cover (1996). Photo by Andrew Scalini. © Significant Other Records.

For the liner notes, Richard solicited tributes to Michael from longtime friends, fellow artists, and admirers of his work including Tony Kushner, Pamela Brandt, Jon Arterton, Holly Near, and Tim Miller. Alongside these brief, loving essays about Michael's music, politics, and activism are dozens of photographs, snapshots, and a reproduction of Billy Quinn's *Mike,* a life-sized gilded painting from *A Plague of Angels* (1992), a series designed to evoke religious iconography but with a pro-sex message.

When all the tracks were mastered and sequenced and the liner notes and packing finalized, Richard sent the materials to Europadisk (75 Varick St.) to have the physical CDs made and the digipacks assembled. Boxes of CDs arrived at Richard's apartment in June 1996, and he planned to sell them on Christopher Street after the annual Gay Pride March and to submit the album for the first annual Gay and Lesbian American Music Awards (GLAMAS).[6] A few days after the GLAMA committee received their copies of *Legacy*, they called Richard with some concerns. When they played the second disc of *Legacy*, the songs did not seem to match the titles listed in the booklet. Confused, Richard put a copy into his CD player and heard Christian rock blaring from the speakers! Europadisk had pressed, packaged, and sent several thousand faulty copies of *Legacy*. Richard quickly returned the defective discs, which had to be opened, the correct disc inserted, then repacked and shipped. In the meantime, he took one of his personal copies of the correct edition of the album to GLAMA founders Tom McCormack and Michael Mitchell.

On 6 October 1996, *Legacy* was honored with an astounding nine nominations and four awards: Album of the Year, Male Artist of the Year, Best Group Recording, and Best Choral Recording. The GLAMA committee awarded its first Michael Callen Achievement Award to "an individual, group, organization, or business committed to the courageous and important work of engendering, nurturing, and furthering gay/lesbian music."[7] Fittingly, the first recipient of the Michael Callen Achievement Award was his friend and fellow musician Cris Williamson.

Looking back, Richard Dworkin thinks that he waited too long to finish the project, which limited its reach and impact. He also believes that because Michael was one of the longest living PWAs in the pre-combination therapy era, he was an icon of hope and survival. His passing demoralized people who looked to him for inspiration and "listening to [his music] was a reminder that he wasn't there."[8] However, Richard also thought

---

6 The GLAMAs were founded by Tom McCormack and Michael Mitchell and lasted for five years, from 1995 to 2000.
7 JD Doyle, "The GLAMA's," Queer Music Heritage, http://www.queermusicheritage.com/awards.html.
8 Richard Dworkin, interview with author, 5 June 2017.

Fig. 3. Michael Callen in vocal booth (1993). Photo by Patrick Kelly. © Significant Other Records.

that even 1994 would have been too late. Mike was already dead and could not tour, perform, or promote the album. Still, Richard has no regrets about the project. "When you make a record, you make it for the world." he told me. "But you also make it for a very few people who are really important to you, who really appreciate what you've done."[9]

9   Ibid.

LOVE DON'T NEED A REASON

Fig. 1. Me & Dickie D. Richard Dworkin (l) and Matthew Jones (r), NYC (2016). Courtesy of the author.

20

Michael Callen's Legacy: A Conclusion

> *Life don't always go the way we planned.*
> *Sometimes you have to take a stand.*
> *And if you stumble, you can take my hand*
> *And feel the healing power of love*
> — Michael Callen and Marsha Malamet

I hope you'll forgive me a few, last-minute theoretical arabesques: As I wrapped up work on *Love Don't Need a Reason* in the spring of 2020, I found myself rereading Eve K. Sedgwick's *Tendencies,* a book suffused with the author's wide-ranging curiosity and sensitivity to the preciousness and precariousness of living with illness. In "White Glasses," a memorial essay about her friend, Canadian AIDS activist Michael Lynch (1944–1991), Sedgwick describes a desire — hers, Lynch's — that arises during the experience of grave illness, a desire

> to entrust as many people as one possibly can within one's actual body and its needs, one's stories about its fate, one's dreams and one's sources of information or hypothesis about disease, cure, consolation, denial, and the state or institutional violence that are also invested in one's illness.

She continues:

> It's as though there were transformative political work to be done just by being available to be identified within the very grain of one's illness (which is to say, the grain of one's own intellectual, emotional, bodily self as refracted through illness and as resistant to it) — being available for identification to friends, but as well to people who don't love one; even to people who may not like one at all nor even wish one well.[1]

I've probably read this essay a dozen times over the years, but it wasn't until I finished writing *Love Don't Need a Reason* that this particular passage really made sense to me.

Michael Callen made himself "available to be identified within the very grain of [his] illness" and "entrust[ed] as many people as [he] possibly [could] with [his] actual body and its needs." Michael made his illness and his body public because he knew that the experiences, knowledge, and participation of PWAs were essential to the quest for solutions to the pandemic and that they were important parts of the history of (homo)sexuality in the last half of the twentieth century. Michael also knew that his lived experience, and whatever record of it he left behind, was his memory, his legacy.

Now, this book is part of that legacy, too.

Memory is messy business, especially as it intersects with trauma. HIV/AIDS is a collective and cultural trauma, an ongoing public health emergency, and something that a lot of people would rather just forget. However, "AIDS has rarely been taken up as one of the most significant cultural traumas of the late twentieth century."[2] Cultural trauma occurs, according to Jeffrey Alexander, "when members of a collectivity feel they have been subjected to a horrendous event that leaves indelible marks upon their group consciousness, marking their memories forever, and changing their future identity in fundamental and irrev-

---

1 Eve Kosofsky Sedgwick, *Tendencies* (Durham: Duke University Press, 1993), 261.
2 Christopher Castiglia and Christopher Reed, *If Memory Serves: Gay Men, AIDS, and the Promise of the Queer Past* (Minneapolis: University of Minnesota Press, 2012), 10.

ocable ways."³ It is an understatement to say that the AIDS crisis changed gay identity in fundamental and irrevocable ways. HIV/AIDS altered the way we have sex; the ways we mobilized politically; and the ways we grieve. HIV/AIDS ushered in new rituals, vocabularies, and identities, and after fifteen years of trauma, it engendered a certain will to forget — which is also a sign of trauma. It has also changed the way we remember.

Looking back at the US AIDS crisis, 1981–1996, Castiglia and Reed found that gay men and lesbians had a lot to forget. "In the wake of assaults on and erosions of memory from the [political] left and right, unremembering became the order of the day. […] The sweeping call to unremember targeted the generation hardest hit by the onset of AIDS, cutting that generation off from younger gays and lesbians who might continue [their] visionary work."⁴ They develop the notion of "de-generational unremembering" to account for the amnesiac effect of AIDS on queer cultural memory. By *de-generation* they mean a form of "temporal isolation" that separates generations of LGBTQ+ folks from their own collective pasts, and by "unremembering," they signal an active, perpetual process of "policed conservativism that followed on the heels" instead of "a once-and-for-all forgetting."⁵

Certainly, there are formal, institutional forces that "de-generate" us. How many families are willing to step outside their comfort zones and engage their LGBTQ+ children or relatives in open discussions of their lived experience? How many high schools teach LGBTQ+ history? How many university professors integrate LGBTQ+ topics into mainstream survey courses in history, politics, or music? How many leave those topics sequestered in niche departments? We still search for diverse images of ourselves in the media, and many of us still battle our own in-

---

3 Jeffrey C. Alexander, "Toward a Theory of Cultural Trauma," in *Cultural Trauma and Collective Identity*, eds. Jeffrey C. Alexander, Ron Eyerman, Bernard Giesen, Neil J. Smelser, and Piotr Sztompka (Berkeley: University of California Press, 2004), 1.
4 Castiglia and Reed, *If Memory Serves*, 9.
5 Ibid., 9–10.

ternalized bullshit — the queer-, homo-, and transphobia we've been force-fed our whole lives.

There are also less formal, though no less powerful, forces that lead to de-generation: homophobia, transphobia, and all the lingering stereotypes that haunt our cultural imaginations; ideas about LGBTQ+ people as perverts or predators; or the reality that for many people, queer sex and sexuality (and, therefore, identity) are uncomfortable, unfamiliar topics, taboos — something "they" do and that "we" would rather not think about. In the 1960s, Michael Callen's mother worried that simply discussing her son's effeminacy would exacerbate his gender trouble, and people still feel that way today. "Ignore it, and it'll just go away…" So, they respond with silence — a technology of violence and a tool of erasure. LGBTQ+ kids still track the gay imaginary, searching for themselves in books, movies, media, and online — looking for traces of others "like them" or a trail of… not breadcrumbs, how dull! No, rhinestones, dazzling glints of light, sparkling like a mirror ball, leading us through the thickets of a heteronormative and homophobic world that would prefer to keep us ignorant of ourselves, our history, and our power. A world that would prefer that we were not here at all. But we do, awkwardly, slowly, inevitably find our way home, to one another and to ourselves, generation after generation. Nevertheless, we must actively and perpetually resist the will toward de-generational unremembering.

The amnesiac effect of HIV/AIDS has also been exacerbated by gentrification, the disappearance of what Pierre Nora calls *milieux de mémoire*. "There are *lieux de mémoire*, sites of memory," he writes, because there are no longer […] real environments of memory."[6] In *The Gentrification of the Mind*, Sarah Schulman contemplates the impact of gentrification and HIV/AIDS on the arts, politics, literature, thought, and memory. She asks:

---

6   Ibid.; Pierre Nora, "Between Memory and History: *Les Lieux de Mémoire*," *Representations* 26 (1989): 7–24.

Do you know what I mean when I refer to 'AIDS' of the past? I am talking about the Plague (the overlapping period between Perestroika and Gentrification). The years from 1981 to 1996, when there was a mass death experience of young people. Where folks my age watched in horror as our friends, their lovers, cultural heroes, influences, buddies, the people who witnessed our lives as we witnessed theirs, as these folks sickened and died consistently for fifteen years. Have you heard about it?[7]

In my experience studying, writing about, and teaching the history of HIV/AIDS, the answer is a resounding, "No."

The will to forget AIDS began in the earliest years of the epidemic when political, cultural, and religious leaders chose to ignore the plight of gay men, injection drug users, non-white minorities, sex workers, and others touched by the disease. It reached an ugly apotheosis in 1996, when gay neoliberal Andrew Sullivan announced "the end of AIDS" then backhanded the urban, gay sexual culture of the '70s as recklessly immature, shamefully dangerous, and ultimately *responsible* for AIDS.[8] Exhausted from a decade of activism and wishing to rinse from their skins the residues of trauma and loss, some gay men — especially those with access to effective treatments — began to believe Sullivan's story, a process facilitated, ironically, by the development of the same medications that kept people living with HIV alive.

In the 1990s, the processes gentrification erased, wrote over, and demolished many of the *milieux de mémoire* of urban gay culture as cities around the country transformed themselves into family-friendly vacation destinations — the Disneyfication

---

7 Sarah Schulman, *The Gentrification of the Mind: Witness to a Lost Imagination* (Berkeley: University of California Press, 2012), 45.
8 In 1996, Sullivan published an infamous op-ed called "When Plagues End," *New York Times*, 10 November 1996, https://www.nytimes.com/1996/11/10/magazine/when-plagues-end.html.

of Times Square, for example.⁹ Such gentrified thinking continues into the present because the present moment looks so different from the crisis years. As Schulman writes:

> We went through a cataclysmic disaster and then we took a break. Instead of constant morbidity, there was puking, diarrhea, never-ending adjustments to toxic drug combinations, a lot of swallowing, and a certain facsimile of robustness, everyone feeling 'great.' Back to the gym. The funerals slowed or stopped, and the neighborhoods were changed, a new kind of AIDS body modification came into being [...]. We grow weary, numb, alienated, and then begin to forget, to put it all away just to be able to move on.¹⁰

But we — the generations that came after and who benefit from the political and artistic work of Michael's generation — must not move on. We cannot forget.

Oral history and survivor testimony are tools we can use to ensure remembrance, antidotes to amnesia, unremembering, and the gentrification of our collective memory. Oral history "facilitates the activation of public memories, literally the collective, communal practice of facing loss while transforming it into processes of healing," according to Horacio Roque Ramírez.¹¹ We can use oral history to excavate "layers of memory and truth" and to "make public our memories of the missing [or the dead], claiming their loss as part of our histories of the present."¹²

From the men and women whose oral histories are threaded into this book, I learned about our shared past. They told me

---

9   Samuel R. Delany captures this process of transformation in his book *Times Square Red, Times Square Blue* (New York: New York University Press, 1999).
10 Schulman, *The Gentrification of the Mind*, 58–59.
11 Horacio N. Roque Ramírez, "Memory and Mourning: Living Oral History with Queer Latinos and Latinas in San Francisco," in *Oral History and Public Memories*, eds. Paula Hamilton and Linda Shopes (Philadelphia: Temple University Press, 2008), 165–86.
12 Ibid., 166.

more about the late twentieth century than any graduate seminar or college textbook and taught me more about LGBTQ+ history than any documentary or book. They also taught me about Michael as a living, breathing, vibrant person, an activist, an author, a critical thinker, a public figure, a gourmet cook, a camp wit, a loyal friend, and a complicated lover. As each interview came to its conclusion, I posed one question: What is Michael Callen's legacy?

Activist and musician Holly Near considers feminism and music intertwined elements of Michael's legacy. "There has always been a tradition of music that comes out of social change in this country," she told me. "Music is a way of educating and inspiring. It can give courage and hope. Michael understood that. And he saw how profoundly linked the music of feminists and lesbians was not only to activism but to personal transformation. Lesbian music and feminist music gave women the courage to discover themselves […]. I think men like Michael and The Flirtations understood that."[13]

Douglas Sadownick published an essay around the time of Michael's death in which he meditates on Michael's strong sense of ethics, lovingly referring to him as "Ellie Ethical." Michael's words linger in his memory: "'There's nothing wrong, my dears, with feeling good about yourselves' […]. Maybe this is what Mike meant when he said, over and over again, without his usual tongue-in-cheek that 'being gay is a great gift.'"[14]

Joy is a hallmark of lesbian chanteuse Suede's memory of Michael as a "visionary in his activism and musically speaking" and for his willingness to bring lesbians and gay men together. "The women and the men's communities were really pretty separate at that point, and Michael said, 'No, no, no. We have all these shared battles and are stronger as a coalition.'" And for her, his spirit lives on in his insistence on having joy in life. "He was just

---

13 Holly Near, p.c., 30 October 2012, email.
14 Doug Sadownick, "Surviving Life: An Interview with AIDS Diva Michael Callen," *Frontiers*, n.d. (but likely early 1994 after Callen's death), Cliff Townsend's scrapbooks.

so OUT there. There were times when I thought it was too much, too much, but he was right on. He never let up, and I don't know where that spirit came from."[15]

For Tim Miller, Michael's legacy can be found in "the traces left behind in his music, his writings, and his life [...]. Mike keeps passing these notes on to faggot Hansels and dyke Gretles there in the scary forest so they can find their way home."[16]

Jon Arterton and Aurelio Font of The Flirtations heard Michael's legacy in "the comments we would get back; the audience reactions we would get. There were so many times when people would come up and tell us how meaningful a performance was — people who were struggling with their own identities or relationships in the world."[17] Michael's foregrounding of gay identity and experience as part of his music fed the souls of listeners who were sometimes "desperate to hear that message in those days."[18]

In his touching obituary published in *Gay Times* in 1993, Simon Watney wrote that the news of Michael's death made him think of how glad his "old friend film-maker Stuart Marshall would be to see him again. And Michael could continue his ceaseless, fascinated quest to find out whether everyone around him was 'really' a top or a bottom. Michael Callen was a brave, far-sighted, funny, sexy, clever, richly gifted gay man, who found his voice (like many others) in a crisis."[19] In the wake of Michael's death, and those of so many others, "gay life continues, the richer for [Michael's] great contribution to our collective struggle

---

15 Suede, interview with the author, 28 March 2017.
16 Matthew J. Jones, "How to Make Music in an Epidemic: Michael Callen, AIDS Activism, and Music," *Threads Radio/Subtext Radio*, broadcast 26 April 2020, available on SoundCloud, https://soundcloud.com/threadsradio/how-to-make-music-in-an-epidemic-w-dr-matthew-j-jones-26-apr-20-threadssub_xe.
17 Jon Arterton, interview with the author, 5 April 2013; Aurelio Font, interview with the author, 9 March 2016.
18 Ibid.
19 Simon Watney, *Imagine Hope: AIDS and Gay Identity* (London: Routledge, 2000), 114–15.

against AIDS, which Michael Callen also always recognized as a struggle *for* our pleasures."[20]

For Marsha Malamet, Michael's legacy is an all-encompassing celebration. "When I think of Michael, I think 'let's write a song, let's go out to dinner, let's have a great time! It's the man, the music, the activism, the love. The total package! I met my musical match with him. His lyrics were heartfelt and flowed out of him. He was a sensational human being. His brilliance. His politics. All things AIDS related. He was a charmer! He charmed the pants off people! You just had to embrace him, figuratively and literally. He was a very compelling soul."[21]

For Michael's biological family, his legacy has been more complex. After Michael's death, Barry was grief stricken. Having spent so much of his life protecting his younger brother and being asked to help him die at the end of his life was, in Barry's words, "a real mindfuck," and it took him many years to process the grief.[22] After bouncing around the country, Barry now lives in Madison, WI where he continues to make music, draw, and paint. He released his own album, *The Gospel of Fun*, in 2011.

For Cliff and Barbara, Michael's decision to come out as gay and as a PWA impacted their lives in Hamilton. In 1993, Michael appeared in an episode of *American Undercover* called "Why Am I Gay?" in which he drove around his hometown with a camera crew, pointing out the high school where he was tortured by his male classmates and other sites of childhood trauma. Barry characterized Michael's segment in the show as his brother's "platform to kick the ass out of everyone, for revenge against Hamilton."[23] While nothing Michael said was especially confrontational and he stopped short of naming names, it was enough to anger the congregation at the church Cliff and Barbara attended. They were pressured to leave the church. Several years afterward, Cliff was reading the paper one afternoon when

20 Ibid.
21 Marsha Malamet, interview with the author, 14 July 2017.
22 Barry Callen, interview with the author, 30 August 2020.
23 Ibid.

the episode aired in syndication. He watched the whole thing, and as Barry described his father's change in demeanor afterward, "it broke his heart."[24] Cliff, who had been so stubborn while Michael was alive, had a belated change of heart. He called Barry, still crying, and told him that "I realize now that I was too hard on Michael. I really regret my attitude and treatment of him. I hope, at least, you can forgive me."[25] Mr. Callen called a minister he knew who had a lesbian daughter and asked him to come pray with him. Afterward, he tried to think differently about homosexuality and about Michael. Cliff passed away at the age of 82 in 2007.

As she had while Michael was alive, Barbara Callen continued to struggle with her love for her son and her faith, though, like her husband, she could, regrettably, only resolve this tension after Michael died. She passed away at the age of 82 in 2014.

For Richard Dworkin, Michael's legacy can be summed up in the words of Robert Woodruff Anderson: "Death ends a life, but it does not end a relationship, which struggles on in the survivor's mind toward some final resolution, some clear meaning, which it perhaps never finds."[26] This, he thinks, is what Michael meant when, on his deathbed, he uttered, "No regrets."[27]

Michael's legacy endures in other ways. The New York City Community Health Project (the only primary care center in the city that specifically serves the LGBTQ+ community) honored his contributions to gay and lesbian healthcare activism by renaming their organization The Callen-Lorde Community Health Center (356 W 18th St.). Dedicated to providing "sensitive, quality healthcare and related services [...] regardless of their ability to pay," Callen-Lorde offers a full range of services ranging from general adult medicine to women's, children's, and

---

24 Ibid.
25 Ibid.
26 Robert Woodruff Anderson, *I Never Sang for My Father: A Play in 2 Acts*, first edition (New York: Dramatists Play Service, 1968).
27 Richard Dworkin, interview with the author, 5 June 2017.

trans*--specific services as well as mental and behavioral programs and HIV/STI testing and treatment.[28]

Parts of Michael's story have been told in books by Sean Strub, David France, Richard Berkowitz, and Martin Duberman, and his personal papers are accessible to anyone who can visit the New York City Lesbian, Gay, Bisexual, and Transgender Community Center's National History Archive. Regrettably, no anthology of his writings has been produced. However, *How to Have Sex in an Epidemic: One Approach* is available on the Internet, and copies of *Surviving AIDS* can be found in used bookstores and online. Likewise, many of his speeches have been archived on the Posthumous Homepage of Michael Callen (http://www.michaelcallen.com). While much of the specific healthcare advice in those pages is now decades out-of-date and should not be followed, Michael's reflections on living with AIDS, his investigations of contemporary gay life, observations on activism, and the interviews with long-term survivors as well as his own biographical anecdotes offer a fascinating glimpse into the realities of living with AIDS during the US AIDS crisis.

Of course, Michael's music is also his legacy. A few months before his death, Michael described the significance of music to his sense of self to filmmaker Deborah Wasser:

> The spirit descends when I sing. I could be sick with a fever and not know whether any sound is going to come out. But when the music starts, it just fills my body with passion and love, and I am able to reach down into what's left of my lungs and my heart and my soul and out it comes.[29]

Quite a statement from the self-proclaimed atheist, though I do not take these words as evidence of a late in life religious conversion. Rather, I think they speak to Michael's hope and optimism,

---

28 "About Us," *The Callen-Lorde Community Health Center*, https://callen-lorde.org/about/

29 Deborah Wasser, dir., *Legacy*, 1993. Richard Dworkin Private Archive (henceforth RDA).

his deep sense of music's power to voice his own experiences as a metonym for many PWAs and as a voice of resistance to ignorance, stigma, fear, and the myriad forms of interpersonal and state violence directed at PWAs.[30]

Thanks to Richard Dworkin's ongoing efforts, *Purple Heart* and Legacy remain available for purchase as CDs, MP3 downloads, streaming services, and YouTube. Richard also hopes to release a final album of tracks from the *Legacy* sessions in the near future.

The Flirtations' discography remains a touchstone of the *a cappella* revival and a crucial part of our shared queer music heritage. Historian and archivist JD Doyle has also assembled pages about Michael and The Flirtations in the archives of his long-running radio show "Queer Music Heritage," and Doyle's entire archive of LGBTQ+ music history was selected for inclusion in the permanent collection of the Library of Congress, ensuring that Michael, too, is now part of our national collective memory.[31]

There have been a few songs and compositions about Michael Callen. In his song "Michael," gay singer-songwriter Grant King offers a touching tribute, imagining him with "arms held high like wings, Michael, archest angel. Michael, queen of kings." King composed the song "on the occasion of [Michael's] farewell performance with The Flirtations," and he recorded it for his album *Let Love Out* (1995). Experimental composer and Columbia University neuroscientist Dave Soldier composed a string quartet with soloist, backup singers, and piano called "Michael Callen" (1995). Soldier's original text imagines the way famous queer figures would render Michael had he lived in their eras. "Courbet could paint your eyes [...] Genet would send you a thousand pretty lies" while "someone would write lyrics like Porter and bring them to you on his knees." Soldier's music is an eclectic

---

30 I have explored the role of hope in Michael's music in my essay, "Luck, Classic Coke, and the Love of a Good Man: The Politics of Hope and AIDS in Two Songs by Michael Callen," *Women and Music: A Journal of Gender and Culture* 21 (2017): 175–98.

31 JD Doyle, *Queer Music Heritage,* http://www.queermusicheritage.com.

Fig. 2. "Tart with a Tart" (c. 1984). Photo by Richard Dworkin. © Richard Dworkin.

mixture of post-tonal chromaticism and nostalgic elements of pop music from bygone eras, a fitting tribute to Michael, who possessed his own eclectic literary and musical tastes.

On 16 July 2012, Richard Dworkin and I attended a staged reading of Jim Bredeson's *Even for One Night*,[32] a theatrical-musical work based on Michael's words and conceived as a celebration of his status as "a hero — and a heretic." Five actors portrayed Michael at different stage of his life, speaking Michael's own words and singing his songs. The play is still in development, but it promises to bring Michael's compelling life story to audiences in the future. As we approached the theater at Dixon Place (161A Chyrstie St.), Richard, who had seen earlier rehearsals and read-throughs, expressed some anxieties, and we discussed them afterward. "When it was over, it was really hard for me cause that was the first time people could buy a ticket to it, total strangers could come to it, or people who knew me sepa-

---

32 Jim Bredeson, *Even for One Night*, 2012, http://www.evenforonenight.com/show.html.

rately from Mike, or anyone who was sort of involved with ACT UP, who sort of knew Mike. It was hard for me. It was difficult. Someone said, 'Well, what's the worst that could happen?' And I said, 'someone could judge me harshly, not to mention Mike, who I'm so protective of.'"[33]

Hero and heretic, Michael Callen shaped the history of the AIDS epidemic with his activist work, community organizing, and his music. Michael loved gay people fiercely and envisioned a world where everyone could love and live their best gay life. He was hopeful that this future would arrive, though he did not live to see it and, sadly, there is still so much work to do.

The processes of de-generational un-remembering and gentrification of the mind, however, were never quite complete. Like a cassette tape that's been recorded over time and again, the past left traces, ghostly voices audible in the playback. Although the physical body from which his voice emanated has been lost, Callen's *archival voices* can be heard in thousands of pages of written documents, videos of his television and live appearances, and audio recordings of his music. Listening again to his voice in these works, we hear our own history, our own story. Michael Callen taught us how to have sex in an epidemic, and his legacy reminds us that, above all, *Love Don't Need a Reason*.

---

33   Richard Dworkin, interview with the author, 2 June 2012.

Bibliography

Books and Articles

Alexander, Jeffrey C., Ron Eyerman, Bernhard Giesen, Neil J. Smelser, and Piotr Sztompka. "Toward a Theory of Cultural Trauma," in Jeffrey C. Alexander et al., *Cultural Trauma and Collective Identity*. Berkeley: University of California Press, 2004.

Altman, Dennis. *AIDS in the Mind of America: The Social, Political, and Psychological Impact of a New Epidemic*. Garden City: Anchor Books, 1986.

Aral, Sevgi, Kevin Fenton, and King Holmes. "Sexually Transmitted Diseases in the USA: Temporal Trends." *Sexually Transmitted Infections* 83, no. 4 (2007): 257–66. DOI: 10.1136/sti.2007.026245.

Auslander, Phillip. *Performing Glam Work: Gender and Theatricality in Popular Music*. Ann Arbor: University of Michigan Press, 2006.

Averill, Gage. *Four Parts, No Waiting: A Social History of Barbershop*. Oxford: Oxford University Press, 2010.

Berkowitz, Richard. *Stayin' Alive: The Invention of Safe Sex*. New York: Basic Books, 2003.

———. "AIDS — One Man's Odyssey." In *The Sourcebook on Lesbian/Gay Healthcare: A Handbook for the First International Lesbian and Gay Health Conference 16–19 June, 1984*.

Washington, DC: National Gay Health Education Foundation, 1984.

Bordowitz, Gregg. *The AIDS Crisis is Ridiculous and Other Writings: 1986–2003*, ed. James Meyer. Cambridge: MIT Press, 2004.

Boyd, Nan Alamilla, and Horacio N. Roque Ramírez, eds. *Bodies of Evidence: The Queer Practice of Oral History*. Oxford: Oxford University Press, 2012.

Callen, Michael. *Surviving AIDS*. New York: Harper Perennial, 1990.

Callen, Michael, and Dan Turner. "A History of the AIDS Self-Empowerment Movement." *Lesbian and Gay Health Education Foundation Program Booklet* (1988), 288–95.

Callen, Michael, Richard Berkowitz, and Joseph Sonnabend with Richard Dworkin. *How to Have Sex in an Epidemic: One Approach*. New York: Tower Press, 1983.

Castiglia, Christopher, and Christopher Reed. *If Memory Serves: Gay Men, AIDS, and the Promise of the Queer Past*. Minneapolis: University of Minnesota Press, 2012.

Cervini, Eric. *The Deviant's War: The Homosexual vs. The United States of America*. New York: Farrar, Straus, and Giroux, 2020.

Chambré, Susan. *Fighting for Our Lives: New York's AIDS Community and the Politics of Disease*. New Brunswick: Rutgers University Press, 2006.

Cohen, Howard. "Feminist, Rock Musician and Food Writer Pamela Brandt Dies at 68." *Miami Herald*, 4 August 2015. https://www.miamiherald.com/news/local/obituaries/article30104304.html.

Crimp, Douglas. *Melancholia and Moralism: Essays and AIDS and Queer Politics*. Cambridge: MIT Press, 2009.

Cvetkovich, Ann. *An Archive of Feelings: Trauma, Sexuality, and Lesbian Public Cultures*. Durham: Duke University Press, 2003.

Davis, Peter. *Hometown: A Portrait of an American Community*. New York: Simon and Schuster, 1982.

Delaney, Samuel. *Times Square Red, Times Square Blue.* New York: New York University Press, 1999.

Duberman, Martin. *Hold Tight Gently: Michael Callen, Essex Hemphill, and the Battleground of AIDS.* New York: The New Press, 2014.

Escoffier, Jeffrey, ed. *In My Time: Essays on Sex, Science, and AIDS.* Unpublished manuscript, 1993.

Fabbri, Franco. "A Theory of Musical Genres: Two Applications." In *Popular Music Perspectives,* eds. D. Horn and Phil Tagg, 52–81. Göteborg and Exeter: International Association for the Study of Popular Music, 1981.

Farber, Celia. *Serious Adverse Events: An Uncensored History of AIDS.* Hoboken: Melville House Publishing, 2006.

Ferraro, Geraldine A. "The Trauma of Living with AIDS." *Congressional Record* 129, no. 69 (28 May 1983). http://michael-callen.com/mikes-writing/congressional-record-on-aids/.

France, David. *How to Survive a Plague: The Inside Story of How Citizens and Science Tamed AIDS.* New York: Knopf, 2016.

Frith, Simon. *Performing Rites: On the Value of Popular Music.* Cambridge: Harvard University Press, 1990.

Gavin, James. *Intimate Nights: The Golden Age of New York Cabaret.* New York: Grove Weidenfeld, 1991.

Gilman, Sander. *Disease and Representation: Images of Illness from Madness to AIDS.* Ithaca: Cornell University Press, 1988.

Goffman, Erving. *The Presentation of Self in Everyday Life.* New York: Anchor Books, 1959.

Gray, Fred. *The Tuskegee Syphilis Study: An Insider's Account of the Shocking Medical Experiment Conducted by the Government against African American Men.* Montgomery: NewSouth Books, 2002.

Gould, Deborah. *Moving Politics: Emotions and ACT UP's Fight against AIDS.* Chicago: University of Chicago Press, 2009.

Hagan, Sean, ed. *Bowie on Bowie: Interviews and Encounters with David Bowie.* Chicago: Chicago Review Press, 2015.

Halberstam, J. *Trans*: A Quick and Quirky Guide to Gender Variability.* Berkeley: University of California Press, 2018.

Halperin, David. *How to Be Gay.* Cambridge: Harvard University Press, 2014.

Harden, Victoria. *AIDS at 30: A History.* Lincoln: Potomac Books, 2012.

Hersch, Fred. *Good Things Happen Slowly: A Life In and Out of Jazz.* New York: Crown Archetype, 2017.

Humphreys, Laud. *Tearoom Trade: Impersonal Sex in Public Places.* Piscataway: Adline-Transaction Publishers, 1970.

Jones, James. *Bad Blood: The Tuskegee Syphilis Experiment.* New and expanded edition. New York: The Free Press, 1993.

Jones, Matthew J. "Anglophone Songs about HIV/AIDS." In *The Oxford Handbook of Music and Queerness,* edited by Sheila Whiteley and Fred Maus. Oxford: Oxford University Press, 2018. DOI: 10.1093/oxfordhb/9780199793525.013.100.

———. "Enough of Being Basely Tearful: 'Glitter and Be Gay,' Camp, and the Politics of Queer Resistance" *The Journal of the Society for American Music* 10, no. 4 (2016): 422–45. DOI: 10.1017/S1752196316000341.

———. *How to Make Music in an Epidemic: Popular Music-Making during the AIDS Pandemic, 1981–1996.* London: Routledge, forthcoming.

———. "'Luck, Classic Coke, and the Love of a Good Man': The Politics of Hope and AIDS in Two Songs by Michael Callen." *Women & Music: A Journal of Gender and Culture* 21, no. 1 (2017): 175–98. DOI: 10.1353/wam.2017.001.

———. "'Something Inside So Strong: The Flirtations, Queer Politics, and *A Cappella.*" *The Journal of Popular Music Studies* 28, no. 2 (2016): 142–85. DOI: 10.1111/jpms.12168.

Kinsella, James. *Covering the Plague: AIDS and the American Media.* New Brunswick: Rutgers University Press, 1989.

Kramer, Larry. *Reports from the Holocaust: The Making of an AIDS Activist.* New York: St. Martin's Press, 1989.

Lorde, Audre. *Sister Outsider: Essays and Speeches by Audre Lorde.* Berkeley: Crossing Press, 2007.

May, Elaine Tyler. *Homeward Bound: American Families in the Cold War Era.* 20th Anniversary Edition. New York: Basic Books, 2008.

Monette, Paul. *Borrowed Time: An AIDS Memoir*. San Diego: Harcourt, Brace, and Jovanovich Publishers, 1988.

Nagle, Jill. "Skinny, 'White' Chicks and Hung, Buff Boys: Queer Sex Spaces and Their Discontents." In *Looking Queer: Body Image and Identity in Lesbian, Bisexual, Gay, and Transgender Communities,* edited by Dawn Atkins, 439–44. New York: The Haworth Press, 1998.

Newton, Esther. *Margaret Meade Made Me Gay: Personal Essays, Public Ideas*. Durham: Duke University Press, 2000.

Nora, Pierre. "Between Memory and History: *Les Lieux de Mémoire.*" *Representations* 26 (1989): 7–24. DOI: 10.2307/2928520.

Ocamb, Karen. "Who's History? My Curious Encounter with Radical Faeries." *The Bilerico Project,* 20 February 2009. http://bilerico.lgbtqnation.com/2009/02/whos_history_my_curious_encounter_with_t.php.

Perlstein, Rick. *Nixonland: The Rise of a President and the Future of America*. New York: Charles Scribner and Sons, 2009.

———. *The Invisible Bridge: The Fall of Nixon and the Rise of Reagan*. New York: Simon and Schuster, 2015.

Pillard, Richard, and James D. Weinrich. "Evidence of Familial Nature of Male Homosexuality." *Archives of General Psychiatry* 43, no. 8 (1986): 808–12. DOI: 10.1001/archpsyc.1986.01800080094012.

Reuben, David, MD. *Everything You Always Wanted to Know About Sex: But Were Afraid to Ask*. New York: David McKay Publishers, 1969.

Roque Ramírez, Horacio N. "Memory and Mourning: Living Oral History with Queer Latinos and Latinas in San Francisco." In *Oral History and Public Memories,* edited by Paula Hamilton and Linda Shopes, 165–86. Philadelphia: Temple University Press, 2008.

Rosenthal, Elizabeth. *His Song: The Musical Journey of Elton John*. New York: Billboard Books, 2001.

Roth, Benita. *The Life and Death of ACT UP/LA: Anti-AIDS Activism in Los Angeles from the 1980s to the 2000s*. Cambridge: Cambridge University Press, 2017.

Russo, Vito. *The Celluloid Closet: Homosexuality in the Movies*. New York: Harper & Row, 1987.

Sadownick, Douglas. *Sex between Men*. San Francisco: Harper San Francisco, 1996.

Schulman, Sarah. *The Gentrification of the Mind: Witness to a Lost Imagination*. Berkeley: University of California Press, 2012.

Sedgwick, Eve Kosofsky. *Tendencies*. Durham: Duke University Press, 1993.

———. *The Epistemology of the Closet*. Durham: Duke University Press, 1990.

Shilts, Randy. *And the Band Played On: Politics, People, and the AIDS Epidemic*. 20th Anniversary Edition. 1987; rpt. New York: St. Martin's Press, 2007.

Stone, Amy L., and Jamie Cantrell, eds. *Out of the Closet, Into the Archives: Researching Sexual Histories*. Albany: SUNY Press, 2015.

Strub, Sean. *Body Counts: A Memoir of Politics, Sex, AIDS, and Survival*. New York: Scribner Books, 2014.

Vrabel, Jim. *A People's History of the New Boston*. Amherst: University Massachusetts Press, 2014.

Wallace, J. Felice S. Coral, Ilonna J. Rimm, Heather Lane, Herbert Levin, Ellis L. Reinherz, Stuart F. Schlossman, and Joseph Sonnabend. "T-Cell Ratios in Homosexuals." *The Lancet* 319, no. 8277 (1982): 908. DOI: 10.1016/s0140-6736(82)92177-8.

Watney, Simon. *Imagine Hope: AIDS and Gay Identity*. London: Routledge, 2000.

Weston, Kath. *Families We Choose: Lesbians, Gays, Kinship*. New York: Columbia University Press, 1991.

———. "Get Thee to a Big City: Sexual Imaginary and the Great Gay Migration." *GLQ: A Journal of Gay and Lesbian Studies* 2, no. 3 (1995): 253–77. DOI: 10.1215/10642684-2-3-253.

White, Edmund. *City Boy: My Life in New York during the '60s and '70s*. New York: Bloomsbury, 2010.

———. *States of Desire: Travels in Gay America*. Ann Arbor: University of Michigan Press, 2014.

Whiteley, Sheila, and Jennifer Rycenga, eds. *Queering the Popular Pitch*. New York: Routledge, 2006.

Wilson, Sloan. *The Man in the Gray Flannel Suit*. New York: Simon and Schuster, 1955.

Woubshet, Dagmawi. *The Calendar of Loss: Race, Sexuality, and Mourning in the Early AIDS Era*. Baltimore: Johns Hopkins University Press, 2015.

Wright, Richard. *Black Boy: American Hunger*. Restored edition. New York: HarperCollins, 1998.

Journalism and Other Sources

BettyByte, "AIDS and promiscuity - (1) point counterpoint - introduction - Vito Russo - 1983." *YouTube,* 19 October 2011. http://www.youtube.com/watch?v=PgZh7Kk8cnI.

———. "AIDS and promiscuity - (2) point - Charles Jurrist - 1983." *YouTube,* 19 October 2011, http://www.youtube.com/watch?v=-ltMm3bMnMY.

———. "AIDS and promiscuity - (3) counterpoint - Michael Callen - 1983." *YouTube,* 19 October 2011. http://www.youtube.com/watch?v=zVlE7Vk4Ivg.

Brandt, Pamela. Interview with JD Doyle. *Queer Music Heritage,* March 2013. http://queermusicheritage.com/mar2013s.html.

Brass, Perry. "A Prophecy Before Our Time: The Gay Men's Health Project Clinic Opens in 1972." *New York Public Library Blog,* 7 November 2013. https://www.nypl.org/blog/2013/11/07/gay-mens-health-project-clinic-1972.

Bucchino, John. "Interview with and JD Doyle." *Queer Music Heritage,* April 2009. http://www.queermusicheritage.com/apr2009s.html.

Buckley, William F., Jr. "Crucial Steps in Combating the AIDS Epidemic: Identify all the Carriers." *New York Times,* 18 March 1986.

Burr, Chandler. "Homosexuality and Biology." *The Atlantic* 271, no. 3, March 1993, 47–65.

Callen, Michael. "Are You Now, or Have You Ever Been." *PWA Coalition Newsline* 40, January 1989, 34–36.

———. "Crashing." *PWA Coalition Newsline* 32, March 1988, 35–37.

———. "Dinosaur's Diary: In My Time of Dying." *QW,* 30 August 1992, 46–47.

———. "Farewell." *PWA Coalition Newsline* 47, September 1989, 2.

———. "Wading the Deep, Messy Waters of Sex: Wear Your Rubbers." *QW,* 7 June 1992, 44.

Callen, Michael, Richard Berkowitz, and Richard Dworkin, "We Know Who We Are: Two Gay Men Declare War on Promiscuity." *The New York Native,* 8–21 November 1982.

Centers for Disease Control and Prevention. "A Cluster of Kaposi's Sarcoma and Pneumocystis Pneumonia Among Homosexual Male Residents of Los Angeles and Orange Counties, California." *Morbidity and Mortality Weekly Report* 32, no. 23, 18 June 1982, 305–7.

———. "Kaposi's Sarcoma and Pneumocystis among Gay Men—New York City and California." *Morbidity and Mortality Weekly Report* 30, no. 24, 4 July 1981, 305–8.

———. "Pneumocystis Pneumonia—Los Angeles." *Morbidity and Mortality Weekly Report* 30, no. 21, 5 June 1981, 1–3.

———. "U.S. Public Health Service Syphilis Study at Tuskegee." https://www.cdc.gov/tuskegee/index.html.

Chesley, Robert. Letter to the editor. *The New York Native,* 22 November 1981.

Christagau, Robert. "The Deadly Nightshade" album review (1975). http://www.robertchristgau.com/get_artist.php?name=The+Deadly+Nightshade.

Coates, Ta-Nehisi. "The Case for Reparations." *The Atlantic,* June 2014. https://www.theatlantic.com/magazine/archive/2014/06/the-case-for-reparations/361631/.

Cohen, Howard. "Feminist, Rock Musician and Food Writer Pamela Brandt Dies at 68." *Miami Herald,* 4 August 2015. http://www.miamiherald.com/news/local/obituaries/article30104304.html.

"Curable Disease." *Time* 68, no. 24, 10 December 1956, 76.

Davis, Curt. "A Mixed Bag, or a Mistaken Identity." *New York Post,* 9 October 1981.

D'Entremont, Jim. "Pilgrim's Progress: Boston's Gay History." *The Guide,* November, 2007. https://web.archive.org/web/20160203060339/http://archive.guidemag.com/magcontent/invokemagcontent.cfm?ID=211D6820-56B6-41CB-8DF1503C48C70284.

D'Eramo, James E. "Whose Guidelines?" *New York Native* 76, 7–20 November 1983.

Doyle, JD. *Queer Music Heritage Website.* https://www.queermusicheritage.com/.

Dworkin, Richard. "Patrick Kelly, Dancer and Writer, Dies at 40." *New York Times,* 13 December 1993. http://www.nytimes.com/1993/12/13/obituaries/patrick-kelly-dancer-and-writer-dies-at-40.html.

Eder, Bruce. "Lowlife Laughs." *The Village Voice* 29, no. 35, 28 August 1984.

"Fire in the Everard Baths." *StevenWarRan,* 15 July 2014, https://stevenwarran.blogspot.com/2014/07/fire-in-everard-baths.html.

Foucault, Michel, with R. de Ceccaty, J. Danet, and J. Le Bitoux. "De l'amitié comme mode de vie." *Gai Pied* 25, April 1981, 38–29.

"From 1975 to Now, How's New York City Doing?" *New York Times,* 10 April 1983.

Gay Men with AIDS. "A Warning to Gay Men." Advertisement, *New York Native,* 22 November–5 December 1982.

Glueck, Grace. "The Downtown Scene, When It Was Still Dirty." *New York Times,* 13 January 2006.

Gross, Terry. "Michael Callen on 'Surviving AIDS' Long Term." *Fresh Air*, 16 November 1990.

Hajdu, David. "Giant Steps: The Survival of a Great Jazz Pianist." *New York Times*, 28 January 2010. http://www.nytimes.com/2010/01/31/magazine/31Hersch-t.html.

Holden, Steven. "Reno Sweeny Alumni to Stage AIDS Concert." *New York Times*, 7 April 1988. https://www.nytimes.com/1988/04/07/arts/reno-sweeney-alumni-to-stage-aids-concerts.html.

Jewell, Geri, David Zimmerman, and Marsha Malamet. "Lesson to Be Learned." *ABILITY*, https://abilitymagazine.com/marsha-malamet-music-legend/.

Johnston, Laurie. "9 Killed in Fire Identified by Friends." *New York Times*, 27 May 1977.

Jones, Matthew J. "How to Make Music in an Epidemic: Michael Callen, AIDS Activism, and Music." *Threads Radio/Subtext Radio*, broadcast 26 April 2020. Available on SoundCloud, https://soundcloud.com/threadsradio/how-to-make-music-in-an-epidemic-w-dr-matthew-j-jones-26-apr-20-threadssub_xe.

Kilday, Gregg. "Barbara Streisand on 'The Normal Heart': 'I Tried Very Hard to Get It Made.'" *The Hollywood Reporter*, 9 April 2014. https://www.hollywoodreporter.com/news/barbra-streisand-normal-heart-i-694691.

Koch, Edward. "Senator Helm's Callousness toward AIDS Victims." *New York Times*, 7 November 1987. https://www.nytimes.com/1987/11/07/opinion/senator-helms-s-callousness-toward-aids-victims.html.

Lieberson, Jonathan. "Anatomy of an Epidemic." *New York Review of Books*, 18 August 1983.

Malamet, Marsha. Interview with JD Doyle. *Queer Music Heritage*, May 2013. http://www.queermusicheritage.com/may2013s.html.

Mass, Lawrence. "Disease Rumors Largely Unfounded." *New York Native*, 18 May 1981.

Markovitz, Adam. "Barbara Streisand and Larry Kramer Trade Blame for Failed 'Normal Heart' Film." *Entertain-

ment Weekly, 7 May 2011. https://ew.com/article/2011/05/07/streisand-normal-heart/.

"Michael Callen." *Gay New York,* February 1980.

Nahmod, David. "Heart to Heart: Singer/Activist Michael Callen Talks about Politics, AIDS, and Music as Warfare," article in an unknown magazine, 1988.

Neyfakh, Leon. "How Boston Powered the Gay Rights Movement." *The Boston Globe,* 2 June 2013.

Ortleb, Charles. "Editorial Introduction." *New York Native* 50, 8–21 November 1982.

"Patrick Kelly, Dancer and Writer, Dies at 40." *New York Times,* 13 December 1993. https://www.nytimes.com/1993/12/13/obituaries/patrick-kelly-dancer-and-writer-dies-at-40.html.

Pilshaw, Elliot. Interview with JD Doyle. *Queer Music Heritage,* July 2008. http://www.queermusicheritage.com/jul2008s.html.

"Review of Lowlife." *Ms. 13,* 10 April 1985.

Rosenberg, Kenneth Paul. *America Undercover,* Episode 10: "Why Am I Gay?" HBO, 10 August 1993.

Sadownick, Douglas. "Doug Sadownick's Response to Karen O. (Section 2)." *Gay Psyche Politics,* 24 April 2010. http://gaypsychepolitics.blogspot.com/2010/04/douglas-sadownicks-response-to-karen.html.

———. "Surviving Life: An Interview with AIDS Diva Michael Callen." *Frontiers,* n.d.

Seitzman, Peter. "AIDS and Luck." *New York Native* 50, 8–21 November 1982.

Shenon, Philip. "A Move to Evict AIDS Physician Sought by State." *New York Times,* 1 October 1983.

Shewey, Don. "Cabaret!" *The Advocate,* 5 October 1977.

Sloan, David. "A New Vocalist for the Rest of Us." The New York City News 11, no. 23, 1 December 1981.

Stanley, Bob. "Heart Carny: Marsha Malamet, Coney Island Winter." *Mojo Magazine,* n.d., 128.

Strub, Sean. "The Good Doctor." *POZ Magazine,* July 1998.

Sullivan, Andrew. "When Plagues End." *New York Times*, 10 November 1996. https://www.nytimes.com/1996/11/10/magazine/when-plagues-end.html.

"The City: AIDS Doctor Gets Stay of Eviction." *New York Times*, 15 October 1983.

"The Homosexual in America." *Time* 87, no. 3, 21 January 1966, 52–57.

Thomas, Evan. "The New Untouchables." *Time*, 23 September 1985. http://content.time.com/time/magazine/article/0,9171,959944,00.html.

United Press International. "Helms Calls for AIDS Quarantine on Positive Tests." *Chicago Tribune*, 16 June 1987. https://www.chicagotribune.com/news/ct-xpm-1987-06-16-8702140384-story.html.

United Nations Programme on HIV/AIDS. "Global HIV & AIDS Statistics—2020 Fact Sheet," 2020. https://www.unaids.org/en/resources/fact-sheet.

Walter, Kate. "High Spirits." *New York Native*, 26 August 1984.

———. "Rock'N'Roll Lowlife with a Gay Conscience." *The Advocate*, 3 October 1984.

Warran, Steve. "Fire in the Everard Baths." *SteveWarRan*, 15 July 2014. https://stevenwarran.blogspot.com/2014/07/fire-in-everard-baths.html.

Interviews

Between 2012 and 2020, I conducted interviews with a number of people who knew Michael Callen personally. These interviews took place in person, over the telephone, via social media, and over email, totaling more than 50 hours of audio recording and dozens of emails and social media messages.

Jon Arterton, 17 October 2013.
Richard Berkowitz, 8 June 2020.
Barry Callen, 21 September 2013.
Richard Dworkin, 6 February 2012; 4 September 2012; 2 June 2012; 12 January 2014; 5 June 2017; 25 July 2020.

Aurelio Font, 9 March 2016.
Joel Jason, 23 May 2020.
Grant King, 2 July 2017.
Marsha Malamet, 14 July 2017.
Tim Miller, 5 July 2017; 8 April 2019.
Holly Near, 29 June 2017, 21 March 2020.
Karen Ocamb, 17 May 2020.
Suede, 25 April 2017.
Terry Tincher, 22 June 2017.
Clifford Townsend, 2 July 2014.

Archives

MCP: Michael Callen Papers at the New York City Gay, Lesbian, Bisexual, and Transgender Community Center's LGBTQ National History Archives. A collection of literally thousands of pages of letters, musical scores, handwritten lyrics, medical papers, and other ephemera as well as archival recordings and home videos, this resource has been essential to my work. Unless stated otherwise, all correspondences between Michael Callen and other parties can be found here.

RDA: Richard Dworkin Private Archive. Michael's surviving partner, producer, and musical collaborator, provided access to photographs, concert recordings, unreleased studio recordings, and a variety of other documents.

Select Discography

Michael Callen
Purple Heart. Significant Other Records, 1988.
Legacy. Significant Other Records, 1996.

The Flirtations
The Flirtations. Significant Other Records, 1990.
Live: Out on the Road. Flirts Records, 1992.
Three. Flirts Records, 1996.

Jon Arterton and James Mack
Legally Married…And the Sky Didn't Fall! J&J Records, 2011.

Marsha Malamet
Coney Island Winter. Decca Records, 1969.
The Natural Thing to Do. Mouton Music Canada, 2017.
Vintage. Mouton Music Canada, 2017.
You Asked Me to Write You a Love Song. Cool Sound, 2003.

Suede
Easily Suede. Easily Suede Music, 1988.
Barely Blue. Easily Suede Music, 1992.
On the Day Met. Easily Suede Music, 2001.
Dangerous Mood. Suede Wave/Easily Suede Music, 2008.

Cliff Townsend
Out Here on My Own. Risco Records, 1994.

www.ingramcontent.com/pod-product-compliance
Lightning Source LLC
Chambersburg PA
CBHW071734150426
43191CB00010B/1568